Peace, War and the European Powers,

# European History in Perspective
## General Editor: Jeremy Black

# Peace, War and the European Powers, 1814–1914

C. J. Bartlett

*Professor of International History, University of Dundee*

St. Martin's Press
New York

PEACE, WAR AND THE EUROPEAN POWERS, 1814–1914

Copyright © 1996 by C. J. Bartlett

St. Martin's Press, Scholarly and Reference Division,
175 Fifth Avenue, New York, N.Y. 10010

First published in the United States of America in 1996

Printed in Hong Kong

ISBN 0–312–16137–9 cloth
ISBN 0–312–16138–7 paperback

Library of Congress Cataloging-in-Publication Data
Bartlett, C. J. (Christopher John), 1931–
Peace, war and the European powers, 1814–1914 / C. J. Bartlett.
p.   cm. — (European history in perspective)
Includes bibliographical references and index.
ISBN 0–312–16137–9. — ISBN 0–312–16138–7
1. Europe—Politics and government—1815–1871.   2. Europe–
–Politics and government—1871–1918.   3. Europe—History,
Military—19th century.   I. Title.   II. Series.
D363.B34   1996
940.2'8—dc20                                          96–6785
                                                          CIP

'Civilization is only savagery silver-gilt.'

H. Rider Haggard, *Allan Quatermain*, (1887)


'The past is a foreign country. They do things
differently there.'

L. P. Hartley, *The Go-Between*, (1953)

# CONTENTS

# PREFACE

The outbreak of the First World War marked the end – by European standards – of a relatively peaceful era between the great powers. A number of mid-nineteenth century conflicts (the Crimea, the Italian and German wars of unification) had been preceded by 39 years of peace, while France's defeat in 1870–1 ushered in a spell of no less than 43 years – a record which stood until 1988. Many scholars see the 1914 war as the cataclysmic breakdown of a sophisticated state system dating from 1814–15 – or even from 1648. While one may be a little sceptical concerning efforts to quantify the differing intensities of conflict in the eighteenth, nineteenth and twentieth centuries, there can be no doubt that by any criteria the middle era was markedly more peaceful than what went before or followed after. In particular the mid-nineteenth century conflicts were in no way comparable to the wars of 1792–1815, 1914–18, or even to the American Civil War. Raymond Aron argues that 'What needs to be explained is not how the war of 1914 became "hyperbolic" ... ', but how peaceful relations between the powers in Europe were interrupted by no more than relatively limited and only moderately destructive wars.

It is evident that answers to this question do not lie simply in the statecraft of the era, but scholars nevertheless have devoted not a little attention to what Richard Langhorne describes as 'the heyday of diplomacy'. Although this was no 'golden age', he argues that here was a time when the 'instinctive responses of statesmen ... [had been] conditioned by their surprisingly common conception of an existing European international system'. This had declined rapidly from 1890, so that by 1914 'the old ways survived more by inertia than the conscious will of statesmen'. Nevertheless even before 1890 he stresses the elusiveness of the so-called Concert of Europe, and its reliance on 'attitudes of mind' and the fears generated by recent revolutions and wars. It is the aim of the present extended essay to examine European statecraft from Metternich to Bethmann Hollweg and to test some of the more extravagant claims made on behalf of what Paul Schroeder has described as 'consensual politics'.

I should like to take this opportunity to express my thanks to Dr Mark Cornwall for providing me with so many useful references, ideas and information on Austria–Hungary, and for listening so patiently as I held forth on certain sections of this book. He was a most constructive, yet sympathetic critic. Meanwhile our ever cheerful Departmental Secretary, Helen Carmichael, provided moral support and the all-important coffee and biscuits.

*C. J. Bartlett*
*Broughty Ferry*

# 1

## THE 'CONGRESS SYSTEM'

...in a condition of Warre, wherein every man to every man, for want of a common Power to keep them all in awe, is an Enemy, there is no man can hope by his own strength, or wit, to defend himselfe from destruction, without the help of Confederates: ...
(Thomas Hobbes, *Leviathan*, Cambridge UP edition, 1904, p. 99)

### To the Vienna Settlement

The eighteenth century has often been described as a classic era of limited war. Martin Wight, for instance, comments on the degree of attention devoted to the concept of the balance of power. This was invoked for several purposes, and not simply to justify new alignments against over-mighty states. Some welcomed it as a means to promote orderly change and to provide a yardstick against which states could be ranked in relation to each other. In addition the period saw the standardisation of diplomatic practice and a growing interest in international law. Edmund Burke wrote of the existence of a 'secret, unseen, but irrefragable bond of habitual intercourse' which encouraged some degree of restraint among the powers.[1] Indeed the scale of the conflicts fought in the era of the French Revolution and Napoleon, together with their large-scale consequences, led some to look back to what they believed had been a less violent and more rational world for ideas in the creation of a more orderly world.

More recently, however, a number of historians have begun to take a more sceptical view of the bigger claims concerning the relative

1

moderation which had supposedly governed eighteenth-century diplomacy and war. Jeremy Black, for instance, argues strongly that the 'conduct of military operations frequently reflected the desperate issues at stake in wars. Armies aimed to win, while civilians were often acutely affected by the conflict.' Furthermore there was less respect for the maintenance of the balance of power than many have suggested. The attempts by the congresses of Cambrai and Soissons in the 1720s to moderate international rivalries were soon put in perspective by later conflicts. 'The arbiter of disputes remained the battlefield.' The same author also questions whether the 'modern impersonal state' was well established by the end of the century. He prefers to stress the continuing importance of dynastic and – to a lesser extent – even religious rivalries.[2]

Matthew Anderson agrees that 'for all its copiousness and variety', the speculative work of eighteenth-century theorists on the sources of international peace made little or no impression on the contemporary practitioners of power politics. It is also interesting to note the views in 1800 of one of the former optimists, Friedrich von Gentz, who – once the utopian promises of the idealists of the French Revolution had turned to dust – bleakly concluded that war was both necessary and natural. He consoled himself with the hope that intense conflict itself might bring occasional spells of peace – if only because of the physical exhaustion of the belligerents and the temporary satisfaction of the most bloodthirsty and ambitious of spirits. It was idle to think that sovereign states would ever accept any form of supranational authority. As it happened Gentz went on to serve as secretary, adviser and intermediary when the leaders of the great powers met occasionally in congress to try to resolve or at least moderate their differences in the years immediately following 1814. In the end, as will be shown later, Gentz became as disillusioned with the practitioners as he had been by the theorists.[3]

Nevertheless the shock of the French Revolution and the duration and intensity of the wars from 1792 persuaded some of those in authority well before 1814 that some amelioration in the conduct of international affairs was essential. Thus the years 1797–9 found a British foreign minister, Lord Grenville, toying with ideas on some form of allied cooperation in peace as well as in war.[4]

Much more ambitious (it was an extravagant mixture of idealism and self-interest) were the proposals which the young Tsar Alexander I of Russia dispatched to the British government at the end of 1804. He aspired to a new Europe based on principles of justice and humanity, and made up of a league of liberal and constitutional states under the enlightened guidance of Russia and Britain. He looked for a strengthening of international law as one of several means to reduce the risk of war. The paper ranged over such diverse subjects as the rights of man to collective security.[5] Yet a careful reading of the proposals as a whole shows that material interests had not been forgotten. Russia, for instance, could be expected to benefit from the proposed creation of a new and loose German confederation, an innovation likely to prove susceptible to outside influences and to limit the roles of Austria and Prussia. Alexander made provision, too, for the collapse of the Ottoman Empire, with Russia and Britain having the decisive voice in its partition.

William Pitt, the British prime minister, responded warily to this remarkable document. He was naturally alarmed by the tsar's challenge to British use of their navy to stop and search neutral shipping in time of war (Russia had been involved in the leagues of Armed Neutrality against Britain in 1780 and again at the turn of the century). The British had long treasured this formidable instrument of economic warfare in order to weaken their enemies and manipulate neutrals. Pitt would make no concessions on this point. Nevertheless in his reply he too was moved by a desire to dampen down great-power rivalries as well as by the expediency of offering some positive thoughts of his own.

Thus he suggested that a concert of the powers, having reduced France to 'its former limits', should attempt to give solidity and permanence to a new post-war order or 'System'. This could best be achieved through a treaty binding the principal powers of Europe 'mutually to protect and support each other against any attempt to infringe' their rights and possessions. 'It should re-establish a general and comprehensive Public Law in Europe, and provide, as far as possible, for repressing future attempts to disturb the general Tranquillity, ...' Above all it was necessary to prevent a renewal of the calamities caused by the French Revolution.[6] Pitt hoped that Britain, Russia, Austria and Prussia might enter into 'a separate engagement ... [binding themselves jointly] to take an active part in preventing its being infringed ...' Ten years later Castlereagh as foreign secretary was to build on these ideas in his search for long-term securities against France, while Alexander carried his youthful idealism to even dizzier heights with his ideas for a Holy Alliance to unite the powers in the pursuit of a new Christian order. He saw himself as a great ruler, righting wrongs and dispensing justice on the largest possible stage.

Although – as the murder of Alexander's father and grandfather had demonstrated – no tsar was omnipotent, his powers to influence Russian policy were considerable. It mattered greatly, therefore, that he was so truly 'cosmopolitan in his attitudes and European in his frame of reference'. In his youth he had become somewhat superficially acquainted with the ideas of leading thinkers of the eighteenth-century 'Enlightenment' through his Swiss tutor, La Harpe. It is interesting to note during his reign that, of his several advisers on foreign affairs, only one was of Russian descent and even he was not representative of the 'Muscovite traditions of Mother Russia'.[7] Alexander, however, lacked consistency and application. The Russian writer, Alexander Herzen, thought him a 'Hamlet crowned'. Many of his actions bore the hallmark of a practitioner of *realpolitik* even as he spoke the language of an earnest reformer or a Christian visionary. He was both a Russian patriot (though never a chauvinist) and a cosmopolitan European: he was successively 'the tsar liberator' and the ally of Metternich against revolution. His contemporaries were often unsure how to handle him, but given the size of the Russian army he had to be taken seriously. Castlereagh and Metternich both resorted to a form of mental siege warfare to wring concessions from a man who liked to be loved. Yet for a leading nineteenth-century Russian historian, Sergei Soloviev, he remained 'the Agamemnon of tsars' – the peer of Peter and Catherine the Great.[8]

Certainly there can be no question but that, for all his changes of mood and mind, Alexander was a key player in many of the seminal events which followed the retreat of Napoleon from Moscow. He overruled those who wished to delay the Russian advance into Prussia in 1813. As early as February he was convinced that he was entrusted with 'a mission to save Europe and her oppressed people (including the French) from the tyranny of Napoleon'. Thus his personality, coupled with the exceptional circumstances which prevailed between 1792 and his death in 1825, ensured that imperial Russia was, in the view of Patricia Grimsted, more closely associated with general European developments than at any other time in its history. Alexander was 'genuinely devoted to a stable, peaceful, well-coordinated community of Europe'. At a practical level and in matters of detail, the tsar might have supplied less to this 'community' than Metternich or Castlereagh, yet his overall commitment to international cooperation and harmony made him an invaluable and indispensable ally.[9]

The degree to which Alexander was his own master can be seen in the private discontents of those of his advisers who did not share his eagerness to be so deeply involved in 'Europe'. They desired a more single-minded pursuit of Russian interests. They would have welcomed an escape from the constraints imposed by what Capodistrias, one of his advisers, described as 'this kind of directory', the Concert of Europe, and above all the great congresses at which the tsar's critics thought him all too susceptible to the insidious arguments and flattery of Metternich and the pertinacity of Castlereagh. Frustrated Russian advisers could even forget or belittle the occasions when the tsar did assert himself, as in the creation of the post-war satellite kingdom of Poland. This represented a considerable advance beyond the boundaries drawn at the time of the Polish partitions in the later eighteenth century.[10]

Alexander's stress on the duties of Christian monarchs could also be turned to practical advantage in Russia's quarrels with the Turks, just as a constitution softened the appearance rather than the reality of Russian rule over Poland. At the same time he was looking for a new order in Germany to help contain France without creating too powerful a presence on Russia's own borders. The tsar found he could capitalise on his personal influence over the impressionable and cautious Frederick William III of Prussia – a relationship which had begun in 1805 but which was greatly reinforced when Russian troops extended their pursuit of Napoleon into Germany in the winter of 1812–13. Allied with Russia by the Treaty of Kalish (January 1813), the Prussians were able to reverse the Treaty of Tilsit which had robbed them of nearly half their territory. At times the grateful king of Prussia became an almost uncritical ally.

Meanwhile it had been far from evident in 1813 that the great Napoleonic empire was about to collapse. Its opponents were by no means united, yet only by consistent and concerted efforts could they hope to defeat France. Metternich, the key figure in the Habsburg Empire, had yet to be persuaded that this was a desirable objective. For some time he clung to the hope that Bonaparte might be content to rule over a somewhat reduced but still formidable France. He had no wish to assist in the removal of one great empire only to have it replaced by another – that of Russia. Far better for a chastened Napoleon to survive so that a strong (but not too strong) France would play her part in maintaining a satisfactory equilibrium in Europe. Metternich was understandably wary of Russia, a power which in the last hundred years had made such striking advances at the expense of Sweden, Poland and the Ottoman Empire. Nor could he ignore the size of the Russian army and the evident determination of the tsar himself to bestride the European stage. Finally Metternich (given Austria's disastrous experiences in previous wars with France) had reason to explore other options before resorting to arms again. To his dismay he found that Napoleon was not interested in abandoning his imperial dream to assist in the creation of a genuine balance of power in Europe, or to reduce himself to the level of a cooperative son-in-law of the Austrian emperor.

Metternich did not give up all hope of a compromise peace even after Austria's entry into the war on 12 August 1813. Apart from his personal interest in a European equilibrium, he feared those elements in Germany which looked to the struggle of liberation against France as a step towards a more 'united Germany'. Here too Russian meddling at the expense of Austria had to be considered a probability. Metternich's own preference was for a central Germany made up of a number of small states led by princes who would be susceptible to Austrian influence and who would be less likely to threaten the conservative cause with ideas of constitutions and suchlike subversive novelties. The financial and military weaknesses of the Habsburg Empire compelled Vienna to see how far these could be offset by astute diplomacy. Its security would be enhanced the more its survival was seen to serve the interests of other powers or was at least deemed preferable to any other disposal of its territory. To the same end Metternich wished to create as perfect a balance as possible between the leading states of Europe and thus maximise Austria's value as an ally, mediator or possible opponent. But still Napoleon would not compromise, despite heavy defeats and huge losses.

This worked to the advantage of the British, whose interests had not much concerned Metternich in 1813. Napoleon's persistence and skill began to make the allies more sensitive to their demands. The continuing war forced the continental powers to respect Britain as a land as well as a naval, trading and financial power. She became more than the great provider of subsidies to the usually hard-up continental powers. Her position was further improved in the winter of 1813–14 when an army under the Duke of Wellington invaded south-west France from Spain, while the British foreign secretary travelled to the continent to argue the British case in person with the other allied leaders. Indeed Metternich was soon welcoming Castlereagh's presence not only to help combat Napoleon, but also – he hoped – to act as another restraint on the unpredictable tsar. Gentz recorded on 5 February that 'the intimate contact that seems to have been established between the two ministers is, for all present and future relations, one of the most auspicious and reassuring events for the great common interests of Europe'.

Castlereagh, for his part, was looking beyond the defeat of Napoleon. He believed that Britain was in desperate need of a long period of peace, and to this end he was eager to cultivate durable personal ties with the leaders of the other powers. From London in September 1813 he had urged the conclusion of a comprehensive alliance both to accomplish the defeat of France and to provide lasting mutual security for the future. Nor was his as yet so isolated a voice on this subject in Britain as it was to become later. Lord Grenville (whose ideas as Pitt's foreign minister have already been noted) argued in the House of Lords on 4 November 1813 that there was 'neither safety nor peace for England ... [to be found] but with the safety and peace of Europe'.

Any British enthusiasm for enduring continental commitments, however, was bound to be precarious. To understand why so much survived and was perpetuated for some years after 1814 one must look in particular to the personal role and influence of Castlereagh. Another person in his place might have shown less stamina, determination and patience abroad, or been less resistant to critics in the cabinet at home. Nor was it long before strident opponents appeared in Parliament as the usual post-war upsurge of insularity took effect. Many were strongly averse to association with the continental autocracies (though this line of argument was also a means of demonstrating progressive credentials at home). In practice, however, Castlereagh was largely sheltered from effective pressure by the interest of the majority of MPs in the survival of the Liverpool cabinet. They feared that any alternative ministry (one made up of Whigs and Radicals) would follow insufficiently conservative and orthodox policies at home. As long as Castlereagh was deemed 'safe' in home affairs (as well as serving as the cabinet's indispensable spokesman in the Commons), many were prepared to allow him some discretion in Europe.

In the course of a journey from Frankfurt to Basle early in 1814 Castlereagh outlined his hopes to an aide. He believed that the alliance could achieve lasting success only if there developed

> ... an habitual confidential and free intercourse between the Ministers of the Great Powers, *as a body*; and that many pretensions might be modified, asperities removed, and causes of irritation anticipated and met, by bringing the respective parties into unrestricted communications common to them all, and embracing in confidential and united discussions all the great points in which they were severally interested.[11]

Over the next eight years personal ties – even when maintained only by letter – were to remain for Castlereagh one of the essential means to sustain a measure of cooperation with continental statesmen – notably with Metternich and Alexander.

With Metternich, early in 1814, he soon established a good working relationship. The tsar was less malleable until a military setback late in February temporarily dented his confidence. This helped to open the way to the Treaty of Chaumont of 9 March. Under this instrument the allies agreed to act together for no less than 20 years after the defeat of Napoleon to defend Europe and themselves against any further French challenge. Articles V and XVI more vaguely promised that they would strive to secure the 'equilibrium of Europe' and to 'concert together ... as to the means best adapted to guarantee ... the continuance of peace'. This was also a plain signal that the great powers intended to elevate themselves above the lesser states such as Spain or Sweden. If inequality was no new thing between the European states, the long and costly wars since 1792 had demonstrated the huge gap that separated the strongest from the medium sized states. Polite fictions and etiquette could no longer hide 'the realities of unequal might'.[12]

Meanwhile even Napoleon's genius could not offset the great superiority of force deployed by the allies. The tsar himself was present in the drive on Paris at the end of March. His personal sense of mission was never stronger, and he had at his disposal the largest army in Europe. Fortunately for Metternich and Castlereagh, he proved receptive to the advice of one of the great survivors in French politics, the astute if devious Talleyrand. He argued that the only realistic solution in France was the restoration of the Bourbon dynasty – tempered by a constitution. Nevertheless the tsar continued to excite alarm with his Polish contacts, and in other ways aroused suspicion as to his ultimate objectives.[13] The Austrians and some Prussians, each with Polish subjects of their own, nervously speculated as to what unpleasant shocks Alexander might have in store for them. Here was more evidence of the hollowness of much of the talk of allied solidarity.

### In Search of a New Equilibrium, 1814–15

Alexander I was naturally not unique in his pursuit of special interests. The crucial question in 1814–15 was whether the great powers were sufficiently disposed to qualify their self-interest and take a broader view of the problems facing Europe. Clausewitz, later to make his name with his famous study, *On War,* was shocked by the determination shown by some Prussians to impose a punitive peace on France. He asked, 'Should we not regard ourselves as the instruments of Providence, which gave us a victory so that we should exercise eternal justice?' This is all the more interesting since Clausewitz counted himself a realist, contending that 'No reading is more necessary than the writing of Machiavelli. Those who pretend to be revolted by his principles are nothing but dandies who take humanist views.'

Yet Clausewitz perhaps also recalled his hero's advice that if an enemy could not be crushed one should try conciliation? He interestingly showed more insight into the thinking of the British than the banished Napoleon who, from St Helena, later expressed his bewilderment over the leniency shown toward the vanquished in the peace settlement. The ex-emperor could explain this only by dismissing the British ministers as mediocrities. Clausewitz, however, expected the latter to play the better role 'because they do not seem to have come here with a passion for revenge ... but rather like a master who wishes to discipline with proved coldness and immaculate purity'.[14] Of course the British, he might have added, had (apart from the royal interest in Hanover) no direct territorial connection with the continent and no wish for any. Yet their self-interest demanded as genuine a balance of power as could be secured, plus the minimising of the presence or influence of great powers in regions such as the Low Countries or the Iberian states which threatened Britain's own security or her trade routes. The continental powers might also have territorial interests and pretensions which were in conflict with the concept of a true or just 'equilibrium in Europe'. Thus the best that could be expected of the rulers of such states would be a recognition that they too had an interest in ensuring that none of their number should attain an intolerable level of eminence and influence.

Other British gains from the war included unparalleled colonial and trading advantages outside Europe, and a reluctant acceptance by the allies of the claims of the Royal Navy to exercise a 'right of search' of neutral shipping in time of war. Fortunately British wishes concerning the distribution of territory in Europe were often broadly compatible with those of the other powers. Thus Austria handed over her share of the Low Countries to the Dutch for additional possessions and influence in northern Italy. Both steps were also designed to provide better security against any future French aggression.

The fate of the region bordering the west bank of the Rhine took longer to determine, but a somewhat hesitant Prussia finally accepted the Rhenish provinces, much to the satisfaction of the British who welcomed this buttressing of the barrier on France's north-eastern border. On the other hand France was allowed to retain the frontiers of 1792, while Prussia's allies refused to countenance her demand for an indemnity. In the end the victors agreed to ask no more of France than seemed necessary for their own security. They also hoped that a lenient peace might reconcile Frenchmen to the return of the Bourbons who, they hoped, would be committed to stability at home and abroad. Some hints were even dropped that a chastened France might be readmitted to the inner circle of European states. Indeed so ostentatious had been the generosity of the tsar that Castlereagh feared that he was looking to make an ally of France. As it happened France was initially kept at arm's length as the allies in the autumn of 1814 resumed the contentious business of devising an overall peace settlement. France was, however, suddenly welcomed as an ally by Austria and Britain in their troublesome dispute with Prussia and Russia over the fate of Napoleon's former ally, Saxony.

More was at stake in this instance than mere territory. This was the climax to a long struggle over the fate of Poland – the largest part of which was coveted by Russia. The tsar sought to woo and compensate Prussia with the award of all of Saxony. The dismay of Austria and Britain at so massive an upset to the eastern balance of power at the expense of the Habsburgs found an echo or two even among the Prussians themselves. Some shared Metternich's desire to avoid yet more gains by an over-mighty Russia led by a wayward tsar. But hopes in October that the two German powers might sink their differences and combine with Britain and Austria to frustrate Alexander were thwarted by the loyalty of the king of Prussia to the ruler who had reunited his realm in 1813. This was an occasion when personal royal ties were of prime importance. The king would not desert his Russian saviour.

The treaty of alliance signed by Britain, Austria and France on 3 January 1815 against Prussia and Russia was never likely to lead to war, yet the episode highlights the extent of allied competitiveness barely six months after the overthrow of Napoleon. Castlereagh had vainly appealed in person to the tsar to make concessions over Poland for the good of Europe. But in this war of words and appeals to sentiment, the Russians enjoyed a military hold over the disputed territory as decisive as anything that was to be enjoyed by Stalin in 1945. They could remark that with such advantages '*on ne négocie beaucoup*'. If they finally relented a little, it was mainly at the expense of the Prussians who had to surrender part of Saxony. Meanwhile the Prussians, though without as yet fully appreciating its significance, were becoming the leading German power on the Rhine.[15]

The balance that was emerging between the powers by the beginning of 1815 was therefore – whatever the professions of interest in an equilibrium – by no means the product of mathematical formulae or great principles. The appetites displayed by each were as evident as those of the Walrus and Carpenter, whatever tears were shed in the course of the share-out. The Germanic powers remained the weakest of the five, despite the recent territorial adjustments. Prussia had to look to Russia or Austria for support. If the Austrian empire looked impressive on the map of Europe, it also bore more responsibilities than it could easily handle. It is true that France would need time to recover her strength and confidence, while her leaders needed to earn the respect and trust of other powers. But in time they could draw hope from the signs of allied divisions, and expect to re-enter the premier league – that is, along with Britain and Russia.

The pre-eminence of the last two inevitably excited some fear and jealousy among the less favoured powers. Yet it was also evident that neither was a rounded 'superpower'. Russia relied primarily on her army, which in turn imposed a heavy burden on a relatively backward economy. In contrast Britain's leading assets were economic and maritime. Each power also had major interests outside Europe which could entail some diversion of their energies. Gentz, however, was one of those who was particularly fearful of Russia. In 1815 he thought her virtually invulnerable and well placed to advance at the expense of others. If she overthrew the Ottoman Empire, Austria herself could soon be at risk. Metternich described the Ottoman Empire (for all its faults and weaknesses) as 'one of the most essential counterweights in the general equilibrium of Europe'.[16] As for the British, while their army was soon in decline and they had no desire for territory in Europe, many – especially in France – complained of their 'tyranny' at sea, their ruthless commercialism, not to mention their overweening belief in their own moral and material superiority.

Meanwhile there was still one scene in the final act of the Napoleonic drama to be played out. The emperor escaped from Elba and for 'One Hundred Days' in the spring and early summer of 1815 France again threatened the stability of Europe. The allies, however, reacted with surprising vigour, burying their differences and uniting to defend the new if flawed settlement. British and Prussian armies narrowly – but decisively – prevailed at Waterloo, thus finally bringing to an end the extraordinary career of Bonaparte. In return Waterloo gave Britain considerable political influence at a decisive moment. Castlereagh and Wellington were able with the support of Metternich and Alexander – and against Prussian protests – to negotiate a second relatively lenient peace with France. Castlereagh bluntly warned cabinet critics at home: '... it is not our business to collect trophies, but to try to bring the world back to peaceful habits'. His fears of future trouble from Russia similarly led him to suggest that France might yet become 'a useful rather than a dangerous member of the European system'.

This reference to 'the system' highlights Castlereagh's belief that the security and stability of Europe lay in the degree to which each power had a vested interest in the status quo, even if it fell far short of an exact (and unattainable) equilibrium. Thus France was merely required to withdraw roughly to her 1790 frontiers, pay an indemnity, and accept an army of occupation. E. J. Hobsbawm, not a scholar readily inclined to give credit to aristocratic diplomats, comments that while the Vienna Settlement was 'no more just or moral than any other', it was also 'realistic and sensible', and it inaugurated a period of skilful international statecraft.[17]

Castlereagh and Metternich did their best to capitalise further on Napoleon's 'Hundred Days'. The experience, for instance, had been a reminder that with only a few successes Bonaparte might have unleashed a horde of troublemakers in Europe. The British and Austrian ministers hastened to strengthen the security arrangements provided by the Treaty of Chaumont. The tsar also came forward with the Holy Alliance whereby he hoped to bind all the monarchs in a great Christian union. At one point during the Congress of Vienna he was driven to protest, 'There is always too much diplomacy around, and I don't like hypocrisy.' Since January 1815 he had been 'inspired by a curious religious ecstasy'. After the defeat of Napoleon he tended to leave the detail of conventional politics to his various advisers while he concentrated upon higher things.

One of these men, Czartoryski, hoped that tsar's belief in his holy mission might give rise to more action in defence of justice and right. But Alexander lacked the energy and ambition to become 'a sort of arbiter of the civilized world' or of 'justice and right in European politics'.[18] Instead he was content to draft the Holy Alliance with its vague references to 'Justice, Christian Charity and Peace' and royal duties. Only the king of Prussia took this alliance seriously. Metternich, though scornfully critical in private, allowed his own emperor to sign: one had to humour a man with one million soldiers at his beck and call. The British politely made their excuses. At the same time the Holy Alliance of 20 September 1815 was further evidence of the tsar's commitment to some sort of European order or 'system'.

The foreign ministers, meanwhile, were at work on the Quadruple Alliance as a more substantial basis for continuing cooperation by the victors. Gentz as secretary to the Congress was a key figure in its creation.[19] He was an adviser and mediator; 'the statesman without a country' according to his biographer. He was totally involved – yet also at times strangely detached. In 1814 he had listened unmoved as the great figures had emphasized the nobility of their aims. Metternich and his ilk he classified as mediocrities intent upon grabbing all they could. Their ambitions, however, were tempered to some extent by the realisation that self-preservation demanded some measure of restraint and cooperation. Gentz himself, having long since cast aside his youthful idealism, believed that a power equilibrium gave the best promise of peace. In 1806 he had even put forward an ingenious mechanistic version; 'a system of *counterpoise*' based upon 'a constant alternate vacillation in the scales of the balance, which, from the application of *counter-weights*, is prevented from ever passing certain limits'.[20] The real world, however, could not be described in such mechanical terms. In his later years Gentz came to rely more and more on working with things as they were rather than engaging in further exercises in political engineering.

Even so he was still anxious to identify dangers before they arose. Gentz feared, for instance, that a united Germany might prove too big for the health of Europe. For the same reason Wilhelm von Humboldt was content with a German confederation, troubled though he was by many flaws in the Vienna Settlement which only some future war might rectify. His wife was yet more pessimistic.[21] For Gentz, however, the continent's stability rested on the survival of the Habsburg Empire. Here was the European power par excellence with its vested interest in the cooperation of all conservative powers. He thought Britain and Russia less predictable, the one being likely to involve herself too little and the other too much in European affairs. Even so, some of his youthful interest in the reform of the management of international affairs was reawakened when Talleyrand professed an interest in a 'European community of states' which would authorise changes to the map of Europe. The Frenchman did add the shrewd reservation that for his country to be a 'loyal' European there would first have to be a fair distribution of power. Gentz himself briefly hoped that such a community would observe binding laws. Meanwhile in the everyday world he continued to serve as the secretary of Europe at subsequent conferences, and to mediate and advise. But disillusionment got the better of him in the end. By 1827 he felt he had dedicated his life to a lost cause, citing the current Greek crisis as proof that no power was prepared to put the good of Europe first.[22]

Back in 1815 the powers had toyed briefly with the idea of a general guarantee of all Europe against aggression. Indeed, the indefatigable Gentz drafted a declaration on these lines. Discussion, however, only excited alarm over the extent of the responsibilities and restrictions which the powers would be undertaking. Castlereagh was soon obliged to reassure a suspicious British Parliament that the draft declaration was not an official document. The other powers were becoming equally reserved, and in the end cooperation was based on the Quadruple Alliance (November 1815). This was to uphold the second Peace of Paris and to exclude Napoleon or any Bonaparte from the French throne. Article VI also provided for periodic conferences of the powers.

> [The powers would meet] ... for the purpose of consulting upon their common interests, and for the consideration of measures which at each of these periods shall be considered the most salutary for the repose and prosperity of Nations, and for the maintenance of the Peace of Europe.

Yet no matter how interesting an innovation in European diplomacy this might seem, its substance and shape were at any one time entirely dependent on the wishes and even the whims of the individual powers and their ministers. The word 'periodic' hinted at a degree of regularity which it never attained. In practice what ensued was far from an 'established diplomatic arrangement', being no more than an option which happened to be exercised several times over the next nine years.[23] Congresses were also held in Paris (1856) and Berlin (1878). Meanwhile the Concert of Europe found further expression in sundry lesser conferences. Thus, for all its mutability, it proved at least an intermittent feature of European diplomacy until 1913. As for the Congress System, this was, as Roy Bridge notes, not the precursor of the League of Nations but of summit conferences (essentially ad hoc, not regular occurrences).[24]

## The Congress System at Work

There were difficulties from the outset. Thus on the specific and vital question of the future governance of France, Castlereagh would (or could) agree to no more than that the allies should 'concert among themselves ... the measures which they may judge necessary' against revolutionary aggression. The British could not commit themselves to an alliance for all seasons. Their reviving detachment from the continent was soon evident, coupled with the fear that Russia and Austria would be only too predisposed to interfere in the internal affairs of other states. Continental rulers were alarmed not only by the effects of the French Revolution and Napoleon upon the lives and thinking of many of their subjects, but also by the conse- quences of the reforms which they themselves had been compelled to introduce in order to boost the power and efficiency of their own societies in the struggle against Napoleonic France. Gentz was one of those who wondered what would happen to all this popular energy once victory had been achieved. Von Humboldt's politically-minded wife argued that the people were not being treated as they deserved. The spirit of the age would ultimately prevail.[25]

British interest, meanwhile, was concentrated upon international stability and a power 'equilibrium' rather than the suppression of revolutionaries wherever they might appear. British ministers in any case could not afford to be seen to be identifying too eagerly with the autocrats in such circumstances (whereas their domestic critics could rejoice over anything which could be described as a popular rising – as in Spain in 1820). The cabinet was soon reminding Castlereagh that only the exceptional events since 1789 had enabled them to accept the treaty as it was. Admittedly it was approved in Parliament by 240 to 77 votes, yet critics of British association with autocracy were already active and would become more so in the near future. Greville summed up the complaints against Castlereagh after his suicide in 1822: 'The result of his policy is this, that we are mixed up in the affairs of the Continent in a manner which we never had before, …'. Furthermore his policy had countenanced the evil doings of the Holy Alliance.[26]

This was, of course, a party political judgement which did not do justice to the subtlety of Castlereagh's diplomacy. He was fully aware of the limitations of the Concert, and between 1815 and 1822 he had cause to qualify his connections with his so-called allies. Yet he con- tinued to believe that Britain's interest in peace and stability in Europe could best be upheld by working through the Concert or by the cultivation of good relations with individual states and ministers. On many questions he and Metternich had much in common, espe- cially in keeping a wary eye on Russia and France lest they should become too assertive. This did not mean that Castlereagh could always give backing to Metternich, as when the latter tried to sup- press every revolution or constitutional change in Europe.[27] On the other hand one must not make too much of the political divide between Britain (with its unreformed parliament) and the European autocrats. In matters of great-power rivalry or the balance of power, the ideological divide was easily bridged – as Canning and Palmerston were subsequently to demonstrate.

For the first few years following 1815 France naturally continued to absorb much of the attention of the powers. Even the restored Bourbons were far from satisfied with the terms of the Vienna Settlement. For the time being, however, France was unable to take positive action without at least one ally, a fact which was not lost on the Russian ambassador in Paris or the influential Capodistrias in St Petersburg. Indeed the latter was critical of the existing alignment of the powers. He complained of 'this kind of directory of four powers' which he feared gave too much influence to Britain and Austria to the detriment of Russia as well as France. Various Russian interests in Europe, the Mediterranean and the Near East (and even further afield) conflicted with those of either Austria or Britain – or in some cases with both. On many issues France and Russia seemed natural partners. Metternich and Castlereagh responded by making the most of their personal links with the tsar. For all his mutability, he was the ultimate authority in Russia. An Austrian diplomat reported in 1818 that the tsar was determined to be the peacemaker of Europe – and to be acknowledged as such.[28]

Alexander himself showed some early interest in the reinstatement of France as a full member of the exclusive great-power club, an objective he successfully pursued at the Congress of Aix-la-Chapelle in 1818. He was even entertaining yet more ambitious ideas for a 'general coalition' of the allies. This was to be guided by 'regulations for all contingencies' to safeguard the Vienna Settlement. He talked of general moral guarantees and favoured the creation of an international army and a maritime league. Metternich found all these ideas highly disturbing. He feared this 'terrible Empereur Alexander' whose moralising, proselytising and intrigues, it seemed, were all part of a grand yet insidious design to enable Russia to extend her influence by invoking her responsibilities as a Christian and European power.[29] Fortunately for him the tsar was usually content with an acknowledgement of the spirit of his proposals. He was, however, able to insist that France should be invited to future conferences summoned under Article VI of the Quadruple Alliance.

Meanwhile the British set out to sabotage Russian proposals for joint action against the slave trade, the Barbary 'pirates' and the revolutions in Spain's South America colonies. In each case it was suspected that such proposals were a cover for Russian ambitions to make gains at the expense of British naval and commercial interests. The British were particularly sensitive on the subject of Latin America – an area of growing commercial possibilities as Spanish colonial rule continued to collapse. At Aix Castlereagh submitted no fewer than 43 objections and questions in reply to calls for allied intervention in that continent. When these failed to silence the Russian ministers, he appealed directly to the tsar. In the end it was only by playing on Alexander's malleability that he was able to so dilute the offer of allied mediation between Spain and her American rebels that it was promptly declined in Madrid. In many ways, of course, British interests were already being secured by naval and commercial power, with the most serious competition coming in fact from the United States. Yet it was still important to put the diplomatic record straight so that the fate of Spanish America was indisputably left in the hands of a weak Spain, the rebel colonists, Britain and (less fortunately) the United States given its commercial and maritime potential.

In general Alexander seemed content to find satisfaction in the praise lavished upon him as a great peacemaker and protector of the weak. Gentz concluded from first-hand experience that despite the tsar's absolute power at home, 'it is probable that he is more eager to acquire a reputation for goodness than merely to win glory'. He was also impressed by Alexander's loyalty to the Quadruple Alliance, and (with a hint of his own earlier idealism) rated him 'the inspiration, the hero' of the Congress. Castlereagh and Metternich, fully alive to Alexander's state of mind, stressed 'moral solidarity', and contrived to entrap him in the silken threads of his own high principles. Metternich, too, was striving to neutralise the influence of Capodistrias who took a disturbingly strong if somewhat ill-defined interest in nationalism and constitutionalism within a 'visionary' new international order.[30]

A year later Metternich was able to follow up his successes at Aix by persuading the king of Prussia to cooperate with Austria in the defence of the conservative order in Germany. Castlereagh secretly informed Metternich that 'we are always pleased to see evil germs destroyed without the power to give our approbation openly'. Yet he also urged the Austrian minister not to interfere too openly or too often in the internal affairs of the south German states. The British for their part lost no time (early in 1820) in countering a French bid for influence in Spain following a military revolt in that country. A revolution in Naples naturally alarmed Metternich not only on its own account, but also because it might provide both Russia and France with opportunities for mischievous intervention. He wanted no more than the moral support and approval of other powers to enable Austria to act as the sole defender of the conservative order in Italy. This claim was acceptable to Britain, but less so to France and Russia.

In the end the persistence of Paris and St Petersburg was rewarded by agreement that the problems of Italy should be discussed at a congress – not the mere conference of ambassadors in Vienna preferred by Metternich and which he might have expected to dominate. Castlereagh suspected that the tsar wished to transform the alliance into a 'general government of Europe' against all revolutionary developments. This was true up to a point, although Alexander for a time also hoped to use the Congress of Troppau (at the end of 1820) as a forum from which he could dispense justice on behalf of the oppressed. Meanwhile Metternich suffered from the absence of Castlereagh who (given the mood in Britain) could do no more than send secret notes of sympathy to the Austrian minister.

In any case Castlereagh for various reasons was beginning to take a less sanguine view of congress diplomacy in contrast to his earlier description of it as 'a new discovery in the European Government, at once extinguishing the cobwebs with which diplomacy obscures the horizon ... and giving the counsels of the Great Powers the efficiency and almost the simplicity of a single State'. Even at the Congress of Aix-la-Chapelle he had to bow to cabinet opinion in London and argue that future assemblages should be 'special, namely that they shall arise out of the occasion and be agreed upon by all the five Courts at the time; in fact, no Power can be considered as pledged a priori to any meeting whatever'.[31] Later, in his famous State Paper of May 1820 he denied that the revolt in Spain posed any threat outside that country's borders. He also warned his allies that the Quadruple Alliance had never been created to serve as 'an union for the government of the world or for the superintendence of the internal affairs of other States'. A conference, 'from the necessarily limited powers of the individuals composing it, must ever be better fitted to execute a purpose already decided upon than to frame a course of policy under delicate and difficult circumstances'.

Thus at Troppau (and later at Laibach) Metternich was left to wage a lonely (though ultimately successful) campaign to protect Austrian interests in Italy against Russia and France. It is true that Capodistrias managed to insist that some form of great-power mediation should precede any forceful intervention in Naples by Austria. He also invoked the interest of 'Europe' in the stability of that particular region. In Britain, however, liberal opinion was mainly excited by and preoccupied with the assertion in the Troppau Protocol of 19 November 1820 that the Alliance was entitled to act against revolutions.

In the interval before the great men reassembled at Laibach in 1821 Metternich did his best to undo what Capodistrias had won at Troppau. He was greatly helped by a regimental mutiny in St Petersburg in November 1820 which left the tsar much less interested in Christian paternalism than in the authority of monarchs. The Neapolitan rebels themselves helped to make the Congress of Laibach almost a formality by their refusal to depart in any particular from the radical constitution of 1812. This left the Austrians free to suppress revolution in Italy. Finally news of a Greek revolt against the Turks reached Laibach in April 1821, a report that was immediately used by Metternich as further proof to the tsar that Paris was the chief of several breeding grounds of revolution around Europe. By the end of the congress the French were totally isolated.[32]

In all of this one cannot but fail to be impressed by the fragility and impermanence of the unity of the powers. Metternich still had reason to fear that the Russians would continue to exploit future revolutionary outbreaks to justify further interventions where they were not wanted. Much as he might speak of Castlereagh as his 'second self', he also thought the British minister too selective in his policies towards Europe. He complained of the inveterate egoism of the islanders when he was denied overt diplomatic support in his struggle against revolutionaries. As it was, Castlereagh's discreet backing of Austria against rebels had more to do with the balance of power and the containment of France and Russia than his fears of revolution per se, just as his opposition to foreign intervention against revolution in Spain was designed to keep Iberia free from the influence of other powers.

Again he reiterated the need for a great-power 'equilibrium'. Britain, he declared, could not act upon 'abstract and speculative principles of precaution'. She would, however, be found in her place when 'actual danger' menaced the 'system of Europe'. His choice of words is interesting. By the 'system of Europe' he meant primarily the settlement and the relationship between the victors which had been created at Vienna. As for the 'equilibrium', this included the continued separation of Russia and France to ensure that Britain and Austria retained the diplomatic initiative. Yet it was often as much as he could do to give Metternich a measure of encouragement and backing in the face of British insularity and passionate dislike of the autocratic powers.

Metternich himself was soon running into trouble as French interest mounted in Spanish affairs. Similarly in the Near East the Greek rising against the Turks was leading to such widespread bloodshed (including the hanging of the Greek patriarch in Constantinople by the Turks) that the struggle seemed bound sooner or later to bring conflict between the Ottoman Empire and Russia. Clearly there were limits to what could be achieved by the diplomatic ingenuity of Metternich and Castlereagh. Nevertheless the two men were able to meet in Hanover in October 1821. If little of substance was achieved, each was reassured by the degree to which they were of one mind on key issues. Metternich in particular stressed the value of a face-to-face encounter as opposed to the slow business of communicating by letter. Their understanding was especially important when the Russians early in 1822 began to seek Austrian support against the Turks. Metternich, anxious to prevent major changes in the Near East, did his best to stall for time.

His position, however, was much weakened by Castlereagh's suicide in August 1822. It is true that Wellington attended the Congress of Verona, but he lacked his former colleague's knowledge and creativity as a statesman. Castlereagh himself had been hoping to draw the powers together in support of limited concessions to the Greeks, including 'the creation of a qualified Greek Government'. He was also hoping for agreement that the recognition of the former Spanish colonies was by now merely a matter of timing and method rather than of principle. Progress might have been possible on both issues. It seems, however, that the revolution within Spain might have defeated even his ingenuity. The French were becoming more anxious to restore the old order in Madrid, a possibility which soon prompted the offer of a Russian army from Alexander I. This provided Paris with further evidence of the disunity of the other powers, and the first major independent French move since 1815 quickly followed. In 1823 an army restored the authority of the king of Spain.

What repeatedly emerges from any study of the congresses between 1814 and 1822 is the importance of special circumstances and personal inclinations and experiences. The Congress System revolved in particular around three personalities: Alexander I, Metternich and Castlereagh. Of the three, Metternich was the most dependent on allies given the special problems faced by the Habsburg Empire. Both the British and Russians could have chosen to be more detached, but thanks to Alexander and Castlereagh they did not. For Alexander the congresses enabled him to act out the beneficent and benevolent tsar in accordance with God's will. He could satisfy his desire to be at the heart of Europe, and still promote Russian interests. Castlereagh's concerns were essentially practical, though once or twice he too spoke in almost visionary terms of what might be done. More realistically he saw that Britain, as a maritime, imperial and commercial power, required a stable equilibrium to minimise any distractions that might emanate from the continent. He found that diplomacy for a time bought much influence at relatively little cost to Britain. His loyalty to the Quadruple Alliance also – perhaps – did something to offset the ill-feeling aroused in Europe by Britain's economic dynamism and lordly domination of the seas.

George Canning, who succeeded Castlereagh as British foreign secretary in 1822, was briefly content to follow existing policies towards Greece and Latin America. But the new minister did not share his predecessor's enthusiasm for personal meetings or his faith in the Alliance. He detested Metternich (which the Austrian fully reciprocated) and he disliked congresses in principle. At home his position was weaker than that of his predecessor given his strained relations with the king and some cabinet ministers. From political need as well as personal inclination he was soon cultivating support in and among the public by ostentatiously playing the 'English' card and distancing himself from the autocratic powers. In an earlier Commons debate (on 11 July 1820) – when Castlereagh had provocatively claimed that 'the honour of every individual power who was a party to that holy alliance ... was untainted' – Canning had emphasised his support for 'the extension of liberty and liberal institutions throughout the world'. Not surprisingly the absolutists viewed Canning with suspicion, while Metternich felt obliged to turn to Russia even if that power seemed likely to go its own way in the Near East – just as the French were about to do in Spain.[33]

F. H. Hinsley states that the 'impressive thing about the behaviour of the Powers after 1815 is that they were prepared as they had never previously been prepared, to waive their individual interests in pursuit of an international system'.[34] There is some truth in this, but what is also evident is just how often they tried to use the international system to further their separate interests. Each compromise was usually a pretty fair reflection of the realities of power. If the conduct of any leading participant was modified, it was usually that of Alexander I. Restraint owed most to memories of the delibilitating effects of an era of war and revolution and fears that the same might easily return. Any moderately intelligent statesman appreciated that this was a time for diplomacy, not ambition, honour or gallantry.

# 2

## COMPETITION SHORT OF WAR

'...every nation for itself and God for us all'. (George Canning)

### The Concert in Abeyance

Something of the old Anglo–Austrian alignment survived to exert a degree of restraint over the Russians in their differences with the Turks until the spring of 1823. But thereafter Canning stood apart, especially when the other four powers held meetings in St Petersburg in 1824–5 to discuss the Near East. He had nothing to fear: the talks hardened rather than eased differences. As the Concert fragmented Canning contentedly remarked that international politics were 'getting back to a wholesome state again'. Yet by and large he had tended to exaggerate the importance of the Congress System. References to the 'one and indivisible alliance' with its 'predominating areopagatical spirit' suggest much greater unity than had actually existed since 1814.

Furthermore, despite Metternich's complaint that he had 'shaken everything and destroyed much', Canning had been one of the lesser causes of the ending of the Congress era. This was mainly brought about by the other powers (especially France and Russia), with Metternich himself soon being driven to admit that a congress could serve no useful purpose. At best an 'accord' could be achieved only by easy stages through 'simple conferences'. Such a process promised to achieve little for the time being. Metternich also had to recognise the strains imposed on Austria's finances by her recent (and limited) military intervention in Naples in 1821. As before his best assets were the usefulness of Austria in the power balance, the suspicion of France and fear of revolution.

Canning, meanwhile, happily noted that there had been a return to 'every nation for itself and God for us all'. Admittedly the British had to look on in 1823 while a French army suppressed the revolutionary movement in Spain. France could now field about a quarter of a million troops, while her navy had sufficiently recuperated to provoke some British attention. But ministers in Paris were soon discovering that their so-called 'Russian policy' had largely exhausted its possibilities. Alexander remained as determined to uphold the Vienna Settlement as he was to see revolutions suppressed. The 1815 settlement, however, did not extend to the Ottoman Empire, and shortly before his death in 1825 the tsar was beginning to concentrate troops on the Turkish border and to show some interest in new contacts with Britain.[1] His successor, Nicholas I, a less sensitive and less complicated man (at least until his last years), was definitely in no mood to be advised and therefore obstructed by Metternich. The latter was rather put out (by November 1826) to find that all his personal attempts to woo the new tsar had failed. He was dismayed to find that Nicholas entertained 'a certain dislike towards me'.[2] In fact the new tsar was beginning to listen to siren voices in London where Canning was beginning to discover the limitations of the slogan 'every nation for itself'.

It is true that the British had found it easy enough to protect their Portuguese interests with the dispatch of a few troops and warships to Lisbon during a short-lived crisis in 1826. Similarly, in so far as the former American colonies of Spain had needed foreign support in the mid-1820s to confirm their independence, British sea and economic power had largely sufficed. On the other hand Canning's boast that his policies in Spanish America had brought the New World into being to redress the balance in the Old lacked substance. If any balance had been improved, it had been British commercial gains at the expense of the United States. In contrast the struggle in Greece seemed no nearer a solution, while the risk of escalation was enhanced by Russia's own disputes with the Turks.

Canning appreciated that these were problems which Britain could not solve unilaterally. Fortunately he had acquired a valuable ally in the person of the influential Dorothea Lieven, wife to the Russian ambassador in London. She greatly admired his intelligence and energy. Already in the summer of 1825 the Lievens had played upon Alexander I's doubts as to the value of Metternich as a friend, while pressing him to consider the merits of an approach to Britain. Matters moved faster under Nicholas I who was prepared to overlook Canning's contribution to the spread of republicanism in Latin America (indeed Canning himself would have preferred constitutional monarchies). By April 1826 relations had sufficiently improved for Britain and Russia to agree to mediate between the Turks and Greeks by proposing the establishment of an autonomous vassal state within the Ottoman Empire. Failure would leave them (singly or jointly) free to establish an independent Greek state. Canning had clinched the deal through Nesselrode – now solely responsible for the execution of Russian foreign policy, and one whom Metternich had recently and complacently described as 'a child at my feet'.[3]

The Turks felt it wise to make some concessions. The ensuing Convention of Akkerman (October 1826), however, dealt only with Russia's grievances, not Greece. Britain and Russia, reinforced by France, therefore proceeded to negotiate the Treaty of London of July 1827. Only a show of force, it seemed, would give credibility to their professed determination to end the fighting in the Morea. A joint naval squadron under a British admiral was assembled in Greek waters, Canning seeing joint action as the best way to restrain the Russians. Unfortunately what began as an interesting attempt at concerted action reached an unintended climax at the battle of Navarino (20 October 1827) – a battle which also soon produced a split among the three allies. The Turks remained defiant, and denounced the Convention of Akkerman. War with Russia followed in April 1828. In London there was considerable uncertainty and division, Canning himself having died shortly before Navarino. All the powers were now either adrift or going their separate ways.

At least there had been some movement in Vienna. Once Metternich recognised that Russia was prepared to fight, he began to accept the need for some modest changes in the Near East. But the fear was now growing in Vienna (and also in London) that a general partition of the Ottoman Empire might be unavoidable. This particularly alarmed those Austrians who believed that the empire was not strong enough to use force in the event of a general scramble for territory. Nor could Austria turn her back on her interests in Italy and Germany. The French opportunistically landed troops to remove the

Turks and their allies from the Morea, but declined a British proposal to impress the Russians with a joint show of naval strength in Besika Bay at the mouth of the Dardanelles. Nevertheless, even by itself, the British fleet was a force to be reckoned with – not least in the Black Sea – in the event of war.

Wellington (the British prime minister from January 1828) began to talk with more than a hint of desperation of the creation of a new Greek empire to replace that of the Ottomans. The latter he believed to have 'gone, in fact; and the tranquillity of the world ... along with it'. Indeed the French in September 1829 prepared to take soundings in St Petersburg in anticipation of the possible disintegration of the Turkish Empire. It was proposed in the 'Polignac memorandum' that Russia might receive the Principalities (modern Romania) and some Turkish territory in Asia; Serbia and Bosnia might go to Austria; various territories from Belgium to Alsace might fall to France; Prussia could take the Netherlands and the rest of Saxony. What remained of Turkey in Europe might become a Greek empire under the unemployed ex-king of Holland, while the Dutch colonies could go to Britain. This remarkable set of proposals is seen by Paul Schroeder as both 'proof of how much old eighteenth-century thinking ... could easily surface' and how impractical it was in the changed character of international relations since 1815.[4] It was also evidence of French revisionism even under the Bourbons.

In fact the memorandum was overtaken by a decision by the Russians to make peace with the Turks at Adrianople. Although their army had finally advanced to within striking distance of Constantinople, it was in no shape to deal with a major international crisis. At the same time a special committee in St Petersburg was arguing that the advantages of the survival of the Ottoman Empire easily outweighed the disadvantages. Further Russian military advances, it was feared, would precipitate major seizures of territory by Austria, Britain and France – all to the detriment of Russia. Even worse would be the outbreak of a great international war which Russia as a whole was in no condition to wage.[5] The committee therefore argued for the maintenance of the current status quo. While one cannot claim that the committee would necessarily have advocated stronger policies if Russia's strength had been greater (given the underlying distrust of France and the fear that a great war might unleash new revolutionary forces), the plea for restraint is revealing.

Under the Treaty of Adrianople (14 September 1829) the Turks once again acknowledged the Convention of Akkerman. The Russians, however, were quick to assure London that no extreme demands would be made on behalf of the Greeks. Encouraged by these promises, Aberdeen (the foreign secretary) began to hope that a solution might be found in the creation of a small Greek state under a 'moderate and prudent Prince'. Some Anglo–Austrian cooperation was also occurring as Metternich came to see that an independent Morea was likely to be less dependent on Russia than an autonomous Turkish province. In short, each power was deeply impressed by the unpredictability of the current situation. None had the resources or allies to take risks. It was time to talk.

In fact the diplomatic process had never been totally suspended during the Russo–Turkish war. From August 1827 the French and Russian ambassadors had been meeting intermittently in conference in London with the British foreign minister to monitor developments. Real progress became possible from the autumn of 1829, and in February 1830 it was agreed by the London Protocol that a small but independent Greek state should be created. Its boundaries were extended in 1832 under Palmerston's influence on the assumption that the larger it was the more likely a Greek state would be to remain independent of Russia. The London conference of ambassadors, though not a full meeting of the Concert, was thus an interesting exercise in international cooperation – though one that was also powerfully driven by fear of the consequences of failure.[6]

Such relative harmony, however, could not withstand a revolution in France. Even before this broke out the Russians, despite working at times with France over the Greek question, had been on the lookout for some sudden revisionist or revolutionary twist to French policy. Given his suspicions even of a legitimist monarchy in France, it is not surprising that Nicholas I should have reacted so strongly to the upheaval in France in July 1830. Admittedly there could have been far worse outcomes than the resultant Orleanist monarchy. Despite a new constitutional Charter and tacit acceptance of the principle of popular sovereignty, this was a conservative rather than a liberal regime. Fewer than three per cent of the male population possessed the vote. This did not reassure either the tsar or Metternich. The former denounced Louis-Philippe as 'a vile usurper'. The revolution reinforced a pre-existing inclination of the Romanovs and Habsburgs to settle their differences, the Russians having already shown some sensitivity to Austrian interests in the Balkans (not least because of their own sense of weakness). A meeting between Metternich and Nesselrode in July 1830 signalled that a new version of the 'Holy Alliance' was possible.

## Eastern Trio and Western Duo, 1830–8

The revolution in France and the establishment of the July Monarchy were viewed by the absolutists as a challenge to dynastic rights and binding treaties – especially the Vienna Settlement. Such was the divide between the Orleanists and Russia that for most of the 1830s relations were conducted by way of chargés d'affaires, not ambassadors.[7] The Russians were even slow to recognise the new government. For the Austrians, too, doomsday at times seemed dangerously close at hand. In contrast, Gentz, though sharing many of the fears of social revolution, showed a greater sense of proportion. He was corresponding, for instance, with Baron James Rothschild (a banker living in Paris). The latter had lost heavily on the exchange during the revolution, and was busily using his contacts with the Orleanists to press for policies which would restore financial confidence. Gentz himself argued that, while in the abstract it would seem that the two systems (legitimism and sovereignty of the people) were incompatible, the British had been proving the contrary for 100 years. Gentz's views were of little practical consequence in themselves (the Austrians being restrained primarily by their financial anxieties and problems elsewhere), yet they are an example of the sober views which could be heard in some conservative circles.[8]

The absolutists accepted that the British (even with Wellington as premier) would try to coexist with a 'revolutionary' regime. British ministers knew that any overt identification with the absolutists over such an issue would provoke widespread criticism at home. Nor did they wish to do anything that might inflate Metternich's influence (let alone his ego). Thus the 'neo-holies' contented themselves with the 'chiffon de Carlsbad' of 6 August 1830 in which they affirmed their determination to uphold the status quo. Recognition of the new French regime would be dependent on its acknowledgement of the Vienna Settlement.[9]

The Wellington ministry fell in November 1830, and its Whig successors were soon much preoccupied with the question of Parliamentary Reform at home. Absolutist suspicions of the new government were further increased when they found themselves confronted by so assertive and outspoken a foreign minister as Lord Palmerston. His earlier travels had left him with a low opinion of most of Europe and its peoples. Even the French, he believed, were not such a potent force as in the recent past. From the outset he was confident enough to make fast-footed and strikingly pragmatic changes of front as he eagerly competed with Metternich for the central role in European diplomacy. Although he was not backed up within the Foreign Office by the smooth and relatively large bureaucracy in the Ballhausplatz (Vienna), he more than offset this by hard work, intuition and inventiveness. True, his freedom was constricted at times by such funds as he could squeeze from the Treasury and Parliament. Yet he was able upon occasion to remind other powers not to take Britain's current armed forces at face value. She, more so than other states, had the economic reserves to fund both herself and allies in a great war. As for the French, they could be reminded that London was the only major European capital where – for the time being – they might expect to gain a sympathetic hearing.

Palmerston was further helped in the longer run by a number of other factors. Ministries in France tended to be relatively short-lived – that is, until the era of Guizot in the 1840s. Metternich, as usual, lacked the raw military and financial backing to take bold initiatives. Prussian activity was most marked in the creation of the *Zollverein*, its army only briefly showing its teeth in 1840. Nicholas I was a figure of some substance, but his fear of France and revolution restricted his options. His ambitious naval building programmes of the 1830s also produced few advantages in relation to their huge costs. He was, however, well served by Nesselrode as foreign minister. Of Rhineland Protestant origins, the latter usually favoured discretion rather than valour. His position in government was closer to that of a senior permanent official in a department than of a minister as understood in the west. As such he served three very different tsars. This suggests not only malleability and obedience but also dedication and mastery of his brief. His hand in policy-making has been identified in a number of instances. Of all Alexander I's foreign policy advisers, his had been the strongest voice in support of great-power cooperation.[10] Yet even his equanimity was shaken at times by Palmerston, a man who all too often seemed intent on upsetting the order which Nesselrode was employed to defend. He reflected, however, that not even Palmerston was immortal or had the power to override Britain's basic national interests. Crude self-interest became even more important when the Belgians rebelled against the union with Holland, and the Poles rose against Russia in the autumn of 1830.

The Dutch king promptly appealed for foreign aid in October 1830. Although the Russians were quick to offer help, the Austrians and Prussians had no desire to see the tsar's armies tramping across Europe and perhaps provoking the French into the bargain. Metternich also had to keep a weather eye on Italy. Although the Polish revolt excited much sympathy in Britain and France, Palmerston and Lord Grey (the prime minister) knew that intervention was out of the question. Nor would this have been expedient given their much more immediate and substantial interest in the fate of Belgium (an area which was bound to attract the attention of the French). Fortunately France proved as receptive as the other powers to a Dutch proposal for a meeting of the Vienna signatories.

An ambassadorial conference was in session in London from November 1830 – a choice of location which put Palmerston at the centre of affairs.[11] He was further assisted by the fact that Britain alone of the powers might act as a friend to France, while the three conservative powers (troubled by the reality or fear of revolution elsewhere in Europe) dared not put too much distance between themselves and the wealth of London. It was only at the end of 1832 that Metternich (jealous of Palmerston's success) tried to assert himself with a vain demand that the final talks on Belgium take place in Aix. Already the powers had agreed that Belgium should have its independence, with no power being allowed to lay claim to any of its territory – a self-denying ordinance which was obviously directed against France. Dutch obstructionism postponed the completion of an international guarantee of Belgian neutrality until 1839.[12]

Even so it is evident that the early 1830s had witnessed not a little useful activity by the Concert of Europe at the level of the ambassadorial conference, together with some attention to the public law of Europe, points much emphasised by F. H. Hinsley. One of the protocols on Belgium went as far as to affirm that 'Each nation has its rights, but Europe also has its rights.'[13] An ambassadorial conference even met to discuss reform in the Papal states. Yet at the same time both Grey and Palmerston in 1831 made it plain to colleagues and to their ambassador in Paris (some of their remarks clearly being intended to reach French ears) that force would be used if the French tried to steal a substantial advantage in the Belgian affair. Metternich, too, hoped for a show of strength by the British Mediterranean fleet to help discourage French meddling in Italy. He even raised the possibility in 1831 of a preventive war against France in order to dishearten the revolutionaries elsewhere in Europe. But he was firmly told by the archduke Charles that Austria was in no financial or military condition to embark on adventures of this kind. The emperor later remarked on the poor state of his army.[14]

In general each power in the early 1830s had good reason to act with caution and to concentrate mainly on its own sphere of influence. Thus Austria was left to assert herself in Italy while Russia did the same in Poland. The British broadly had their way in Belgium while Prussia and Austria kept watch over the lesser German states. The shallowness of the professions of unity was soon revealed by the new developments in the Near East and the Iberian Peninsula, the civil wars in Spain and Portugal in particular tending to range the British and French on one side and the three eastern powers on the other. It is true that some scholars have suggested that the Concert might have been used to handle the latest Near Eastern crisis (the future of the Ottoman Empire being put at risk from 1831 by an Egyptian invasion). But Palmerston was unwilling to let Metternich preside over a conference in Vienna, while the other powers turned down an Austrian proposal for a great-power guarantee of Turkey against Egypt.

The start of this Near Eastern crisis seemingly found Palmerston without any very clear policy. Some of his cabinet colleagues were already disposed to write off the Ottoman Empire. Belgium and Portugal were demanding British naval as well as diplomatic attention, and it was clear that neither cabinet nor Parliament was willing to vote the funds needed to commission extra ships to handle a third crisis. Nor could Palmerston hope to repeat his successful manipulation of the Concert over Belgium. In that particular instance he had held most of the trump cards. Things might well prove very different in the Near East, especially once the Russians were free of the Polish crisis, and with Metternich still looking to seize the diplomatic initiative.[15]

The Egyptians were therefore left to advance through and beyond Syria. The Russians took fright once Constantinople itself seemed threatened. It was not in their interest that responsibility for the Straits should pass from the relatively weak Turks to the more dynamic (and pro-French) Egyptians. Their leader, Mehemet Ali, was already well on the way towards the creation of an 'Arab empire' in Asia Minor. A combination of the 'rebellious' Egyptians and the 'revolutionary' French would have serious implications for the stability of the Near East and perhaps even Europe. Russian thoughts turned to pre-emptive action, the Turks being informed at the end of November 1832 that aid would be sent if requested. Russia's objective was revealingly defined in December 1832 as the maintenance of Turkey 'in the stagnant state in which it finds itself'. A Russian naval squadron arrived off Constantinople in February 1833, and was followed by nearly 20 000 Russian troops. This demonstration of force was effective (the one occasion when the Black Sea fleet was able to act decisively in defence of Russian interests at the Straits). The Egyptians withdrew to Syria, and Count Orlov was able to negotiate the important Treaty of Unkiar Skelessi (9 July) with the Turks.[16]

Belatedly the British and French began to show interest in some form of collective action. Yet the feasibility of a concerted approach seems questionable given – for instance – the deep divide between the eastern and western powers over Russia's actions in Poland and the Iberian civil wars between absolutists and nominal 'constitutional' forces. In any case, with Russian forces in command of the Straits, it was natural that the tsar and Nesselrode should seek unilateral (if defensive) advantages. The Turks were required to depend exclusively on Russia for protection, and to reaffirm the closure of the Straits against any foreign power at war with Russia – although Nesselrode also did his best in a circular despatch of 17 August 1833 to convince the other powers of the limited nature of Russia's objectives.

Overall the Russians had acted with considerable good sense and timing. Yet the British and French still feared the existence of some secret clause which would allow Russian warships to pass through the Straits. Although this was not the case, Russia had established herself for the time being as the leading power in Constantinople – whatever the literal terms of the treaty itself. This was not a happy thought if, as Palmerston argued in the House of Commons on 11 July 1833, the integrity and independence of the Ottoman Empire were indeed 'necessary to the maintenance of the tranquillity, the liberty, and the balance of power in the rest of Europe'. Nor was it in his nature to accept a state of affairs which he still regarded as reversible. He was receiving encouraging reports from the embassy in St Petersburg of the poor state of Russian finances and the Black Sea fleet – this information having been easily procured from poorly paid Russian bureaucrats. Indeed in 1835 Palmerston was to dismiss Russia as a great humbug, and make other confident pronouncements as to what the future might bring.[17]

On the other hand there were times when he gave the impression that he believed that the balance in Europe as a whole was moving in favour of the eastern powers, especially when they drew together with the Austro–Russian agreement at Münchengrätz in September 1833 (Prussia being added under a tripartite convention signed in Berlin a month later). At Münchengrätz Austria and Russia promised to work together to protect the Ottoman Empire, or act in concert in the event of its demise. The tsar signalled his goodwill towards Vienna by withdrawing his garrisons from the Danubian Principalities where they had been stationed since the war of 1828–9. The ensuing Berlin Convention with Prussia implied that the three powers were prepared to act together if a fourth power (namely France) tried to intervene against the absolutist cause in a country such as Spain.[18] In short, the interests of two and sometimes all three powers overlapped in particular areas such as the Near East, Poland, Germany and Iberia. All feared France and, to some extent, Britain. Even in regions where no overlap existed, each power could benefit indirectly from the stability maintained elsewhere. Russia, despite her huge army, needed Austria to police Italy and parts of Germany, while Prussia watched the Rhine. Overall the defence of the status quo east of the Rhine was the surest bond between the three eastern powers. In addition the presence of friendly neighbours made it easier for Russia to build up her navy for security against the western powers.

For the time being, therefore, the eastern and western states appeared squarely ranged against each other. In fact there was more unity within the eastern trio than between Britain and France. It is true that Palmerston often trumpeted the defence of constitutionalism and liberal values against the absolutists. He was also genuinely looking for reform programmes in Iberia which might create political stability and increased trade with Britain. In contrast Tories (such as Aberdeen) welcomed the eastern conservative combination 'against the disorganising and revolutionary policy of the present

Governments of England and France'. But the reality was more complex given Palmerston's anxiety to contain the ambitions of France in Spain as well as to frustrate absolutism.

Once again his position was relatively promising. The French had much more reason than the British to fear the three eastern powers – whatever Palmerston might say about their threat to the Near East or Iberia. A French request for a general defensive alliance showed how far France was inhibited by her fear of the three eastern powers. Palmerston had no hesitation in refusing to guarantee France against attack by the absolutist powers if she sent an army to support the 'constitutionalists' in Spain. He was also able to ensure that the Quadruple Alliance of April 1834 (France, Britain and the Iberian states) strictly limited the ways in which France and Britain would support the 'constitutional' factions against the absolutist claimants to the two Iberian crowns. Portugal remained a British preserve (from which the reactionary Miguelist threat was soon removed) whereas the French had to yield at least equal influence to the British in Spain.

Perhaps in the circumstances it was not surprising that the reactionary Carlists were able to battle on in Spain for some years, or that the British prime minister, Lord Melbourne, should ask Palmerston in 1836 and 1838 why Britain should be involved in what seemed so thankless a task. Why, he asked, should constitutional regimes prove more Anglophile in the long run than any others? Palmerston (in 1836) replied that Europe had been split into 'two camps' by the July Revolution. The conservative powers thought and acted differently from Britain and France, yet they also wanted Britain on their side so that they could dictate to France as they had done in 1814 and 1815. The Britain alignment with France was therefore needed to preserve the 'peace of Europe'.[19]

Claims concerning the unity and utility of the western 'liberal and improving powers' against the 'triple league of the despotic powers' might sound impressive, and perhaps Palmerston personally believed some of them. Yet in practice he was allowing only token French and British forces to fight the Carlists, while Anglo–French differences in Iberia and elsewhere meant that the western alliance had no more than a limited influence upon the balance of power. Indeed, the alliance was effectively at an end as early as 1836, riven by Anglo–French suspicion, rivalry and differing priorities. Tories such as Wellington and Aberdeen would have happily taken a still more detached position. Indeed their comments suggest that Britain and Austria might have found much in common had the Tories been in office. Meanwhile even Palmerston knew he was exaggerating when he claimed in 1834 that Anglo–Russian relations were divided by 'the same principle of repulsion' as that which had existed between Britain and Bonaparte.[20]

In 1836 the French, conscious of the degree to which their freedom was constricted by Palmerston, tried to gain a hearing from Metternich. The latter, however, saw this as an opportunity to probe for weaknesses in the liberal camp, and even to pave the way for a separate Austrian deal with Britain – not France! Thus successive French ministers found themselves repeatedly frustrated by the suspicion which their country still excited in the eastern courts. Even Guizot in the 1840s found that while he personally might find favour to some extent with Aberdeen and Metternich, he could not overcome their distrust of France. For the time being French ministers had to live with the Vienna Settlement while they tried to persuade other powers that France was indeed a state with which they could have normal relations. As Roger Bullen observes, Guizot could only resolve differences, not create new alignments.[21]

Thus when the Carlist War in Spain finally ended, it was soon followed by further Anglo–French rivalries, especially when peace did not produce a stable and effective constitutional order in Madrid. Indeed Iberia seemed to have an extraordinary ability to absorb foreign meddling while offering the intruders little if anything of value in return. British influence in Portugal was strong, yet that country also remained backward and politically volatile. In the end Palmerston perhaps gained most from the Iberian imbroglio by impressing the eastern powers – and especially Russia – with the advantages of British friendship.

Some comment is also called for concerning his bitter rivalry with Metternich. Each man was intent on scoring points off the other. In Palmerston's case this was sometimes done to enhance his popularity with certain groups at home. On the one hand he once seemed hopeful that the alliance against the absolutists might gain advantages as far east as Constantinople, and that the Kingdom of the Two Sicilies might be wrested from the Austrian orbit. In return an exasperated Metternich described Palmerston as 'revolution incarnate'. In fact personal vanity was at stake as well as ideology. On the other hand, in the battle between autocracy and 'liberalism', it is unlikely that Metternich overlooked the degree to which Habsburg interests benefited from the preoccupation of both Russia and Prussia with the defence of absolutism and the status quo. They had fewer opportunities to meddle in areas where they might tread on Austrian toes. Metternich, too, could hope that the Anglo–French alignment might finally be broken by events in Iberia, thereby adding to his own potential choice of friends.[22] Therefore, although from very different starting points, both Palmerston and Metternich were looking to limit the activities of their respective partners even while they were engaged in a conflict of principles and power. Palmerston was particularly mindful of the danger if Russia were joined by 'a more active, ambitious and a *naval* ally' – namely France. As matters then stood, he could not work with the eastern powers 'because their views and opinions are now-a-days the reverse of ours'. Thus he had to put up with the 'little ebullitions of [French] national conceit'.

### The Near East Again, 1838–41

Throughout much of the 1830s the British Admiralty kept a close watch as the Russians continued to expand and exercise their fleets in the Baltic and Black Seas. Their growth gave great satisfaction to the tsar. 'Now let the English come', he remarked in 1836, 'if they want their nose made bloody.' Increases to the British navy duly followed from 1836. Palmerston declared that the extra ships were needed to produce 'a moral effect ... [and] uncertainty in the minds of others', especially in the Mediterranean. They also signalled the readiness of Parliament to vote funds to defend national interests against any challenger.[23] By the end of the decade Anglo–American relations were again causing concern, with some in the Admiralty suggesting that Britain now needed a three-power naval standard for real security.

This cloud in the west was accompanied by a larger one in the east as Palmerston became increasingly anxious to counter Russian interest in Persia by the establishment of a pre-eminent British position in Afghanistan. He justified this by arguing that 'it was inevitable that a European power' would be tempted to exploit any advantage in Asia in order to 'influence a European negotiation'. Caught between these two theatres was the Ottoman Empire where Britain had both major commercial and strategic interests. The Russians (not surprisingly) were unimpressed by Palmerston's proposal for a five-power conference to Europeanise the Eastern Question. They reacted to the conclusion of an Anglo–Turkish commercial treaty and to joint naval manoeuvres in 1838 by organising a force with which to make a dash for the Straits in an emergency.

The British naval estimates had been increased by one-fifth since 1835, yet there was still not enough navy to go round in April 1839 when the sultan (intent on revenge for the defeats of 1831–3) suddenly attacked the Egyptians in Syria. The Turks, however, suffered one disaster after another. On 18 July 1839 Palmerston thought it prudent to ask the sultan's permission for a British fleet to pass the Dardanelles in case the Russians arrived in the Bosphorus. Briefly it seemed as if the Anglo–French alignment might be revived. Yet within a matter of months Britain, in a seemingly dramatic volte-face, was to be found siding with Russia against France. In fact Palmerston in 1830–1 had already demonstrated his readiness to incline towards the three absolutist powers if national interest so dictated. Nor had he entirely forgotten 'the principles of the Great Alliance created at Chaumont'.[24]

The important Brunnow mission to Britain in the autumn of 1839 was preceded by hints of Russian interest in a deal with the British. In fact Nesselrode had been moving in this direction for more than a year. He hoped, for instance, that a buffer zone might be created to temper the rivalries between the two empires in Asia. He was also impressed by the advance of British influence in Turkey, and on 23 April 1839 he warned against a repetition of the Russian expedition of 1833 to the Straits – this time the risk of war with Britain (probably supported by France) would be too great. He further doubted if the Treaty of Unkiar Skelessi would do much to protect Russia at the Straits if push came to shove: it was in any case due to expire in 1841.

Although the five great powers managed to produce a collective note in July 1939, the 'Question of the East' as usual highlighted their differences. Nesselrode concluded that Russia's interests could be best protected by an agreement with Britain. In 1839, for instance, when the tsar was briefly tempted to think of unilateral action at the Straits, it was Nesselrode who came up with a constructive alternative.[25] The tsar agreed to send Brunnow to London to inform Palmerston that Russia would defend Turkey against the Egyptians only as the representative of Europe. Russia was also willing to replace the controversial Treaty of Unkiar Skelessi with an international guarantee to close the Straits to *all* foreign warships and to uphold the 'existence and repose' of the Ottoman Empire. This made good sense given the relatively disappointing outcome to the recent Russian efforts to create the naval and other forces needed to secure the Black Sea and the Straits. Russia could not hope for success through unilateral action.[26]

Part of the appeal to Nicholas of the new initiative lay in the fact that Metternich would be bypassed. The latter would then find it more difficult to climb into the driver's seat and assume his favourite role as the 'coachman of Europe'. Equally, given Britain's very specific and crucial interests at the Straits and in the eastern Mediterranean, it seemed wiser to approach London than allow Metternich to broaden and confuse the agenda at some grand European congress. But above all Nicholas was determined to isolate France. Palmerston responded positively, soon finding merit in the Russian proposals. But among cabinet colleagues some preferred to cling to 'liberal' France on grounds of political principle, while Russophobia was still strong among the public. Melbourne himself remarked as late as August 1840 that the last war had made Russia a land power in Europe: the next might make her great at sea.

In contrast Palmerston's thoughts, like those of Nicholas and Nesselrode, were concentrated on the immediate issues. He was worried by the Egyptian victories which might lead to a major upset in the Near Eastern balance of power at the expense of the Turks. He was troubled, too, by Egypt's connections with France so that there was no telling where a regional crisis might lead. A deal with Russia, on the other hand, might strengthen Turkey and thereby (he hoped) make the Ottomans less dependent on Russia. The latter's bilateral treaty with the Turks might be replaced by a European agreement with the thwarting of French ambitions in the eastern Mediterranean as a bonus. Palmerston conceded that the closure of the Straits would add to the security of southern Russia, but it would also confirm the paralysis of 'the left arm of Russia as a naval power' to the advantage of all British military, political and commercial interests in the Mediterranean from Constantinople westward.[27] He was persuaded that where cooperation with France would at best result in the containment of Russia (but at the price of French and

Egyptian gains in the Near East), partnership with Russia would reduce her influence as well as that of Egypt and France – a much better bargain.

Palmerston finally persuaded the cabinet to opt for an initial four-power solution to the Near Eastern crisis with the convention of 15 July 1840. The plan was to limit Egyptian rule to southern Syria to the lifetime of Mehemet Ali. Refusal would mean coercion by the powers, and the immediate loss of all Syria. Palmerston was confident (as was Aberdeen, unlike some ministers and senior naval officers) that, while the French would protest and show the flag with a large and efficient fleet in the eastern Mediterranean, they would not dare to fight. This was confirmed when Thiers fell from office after an attempt at a bold front had provoked Prussian military preparations on the Rhine. As the French retreat continued, the allies speedily expelled the Egyptians from Syria. Yet Palmerston, although he had secured his objectives, was still intent on humiliating the French. It was if he was intent on validating Talleyrand's criticism that, for all his qualities, he sometimes sacrificed 'the greatest interests to his resentments'.[28]

Nor did the rapprochement with Russia in the Near East inhibit Palmerston elsewhere. He persisted with his bid for British pre-eminence in Afghanistan despite the apparent readiness of Nesselrode to discuss an agreement over spheres of influence. But at least he dissented to a Russian proposal for a permanent four-power alliance against France, sensibly wishing to retain Britain's freedom of action. There would surely come a time when France would have her uses – as in the 1830s. Metternich, meanwhile, had been thwarted whenever he tried to enhance his own role and to broaden the agenda for discussion by the powers. In August 1840 the Austrian, for instance, had proposed a league of all the powers to enforce existing treaties and to keep the peace – an obvious bid to improve the security of the Habsburg Empire and to solidify the status quo. In the spring of 1841 he suggested that the ambassadors in Vienna should act as watchdogs with respect to the Ottoman Empire. Britain and Russia, however, refused to allow their hands to be tied in this way. Prussia and Austria now drew together, each feeling that Britain and Russia had become too assertive and urging the return of France to the Concert. France was in any case too powerful a player to be sidelined for long. Despite Russian objections, France was allowed to join the other powers in the negotiation of the Straits Convention of July 1841, the Straits being pronounced closed to all foreign warships as long as Turkey was not at war.

## Absolutism in the East, Tensions in the West, 1842–7

The relations between most of the powers between the Straits Convention of 1841 and the revolutions of 1848 were relatively tranquil. The tsar was anxious to preserve the status quo in the Near East and to contain France – objectives which suited Britain and Austria. It is true that he did not always see eye to eye with Metternich. The latter showed rather too much interest in the Near East for the tsar's peace of mind, and rather too little eagerness to follow up his anti-revolutionary rhetoric with the appropriate action. Nicholas was also disappointed when a Habsburg–Romanov marriage failed to materialise in 1845.[29]

But such tiffs were of little consequence. In so far as there was real tension this lay between Britain and France. Major differences occurred despite the best efforts of Aberdeen, the foreign secretary of a Tory government under Sir Robert Peel. Aberdeen truly believed that mutual accommodation should be pursued where possible between all of the powers. He was content with the current balance of power, and was among those who feared that war might initiate a new era of revolutions. His colleagues shared his interest in peace, anxious as they were to reduce defence costs and end the budget deficits which they had inherited from the Whigs. Aberdeen saw France as the only likely trouble-maker, especially over the future of Spain, but believed he had an ally for peace in Guizot (the French prime minister). He was thus disposed to make some concessions in order to try to prolong the latter's tenure of power.

Peel was more sceptical. He doubted if so much faith could be placed in a single minister – despite the high esteem in which he was held by Louis-Philippe. French governments and even dynasties of late had not proved good insurance risks. Peel showed more realism than Aberdeen as shown when Anglo–French relations were disturbed by so relatively trivial an episode as French maltreatment of a British Protestant missionary in Tahiti. In each country there were many who needed little prompting to think the worst of the other. The situation was made worse by British fears that the rapid development of the steamship might enable France to attempt a surprise invasion or (at the very least) damaging raids across the Channel. With a growing railway network to facilitate a speedy concentration of troops in the French ports, a 'steam bridge' might be thrown across the Channel. The alarm was such that Peel's ministry, though intent upon economy, increased the naval estimates by nearly a quarter between 1844 and 1846. Aberdeen's objections were overruled. Wellington (now in his mid-seventies) personally surveyed the land defences of south-east England. Peel concluded:

> We ought in my opinion even in the midst of peace to be at ease upon vital points, to be enabled to assert our rights, to maintain a becoming tone in the many instances of unavoidable collision which occur even during peace, ...[30]

The scale of the 'invasion panic' in Britain was an ironic outcome to the most determined effort by any British foreign secretary since Castlereagh to work for better relations among the powers. Perhaps too it was hardly the most appropriate time for William Dyce to paint Neptune transferring the empire of the sea to Britain (1847) when so many seemed to doubt the ability of the navy to command the Channel.

Matters were further inflamed soon after Palmerston's return to office in 1846. He was not prepared to take so tolerant a view as Aberdeen of the French government's aspirations for influence in Spain, and especially not its bid for a share in the management of the marriages of the Spanish queen and her sister. Matters came to a head when Palmerston returned as foreign secretary in 1846. Suspicions on both sides prompted Guizot to pull off a double marriage coup (the queen to a reputedly impotent Spaniard and her sister to a French prince). British influence in Iberia seemed under further threat when radical disturbances in Portugal prompted its government to invoke the Quadruple Treaty of 1834 to secure foreign aid against the rebels. Swift British action was taken to warn off either Spain or France from meddling in Portuguese affairs. These and other matters helped to sustain the invasion panic until France was overtaken by revolution in 1848.

Equally important was the reaction of the conservative powers who could hardly believe their good fortune. Metternich happily com-

mented in 1847 that Britain's resources were not equal to the purposes of her government since she could not make war for any of
her objectives. Nesselrode shared his delight. At worst the eastern
powers could expect the British and French to neutralise each other;
at best they might hope to play one off against the other.[31]
Confronted by mounting unrest in Galicia and Cracow (and fearful
lest this should spread further, especially into Russian Poland),
Metternich and his allies seized their chance to suppress Cracow's
independent status.

Guizot himself was desirous of closer relations with Austria, but he
was hampered by the hostility of French progressives to an alignment with an arch-conservative power. Nor was it easy in any case for
Vienna and Paris to sink their differences in Switzerland and Italy,
while Metternich could not bring himself to trust Guizot. Thus the
tide began to flow a little in Palmerston's favour, notably in
Switzerland where the liberal cantons were ranged against the
Catholic *Sonderbund*. When in 1847 intervention by some of the
powers against the Swiss liberals seemed a distinct possibility, Guizot
was obliged by French progressives to insist on Britain's inclusion in
any great-power talks. Palmerston promptly seized his chance to slow
the proceedings. He was further helped by the lack of unanimity
among the other powers, with Metternich vacillating between intervention and fear of the possible complications (he had steeled
himself to act against Cracow only after much prodding from
Russia). This diplomatic confusion and delay enabled the Swiss
liberal and Protestant cantons to force the Catholics into a Swiss
republic.[32]

Meanwhile the election of a reforming Pope (Plus IX) in 1846 had
increased the risk of unrest in Italy and therefore of a challenge to
Austrian rule and influence. Metternich responded by trying to
tighten Austrian rule in Lombardy–Venetia whereas Palmerston, as
ever, hoped to seize the initiative for Britain (for commercial as well
as political reasons). At the same time he could claim to be working
for peace and stability in Europe. Selective and orderly reform, he
said, would provide the best defence against revolution and thus rob
both France and Austria of any excuse to intervene. In the event of
upheavals in Italy, he warned that French radicals might be able to
force their country to intervene against Austrian efforts at suppression. Such a war might spread to Germany. Britain 'at all events', he
concluded, 'can have no wish to see Austria broken down and

France aggrandized, and the military vanity and love of conquest of the French revived ...'[33]

Lord Minto was sent on a special mission to Italy to preach the need for a middle way between radical republicanism and Austrian-supported reaction. This mission, however, was overtaken by events from January 1848 as revolutionary forces asserted themselves in much of Italy. Palmerston begged the Austrians not to interfere – this would only increase the danger of a European 'war of principles'. But neither his flattery (Austria was the central point of the European balance of power) nor his threats (a war over the future of northern Italy might well find Britain ranged with those who favoured change) made any impression in Vienna. Yet as a statement of British faith and interest in orderly progress and peace it made good sense.

British advice, however, could not stem the revolutionary tide which, in due course, was to envelope all the powers except Britain and Russia – and even the British government faced serious discontent at home. Confronted by a chaotic and unpredictable Europe, the two governments once again found that they had a surprising number of interests in common. Nesselrode, for instance, who had recently described Palmerston's ideas on reform in Italy as a 'veritable plague', was soon pleased to describe the British minister as a fit and proper medical partner in the fight to contain the revolutionary infection. Nicholas I, who had already begun to view the Habsburg Empire as a secondary power given its lack of both confidence and strength, reverted to the policies of 1839 and 1844 when he had favoured an alignment with Britain, a power truly of the first rank and with many fewer political faults than the French.[34]

With respect to the years between 1815 and 1848, some historians have continued to stress the interest of the powers in the 'ideal of peace through collective responsibility' before 1854. Paul Schroeder, for instance, has recently stressed 'the consensual game' which was being played. He cites both the occurrence and early collapse of the 1848 revolutions – 'with every treaty still in force, every state boundary unchanged' – as proof that 'Europe's governments were mainly conservative, legalistic, and peaceful, restrained by treaties and the rules of the essentially cooperative, consensual game they had learned to play'. He goes further and argues that 'this era proved that a political equilibrium in international affairs is possible without balance-of-power methods', and that a 'structurally anarchic [system] ... can none the less be restrained by consensus and bounded by law'. In his view, Metternich and company knew that 'war was revolution' since it would jeopardise the international as well as the internal order.[35]

Various attempts have already been made in the present study to suggest the need to qualify some of the larger claims concerning the strength of this 'consensual' approach. It has been argued that self-interested and negative considerations outweighed the positive ones in sustaining the long peace. Admittedly efforts to avoid war were pursued more purposefully than ever before in modern European history, and the 'ideal' of 'collective responsibility' was occasionally glimpsed. But there was more invocation than sustained and deliberate implementation in practice. Often the powers could do no more than agree to go their separate ways. Sometimes the weaker party had to bow to the threat of superior force. Several times the Austrians were restrained by financial and other internal problems when tempted by thoughts of strong action. Russia, too, was less strong than the size of her armed forces might suggest – a fact highlighted both in 1829 and 1839.[36] Prussia remained the weakest of the great powers and had to behave accordingly. As for the French, it must often have seemed as if 'consensual' politics were a euphemism for hostility towards and cooperation against them to ensure their isolation and paralysis. As for the British, despite some years of alarm and relative weakness, this was – by and large – the period in their history when they were best able to exert influence at least cost and danger to themselves. Given the disunity, as well as the limitations of the other powers, they frequently had the choice of playing the 'consensual' card against France or of breaking ranks to constrain the conservative powers by selective association with France.

In general, special circumstances as well as statecraft do much to explain why the challenges to the Vienna Settlement were so limited in these years. While sensible – if self-interested defensive or consolidationist – motives did much to keep the peace, these were assisted by the fact that the balance of forces normally favoured the status quo. Schroeder himself also supplies important answers with his comment that 'an international system and its constituent rules and practices are in themselves not of intrinsic value'. The rules and practices are 'only instrumental – artificial, manipulable, replaceable', employed for the particular ends of particular states and leaders. 'This was, and is, the heart of "realism".'[37] This is an eminently sound verdict.

# 3

## REVOLUTIONS AND WAR, 1848–56

'… the true thinking of the Emperor [Nicholas I] … is of a higher order than one can comprehend in Constantinople and, perhaps, elsewhere, … [since] His Majesty … obeys his conscience'. (Count Nesselrode)

### Revolutionary Europe and the Balance of Power, 1848–52

Nicholas I's first response to news of revolution in France and the creation of the Second Republic (February 1848), was to talk of marching 300 000 troops to the Rhine. This was in keeping with his deeply held distrust of the Orleanist Monarchy, and his doubts as to the competence and resolve of the rulers of Prussia and Austria to uphold absolutism. Disorder could result from inadequate as well as unjust princes. There was also an echo or two of the thinking of his late brother, Alexander I, when he spoke of the need for both righteous and strong rulers if the legitimate order was to be upheld.

Fortunately the tsar, having given vent to his feelings, was content to reinforce Russia's borders, and to send (somewhat superfluous) warnings to the Prussians and Austrians to be on their guard against a French revolutionary offensive.[1] He also wrote to Queen Victoria asking if a '*union intime*' was needed to save the world. Meanwhile Nesselrode was engaged in a more prosaic search for an anti-French coalition, but one which, he insisted, should confine itself to defensive action unless the French put themselves unambiguously in the wrong. Palmerston was much relieved by this evidence of Russian restraint. He wanted no premature alliances against France despite his own fears that the question of peace or war hung upon the whims of a new and unstable government in Paris. He was unsure of the strength of the moderates there, but noted that Lamartine, the head of the provisional government, seemed anxious both for good relations with Britain and for peace in Europe. Although some French republicans condemned the treaties of 1815, others were quick to offer discreet assurances that revision would be sought only by negotiation with all the interested parties.

Palmerston was thus in the promising position of being courted by both absolutists and moderate revolutionaries. Britain was France's only conceivable friend, while the eastern powers were clearly reluctant to act without her moral and – if it came to the crunch – her financial support. Extremists, of course, might prevail, but in the interim he might hope to encourage and strengthen the moderates in the main capitals.[2]

The overall situation in Europe, however, had to worsen before it could improve. Revolution spread swiftly to the Habsburg Empire and Germany. On 21 March the Prussian king horrified all defenders of the status quo by offering to lead a united Germany. This caused particular alarm in St Petersburg. Apart from the general fear of revolution, Russian interest demanded the preservation of the old configuration of Austria, Prussia and the German Confederation. The Russians were still more dismayed to find that some of the revolutionary leaders in Germany were hoping to promote the unity of their country by means of a crusade to liberate Poland from Russian rule. Some even hoped for support from republican extremists in France. Palmerston, for his part, urged Berlin to keep the peace. Although the Prussian king soon began to take a more cautious line, Palmerston continued to be disturbed by the visionary schemes of the German liberals.

Only in one region did he feel that drastic change might prove beneficial. This was in northern Italy where he hoped that Austria might be persuaded to withdraw from Lombardy and Venetia. Her presence, he believed, not only made for instability (it provoked Italians and Frenchmen alike) but also weakened Austria herself as a great power – not least as a bulwark against Russia in the Near East.[3] Much as he favoured a European equilibrium, it was, he believed, possible to improve on some of the territorial dispositions of 1815. A north Italian monarchy – indeed an all-Italian confederation on the lines of that in Germany – might deprive France as well as Austria of any excuse to meddle in future. Thus in the autumn of 1848 he tried to persuade the Austrian foreign minister that Lombardy should be surrendered, warning that if outside mediation by Britain and France failed, the French would lose patience and (with British approval) would drive the Austrians 'clean over the Alps', the natural dividing line between Germans and Italians.[4]

It was the Austrians, however, who seized the initiative by defeating the Italians at the battle of Novara. At the end of 1848 Palmerston was left with the not entirely comfortable thought that, if the Austrians refused to leave quietly, the ultimate fate of Italy – given the military weakness of the latter's miscellaneous components – might be determined primarily by France. Yet in his usual insouciant manner (and unlike some cabinet colleagues), he continued to insist that, if and when France intervened, Britain should be able to 'prevent any permanently bad consequences from resulting from it'. Palmerston, while always sensitive to realities, preferred to wear the mask of an optimist rather than a fatalist. Something unexpected might turn up to his advantage as had happened on a number of occasions in the past. Flexibility was all. Thus when he redrew parts of the map of Europe, he did so with the lightest of pencils. The lines could easily be erased.

In the course of 1849 the Austrians completely restored their position in north Italy. The same year saw the emergence in Vienna of an ambitious and strong-minded chief minister, Prince Felix von Schwarzenberg. The latter had no time for Palmerston and his pretensions to act as the omniscient adviser to Europe. An Austro–Sardinian peace was signed on 6 August 1849, with Britain and France being limited to a show of diplomatic concern for the government in Turin. Nor was it really to Palmerston's taste when French troops – acting on behalf of the Pope – restored the status quo in Rome by defeating the Italian republicans who had seized control of that city. Yet with the conservative powers confidently reasserting themselves, Britain had no choice but to lean towards France in the interest of the balance of power. Palmerston, as usual making a virtue out of a necessity, claimed that anything else would entail a sacrifice of 'truth, principle, or justice'. It would also be unpopular with many people at home.[5]

At the same time Palmerston's respect for liberal principles remained highly selective. Whatever his views on the internal management of the Habsburg Empire in general and its future in northern Italy in particular, he still rated it an essential component of the balance of power. He wrote at one point that the empire's survival depended upon an energetic ruler to assist in the battle between 'honest men' and the 'turbulent, the poor and the rogues'. With regard to the stability of central Europe, he was plainly at one with those who believed that were it not for the fact that the Austrian Empire already existed, it would be necessary to invent it. Small successor states could not fulfil its vital role in the European states system – especially against Russia.[6] Above all Hungary had to remain part of the empire.

More to the point, the tsar was of the same opinion, although in his case the need was sharpened by the fear that unrest could easily spread from Hungary to Poland. Yet once again he acted more pragmatically and cautiously than the epithet, the 'gendarme of Europe', might suggest. His government's financial position was by no means strong. He also listened to his advisers as he tried to understand the various forces which were at work in Europe. He delayed, too, until he was convinced that an autocratic government would survive in Vienna. He even entered into diplomatic relations with the French Republic in May 1849 under its new president, Louis Napoleon. However suspect as the nephew of the Emperor Napoleon, here was a relatively reassuring figure compared with some of the forces which were still at large in 1849. France's military action against the Roman Republic also ensured that she was conveniently occupied elsewhere. Poland, however, remained the most pressing consideration. This was Russia's Achilles's heel. The 10 000 Poles serving in Kossuth's army against the Habsburgs were obviously inspired by the hope that a Hungarian victory would be a step towards the liberation of their own homeland.[7]

The Russian intervention in Hungary received secret encouragement from Palmerston. Although the latter seized appropriate opportunities to speak out and win liberal and radical support at home, his concern for Austria's place in the European balance meant that in private he could sound very like the Castlereagh of 1815–22. He detected advantages even in the renewed alignment of Russia and Austria. The former would in fact be helping to consolidate an empire whose strength might be vital at some future time against Russia herself in Europe or the Near East. As it was Russian troops had been deployed to insulate the Danubian Principalities from the

European upheavals of 1848. The Russians might talk of temporary occupation, but what did this really mean?[8] The troops were in fact removed in 1851.

At the same time as Russian intervention in Hungary was ensuring the defeat of Kossuth, Britain and Russia were beginning to act broadly in parallel in the disputes between the Germans and the Danes over the fate of the duchies of Schleswig and Holstein. Together in 1848–9 they twice helped to negotiate armistices to end military clashes. Both Russia and Britain feared a change to the balance in the southern Baltic region, a vital window on the world for the Russians, and an area of strategic and commercial importance to the British. Nicholas was also moved by sympathy for the Danish monarchy and hostility towards the rebels. Here again he saw himself as the defender of the treaties of 1815. The two powers were helped by the fact that neither the Prussians nor the leaders of the Frankfurt Assembly showed much capacity for effective cooperation or for running their own domestic affairs. The Prussian king quickly wearied of association with German liberals. He was also being urged by Russia to avoid association with any but true conservative forces in Germany. In due course Russia and Britain, with some assistance from France, were able to bring the question of the disputed duchies to a temporary close in favour of the Danes by the Treaty of London of May 1852.

The events in Prussia and Germany as a whole in 1848–9 prompted Palmerston to have second thoughts about the place of the non-Austrian Germans in his preferred Europe. Earlier, in 1847, he had gone as far as to argue that the 'great interests' of Britain and Germany were the same – even though the *Zollverein* had raised tariff barriers against British trade. Britain, he wrote, had an interest in a Germany (excluding Austria) which was 'rich, united and strong', and served as a barrier to France and Russia, both of them 'aggressive powers' and divided at that time only by the tsar's personal animosity towards Orleanist France. But in 1848–9 the Prussians had turned out to be unexpectedly (if spasmodically) aggressive. German experiments in constitutionalism had proved to be either a facade or a cause of disorder. Palmerston had no time for those who advocated a *Grossdeutsche* solution ('a monster of an empire') with the inclusion of the Habsburg domains. This would upset the balance to the disadvantage of Britain and France. The Germans, if united, seemed unlikely to form a progressive nonexpansionist power in the heart of Europe to complement what he was still hoping would emerge in Italy.[9]

In the end it was the Russians who helped to resolve the competition between Austria and Prussia. They needed both German states as allies in defence of the conservative cause, and the tsar also wanted each to content itself broadly with the distribution of power in Germany as established in 1815. The rise of Schwarzenberg in Vienna, and the vigour with which they had reasserted themselves in Prague and Italy encouraged Nicholas to rate the Austrians above the Prussians as effective defenders of the status quo against nationalism and liberalism. It was therefore natural for Russia to lean towards Austria when Prussia continued to try to expand her influence in Germany after 1848. Russian troops were mobilised and the situation seemed particularly tense in November 1850. The Prussians, however, were too weak to fight and soon gave way. King Frederick William IV, though not lacking in ambition for his realm or his dynasty, also valued Austria as a necessary bulwark against revolution.

Schwarzenberg, too, for all his cynical ruthlessness, recognised the desirability of close cooperation with Prussia – provided the latter knew her place and followed the right political line. He was even prepared to accord Prussia a privileged position in north Germany in return for a full acknowledgement of Austria's overall pre-eminence in the German confederation. Thus, despite the very real competition and tension which preceded the so-called 'humiliation' of Prussia at Olmütz in November 1850, some historians believe that the outcome was in many respects a compromise. It could be taken as a signal that the two powers had agreed to return to the pre-1848 relationship.[10]

William Carr suggests that in so far as there existed any 'basic weakness' among the Austrian policy-makers between 1848–66, this did not arise from personal failings or naivete so much as from 'a propensity to believe, despite ominous signs to the contrary, that Prussia in the final analysis would always agree that dualism would prove the only salvation for conservative monarchy'. What they did not reckon with was the emergence of Prussian leaders – notably Bismarck – who would actually engage in war to achieve mastery in Germany, and would do so in the belief that the old order could best be defended, not by maintaining the status quo, but by seeking more control over the new forces which had become so evident in 1848. In particular they would strive to extend Prussian power in the name of German nationalism.[11]

It did not take Prussia long to emerge from any shadow cast by Olmütz, helped by a brief bid from Schwarzenberg in 1851 to reform the Confederation to Austria's advantage. This incurred Russian displeasure. Soon afterwards (May 1851) the two German powers put on a show of unity at Dresden against revolution and in defence of Austrian integrity. To the Russians this suggested at least a partial return to the triple alignment which had existed intermittently since 1813. Some fellow feeling indeed prevailed until it was exposed to excessive strain in the run-up to the Crimean War. Indeed Frederick William IV himself hankered after the defunct Holy Alliance (and even a revived Holy Roman Empire) under Austrian leadership to form part of a wider European organisation for the security of all against France. Prussia would act as a powerful second-in-command with a special military role. Such ideas, however, belonged to a past age. What signified at this time were Prussia's improving economic and financial circumstances, her leadership of the *Zollverein*, and the fact that Germany remained her prime area of interest whereas Austria had additional commitments in Italy and interests in the Near East. The Habsburgs were also deprived of the services of the ambitious and inventive Schwarzenberg who died suddenly in April 1852.

### Towards the Crimean War

In the early 1850s it seemed that the forces of revolution had been crushed – at least for the time being. In the east something akin to the 'Holy Alliance' was once again in being for the defence of the old order. If there was a threat to the peace, this seemed most likely to originate from the conspiratorial inclinations of Louis Napoleon. This proved to be only partly the case. That matters took such a dramatic turn as early as 1852–4 owed much more to the immoderate behaviour of the ultra-conservative tsar in response to what was in fact a very limited bid for prestige by the new Bonaparte in the Near East. The ensuing war and its outcome thereafter did much to facilitate the drastic challenges to the Europe of the Vienna Settlement by Napoleon himself, Cavor and finally by Bismarck.

Nicholas in his last years was increasingly disposed to see the world in simple but stark terms. Russia's part in the defeat of the

Hungarians in 1849 had left him in a great state of elation and over-confidence. The British ambassador thought him 'drunk with success'. The tsar was more than ever convinced of the superiority of absolutism as a system of government and – of course – the invincibility of his armies.[12] He was also reassured by his relations with and the conduct of Austria and Prussia. The truth was rather different. Russia was by no means so secure and formidable as the tsar and some of his advisers believed. Nor could she take the eastern alliance for granted or confidently assume that France and Britain were incapable of combining against her. The determinants of policy in each capital required constant and objective study, something which Nicholas proved less and less capable of doing.

A short-lived crisis (between Russia and Austria on one side and Britain and France on the other) over the fate of the Hungarian refugees who had fled to Turkey in 1849 provided some warning signals to all the powers. These were not correctly interpreted in St Petersburg – or indeed elsewhere. The crisis demonstrated the ease with which relations could deteriorate in the Near East and provided a sharp reminder that there were issues on which Britain and France might line up on the same side. If Palmerston was in part playing to the gallery of progressive opinion in Britain by taking up the case of the refugees, he was also acting on his usual suspicions concerning Russian intentions towards the Ottoman Empire. Nicholas was infuriated by an Anglo–French naval demonstration in support of the Turks, and began to question whether Russian interests were adequately protected by the Straits Convention of 1841. Thus contingency plans were drawn up for a pre-emptive seizure of the Straits, and for pressure to be put on the Turks to join a defensive alliance. In short, Nicholas was hinting at a return to the era of Unkiar Skelessi. As it happened, the refugee affair was gradually defused, it being found possible to save face all round by agreeing that some diplomats might have behaved with excessive zeal. Shaky finances also encouraged thoughts of compromise in Vienna. Nevertheless the ease with which the crisis had erupted should have been noted by all.[13]

Anglo–French relations were also fragile. The British prime minister, Lord John Russell, had written in May 1850 that while Britain should be careful to avoid any provocation, 'let every calculation be made as to what we could do in an emergency. I believe the French majority wish to divert attention by foreign quarrels, ...'[14] Louis Napoleon's coup in December 1851 to strengthen his hold on the

French presidency caused further alarm despite Palmerston's cheerful insistence that he was preferable to the alternatives – and especially 'the Reds'. But Palmerston's eagerness to accept the new order was so much out of step with opinion in Britain that his cabinet colleagues (much put out by his persistent and cavalier disregard of their views on foreign policy) seized their chance to manoeuvre him out of office. The nation was soon in the grip of another invasion panic, and this was followed early in 1852 by some nervousness as to French intentions towards Belgium. The British Mediterranean fleet was stationed west of Malta with fast steamers at Gibraltar to warn of any hostile French moves, while British consuls in northern France were ordered to report suspicious military and naval preparations. A French agent informed Paris that it would not be easy to regain British trust and goodwill.

Nor were the British alone in their fears of France. Nesselrode, reflecting on the year 1852, bleakly concluded:

> Napoleon's absence of principles makes it impossible to establish true relations of confidence, makes vigilance a law, and puts Europe perpetually on the alert. It is peace, but armed peace with all its expenses and uncertainty. Only the union of the Great Powers is capable of maintaining it.[15]

Little had changed, it seems, since the final struggle against the great Napoleon himself. Aberdeen, who had worked so single-mindedly for good relations with France in the 1840s, now spoke grimly to the Russian ambassador of his fear of Louis Napoleon:

> If he thinks us undivided, he will fall on us. ... We should begin by being beaten even with equal numbers. Fifty thousand Frenchmen would beat fifty thousand Englishmen; and we have not so much to oppose a sudden invasion.[16]

Such opinions must have been music in the tsar's ears, and may well have encouraged him to believe that Britain and France could not unite against him. Palmerston himself concluded that the French emperor was intent on developing the strength 'to strike a stunning blow' whenever and wherever he chose. Napoleon did nothing to reduce the tension with his hint in March 1853 that he no longer regarded the treaties of 1815 as binding and would certainly treat them as void in the event of war.[17]

Matthew Anderson describes Napoleon III as a 'strange man [who] united within himself, in unstable and shifting equilibrium, many of the dominant tendencies of the age'.[18] As a Bonaparte he was anxious to uphold the honour of his family and at the same time to learn from the errors of his great but excessively ambitious uncle. As a Bonaparte, too, he felt he had to be seen to be more successful than his Orleanist predecessors. Above all he had to consolidate his political position at home. This meant paying some attention to Catholic, commercial and other special interest groups. His ministers differed among themselves as to whether their enigmatic master was too cautious or too ambitious in foreign affairs. A recent biographer sees him as 'an unpredictable maverick' and 'a visionary', yet also as a practical leader who preferred diplomacy to war.[19] Yet for all his political guile, the results of his scheming were often very different from his intentions. He was inclined to speak out too boldly when silence might have served him better. He also failed to appreciate just what disturbing memories the name of Bonaparte could conjure up throughout Europe.

Napoleon clearly aspired to gain a place in history as the man who restored France to the level of Britain and Russia, and who revised the detested Vienna Settlement. At the same time he was astute enough to see that the other powers would not tolerate gains in Belgium and the westernmost parts of Germany. To seize the initiative, he had to find a region where he would not automatically provoke a coalition against himself. The Near East seemed to offer interesting possibilities. Indeed F. J. Coppa[20] attributes to him ideas for 'a war against Russia as the mechanism for disrupting the Holy Alliance', thereby opening the way to a comprehensive revision of the map of Europe – including the expulsion of Russia from the Near East, Poland and Finland – and the advance of nationalism. Hints to this effect were dropped in discourses and conversation by the emperor. Yet talk of this kind did not necessarily mean that all-out action would follow. J. F. McMillan for instance is persuaded that by the summer of 1853, when war in the Near East began to seem probable, Napoleon became increasingly wary.[21]

The emperor's initial moves in the Levant were relatively modest. He intervened in the long-established rivalry between Roman Catholic and Orthodox monks over the guardianship of the Holy

Places in and around Jerusalem. But this was promptly (and wrongly) interpreted in St Petersburg as a challenge to Russian influence. The tsar believed he could count on Austrian and Prussian support against France, and he surely took comfort from Aberdeen's appointment as prime minister in Britain in December 1852, with Palmerston being relegated to the humdrum duties of the Home Office. Nicholas had discussed the Near Eastern Question with Aberdeen (then foreign minister) in 1844 and duly persuaded himself that more had been agreed on the future of Turkey than was really the case. It is true that Aberdeen saw eye to eye with the tsar on many matters relating to peace and order in the heart of Europe. Nor did he have any liking for the Turks. But the tsar was wrong to assume that Britain would automatically support him – or at least refrain from hostile action – in the event of a Russo–Turkish dispute.

Russian fears of French activity deepened in 1852 when the Turks yielded more influence to the Roman Catholics at the Holy Places. British talk of compromise and reference to international law was not considered helpful. Even so cautious and pragmatic a figure as Nesselrode was (or had to profess to be) firm on the subject of Russia's Christian mission to the Near East. The tsar himself was becoming even less responsive to warnings from his advisers as to the likely behaviour of other powers. He was increasingly convinced that the collapse of the Ottoman Empire was only a matter of time, and he spoke darkly of the need to accept God's will should this occur. Strong action by Russia would be required, but he did not doubt that she would have right on her side given her protective role over Orthodox peoples under Ottoman rule since the last century. Nicholas, however, failed to see that other powers did not necessarily interpret Russia's treaty claims as generously as he did.

Nesselrode, in contrast, knew that Russia could easily find herself isolated. He noted, for instance, that Austria had interests of her own in the Ottoman Empire, whereas the tsar was surprised and embittered when support was not forthcoming from the Austrian emperor. Nesselrode also appreciated that France did not alarm the other powers so much in the Levant as she did in the heart of Europe. Indeed it was Russia who was the more likely to excite suspicion. The tsar, however, was deaf to such wise words. He saw himself as the defender of absolutism and Orthodox Christianity. Indeed by the start of 1853 the mind of this increasingly emotional and dogmatic man was – according to one historian – beginning 'to go awry'. Nesselrode included in one dispatch in April 1853 (obviously at the behest of Nicholas) the assertion 'that the true thinking of the Emperor ... is of a higher order than one can comprehend in Constantinople and, perhaps, elsewhere, ... [since] His Majesty ... obeys his conscience'. One detects parallels here with Alexander I. Professor Goldfrank in a recent and invaluable study of the Crimean War concludes that the tsar was 'more responsible than any other person' for the 'bizarre' conflict which began in 1854. Based on comprehensive research, he suggests that war would have been avoided if 'the leadership of every major power in 1853 had acted rationally'. But he also poses the testing question, 'But what to do when another Great Power starts to act irrationally against its own interest ...?'[22]

Nicholas I had no desire for war, but saw it as a legitimate instrument with which to protect Russian influence in the Near East. Unfortunately Russia was unduly dependent on force to uphold her interests, this being a region in which she was ill-equipped to compete for trade with other rivals. Nor would independent Orthodox Christian successor states in the Balkans necessarily look to Russia (the land of serfdom and extreme autocratic government) for future guidance and support. Not surprisingly some historians have persuasively argued that Russia from the outset faced such an unfavourable potential 'correlation of forces' in the Near East (a fact well understood by Nesselrode and Brunnow), that policy should have been made accordingly. The tsar, however, feared that Russian interests were being eroded to such an extent that patient diplomacy was not the answer. He hoped for British and Turkish cooperation, but was resolved to fight if necessary.[23]

Such was Nicholas's impatience that the Austrian ambassador began to suspect a plot for the partition of the Turkish Empire. Although the issue of the moment was still that of French support of Catholic claims over the Holy Places, Nicholas was beginning to see Bonapartism and the 'revolutionaries' everywhere. In the winter of 1852–3 military preparations were also begun in case the Turks proved obdurate. Yet some senior Russian officers were already troubled by the prospect of a British riposte at the Straits – not to mention a general war. The Austrian and Prussian monarchs were acknowledging Napoleon III as '*mon frère*' – a clear signal that the new French emperor was not regarded as an untouchable. Nesselrode even regretted the tsar's overture to the British in February 1853 with its frank reference to the desirability for concerted action if the collapse of the Ottoman Empire proved unavoidable. The British foreign secretary (Lord John Russell) replied that there was no imminent danger, and called for restraint and reliance on the 'mutual concert between the Great Powers'. But he also unwisely referred to the 'exceptional protection' afforded to the sultan's subjects by Russia which was 'no doubt prescribed and sanctioned by Treaty'. This, rather than Russell's warnings, was what the tsar wanted to read.

A spurt of diplomatic activity in Constantinople in the spring of 1853 finally produced a compromise over the Holy Places. This was encouraging up to a point. Yet it also deprived the Russians of a grievance without advancing their influence within the Ottoman Empire – their main objective. Their special emissary, Count Menshikov, was bullishly described as an 'envoy-herald of peace or war'. Even the offer to the Turks of a defensive alliance against France could be interpreted as another threat to Ottoman sovereignty. The tsar himself had reached a state of mind akin to that in Vienna in June–July 1914 or London in 1956 (after the nationalisation of the Suez Canal). Nesselrode, however, was increasingly impressed by the warnings from Brunnow in London that a hostile coalition including Britain and France, and perhaps even Austria, might be created against Russia.[24]

Menshikov persisted in his efforts to intimidate the Turks in talks in Constantinople, particularly on the subject of Russia's assumed rights of protection over the Orthodox Christians within the empire, a demand which the Turks needed little or no encouragement from the other powers to reject. As early as 5 May it was the belief of most of the other diplomats on the spot that further Turkish concessions were out of the question, especially given the tone in which the Russian demands were being made. The tsar, it was widely feared, was seeking something akin to a protectorate over the Orthodox Christians in Turkey.

Professor V. N. Vinogradov has recently contended that, while the Menshikov demands were apparently very damaging to the Turks, the 'correlation of forces' (given British and French 'omnipotence' at Constantinople) should have ensured that the sultan suffered no real loss of authority.[25] This, however, may assume more rationality than was normally to be found even in an age of 'classical' diplomacy. Palmerston usually favoured a firm stand over the smallest issues before one began to examine the possibility of a settlement.

The best hope for the Russians at this time was to retain the confidence of Aberdeen.

The latter's willingness to give the tsar (as opposed to Louis Napoleon) the benefit of the doubt is well documented. He was in regular contact with Brunnow until September 1853, and through him tried to impress the Russians with his efforts to moderate French conduct while begging St Petersburg for restraint in return. He did this despite his worries over Menshikov's reported behaviour in Constantinople and despite his own feeling that Russia's demands were unreasonable as early as 30 May. For the time being he refused to think of war, relying instead on the hope that Nicholas was acting in good faith. He did, however, add the proviso that 'if his whole conduct should have been a cheat, the case is altered'. Eight days later he feared that a rapid drift to war was taking place.[26] In July the Russians confirmed his worst fears when they occupied the Danubian Principalities. Aberdeen thought this could fairly be treated by the Turks as a *casus belli*.

This intrusion similarly alarmed the Austrians with their Danubian interests, and left no chancellery in any doubt as to the seriousness of the situation. An ambassadorial conference was soon at work in Vienna under the direction of the Austrian foreign minister. Briefly, at the end of July and the beginning of August, it seemed as if the Concert was about to achieve one of its greatest triumphs. The Vienna Note of 28 July proposed to internationalise the protection of the Christian populations of the Balkans, but did not demand an immediate Russian evacuation of the Principalities. Given the presence of the Anglo–French fleets off Besika Bay, this seemed to leave all the pieces roughly balanced so that each power could begin to back off without losing face. The response of the Russians appeared helpful. They had been careful to say nothing during the preparation of the Vienna Note, which they quickly accepted. Briefly this seemed to reassure even the Russophobes among the British press and public. Briefly, too, the militants within the cabinet (including Palmerston) were disposed to give diplomacy a chance.

Palmerston, according to one witness, had always believed that the Turks could be relied upon not to exacerbate the situation. Aberdeen had rightly been much less certain, and was soon regretting that the British ambassador in Constantinople had not been immediately ordered to press the Turks to accept the Vienna Note. But Goldfrank properly highlights just how much luck, diplomatic skill and actual pressure would have been required for this move to have succeeded. Few diplomats were hopeful at the time, and the Turks duly rejected the Note on 20 August. Aberdeen on hearing the news thought the response 'suicidal, and [that] some fatal influence must be at work'. The Vienna Note, he agreed, was not perfect, but the tsar could not be expected to make further concessions.[27]

Before the powers in concert could decide on their next move, a second blow fell early in September with the arrival of news of the 'violent' interpretation of the Vienna Note offered by Nesselrode (but obviously at the behest of the tsar). The Turks, he stated, must 'take account of Russia's active solicitude for her co-religionists in Turkey'. Russia, it seemed, had reverted to her original position. The incident also highlights the degree to which the Concert rested on personal trust and relationships. Aberdeen felt betrayed having, in his own mind, done his best to work for a fair settlement. Perhaps, too, he felt he had been made to seem weak and naive. His foreign secretary, Clarendon, abandoned his hope that the Russians were following an essentially peaceful policy. Both men now believed that Russia was intent on nothing less than the subversion of the Ottoman Empire. If Aberdeen even now hoped to avert war, Clarendon feared the worst.[28]

Yet once again there were signs that the tsar was anxious to pull back from the brink. In talks with the emperor of Austria at Olmütz late in September, he spoke of requiring only the maintenance of the status quo in the Ottoman Empire (though this would not have precluded lengthy talks over the real meaning of, for instance, the old Russo–Turkish treaties), and he promised to evacuate the Principalities once the Vienna Note was signed. An Austrian attempt to capitalise on this concession was upset when the Turks declared war on Russia. Although the two belligerents hinted in November at an interest in the good offices of the other powers, the slide to a wider war became almost unstoppable with the so-called 'massacre of Sinope' on 20 November when a Russian squadron destroyed a Turkish naval force on the southern coast of the Black Sea.

Although this was a legitimate act of war, it played straight into the hands of the war groups in the British government and the country at large. The French were also outraged. A crucial meeting of the British cabinet on 20 December decided not only that the fleet should be sent into the Black Sea but that the Russian navy must return to and remain within its base at Sevastopol. Gladstone vainly argued that such an extreme and humiliating demand should be balanced by a requirement that the Turks give guarantees concerning their future conduct. Here was yet another crucial mistake in this unhappy saga. Aberdeen's biographer, Maureen Chamberlain, comments that the prime minister must have understood that a demand for 'the fleet of a Great Power [to] return to port was tantamount to a declaration of war'. There might have been a case for the creation in modern parlance of an 'exclusion zone' to ensure that Russian and Turkish warships did not encounter each other. Unfortunately there also existed what seem to have been unfounded fears in London that the French might decide to act unilaterally – that is, they might either send their fleet into the Black Sea or recall it to home waters. Nevertheless it was not long before some British and French ministers were showing a degree of regret or embarrassment over the forthright treatment of the Russian fleet. Gladstone remained critical while Aberdeen, much affected by the nightmarish sequence of events, reflected on the occasions (and notably the Olmütz proposals) when a diplomatic breakthrough had seemed within reach.[29] No one had worked harder for peace or a 'consensual' solution.

### War and Peace, 1854–6

An Anglo–French ultimatum was dispatched to Russia on 27 February 1854. It demanded the evacuation of the Principalities by the end of April. Austria was equally anxious to see Russian troops removed from the region of the Danube. Here was a further example of the failure on the Russian side to evaluate the international environment with due care and attention. Austria of all the powers was most anxious to avoid war in the Near East. Yet whatever the unease of ministers in Vienna over the erratic conduct of Britain and France, they feared Russia in the Principalities, especially as she was already opposing improvements to the lower Danube to protect her trade from Austrian competition. Although some Austrians in 1854 believed that a deal might be struck with Russia to partition the Balkans, Buol (the foreign minister) argued that Russia as the stronger party must always be the main beneficiary in the long run. He had some reason to be wary of Russian overtures. The tsar was soon to define his war aims as the release of the Christian parts of Turkey so that they could 're-enter the family of Christian states of Europe'.[30]

Once the war began, Buol insisted on the removal of the Russian army from the Principalities. In return he promised the tsar that an occupying Austrian army would exclude British and French forces from this sensitive region. The tsar, however, complained bitterly of 'the faithlessness of the Austrians' in return for his assistance against the Hungarians in 1849 (forgetful of his own Polish self-interest in that affair). More to the point, the Russians could never feel really certain that Austria would remain a non-belligerent on their south-western borders for the rest of the war. Numerous Russian troops were consequently tied up in this region.

Buol, too, had his problems. If he opted to do as little as possible, this would be widely regarded as a role unworthy of a great power. Austria would gain credit with no one. It was also impossible to ignore Austria's interest in some weakening of Russia's position around the lower Danube. He was thus unable to play the totally dis-interested peacemaker, and had to associate himself to some extent with the war aims of Britain and France. Thus the 'Four Points' which emerged as a possible basis for peace in August 1854 required significant Russian concessions in the Near East.[31] Austria also con-cluded an alliance with Prussia in April 1854 only to find that Berlin's main objective was to prevent a firm Austrian alignment with the western powers. This might lead to a more general war in-cluding Germany. At the same time Prussia intended to use her neutrality to seek advantages in the German confederation and in trade with Russia. Only from the end of 1855 did Prussia exert pres-sure on Russia in favour of peace.

Buol continued his search for a compromise. Under the 'Four Points' Russia was required to renounce any special rights of inter-vention in Serbia or the Principalities; to accept the free navigation of the Danube; to agree to the revision of the Straits Convention of 1841 'in the interests of the balance of power'; and lastly to give up all claims to protect Christians in the Ottoman Empire. Three months of talks in Vienna collapsed in June 1855 when the Russians refused to accept the critical third 'Point', especially once the allies made it clear that this must include the neutralisation of the Black Sea. Buol, meanwhile, was not only continuing to alienate Russia (the power which before the Crimea had had many reasons to support Austria as an ally in central Europe), but was disappointing the hopes of the western powers of direct Austrian support in the war. Buol in return complained that the British and French were too inflexible over the peace terms. Much more damaging, however, was the probability that whatever Buol did he was unlikely to forge permanent links with the western powers, links which were needed to help protect Austrian interests in the Balkans, Italy and Germany.

The French and British finally managed to compel the Russians to admit defeat. It had been necessary to confine the fighting to accessible parts of the Russian periphery – that is from the Baltic and Black Seas. Neither partner found these operations easy or cheap, but the strains imposed upon them were tolerable compared with the huge difficulties experienced by the Russians. Whereas the attackers' lines of communication by sea were hampered only by the weather, the Russians had the utmost difficulty in moving troops and supplies overland to the Crimea. They had few railways even in the north. Their large formations of infantry began the war with few modern weapons. Numerous units were tied down by the allied naval threat in the Baltic. Others had to watch the common border (more than 400 miles in length) with the Habsburg Empire in Galicia. Customs revenue as well as the economy as a whole suffered from the allied blockade. Exports fell by 80 per cent and imports by nearly 35 per cent. The government also lacked a modern financial system to sustain a long war. Inflationary pressures developed, and fears soon followed for the internal stability of the empire. The war underlined just how far Russia lagged behind Britain and France in modern institutions and equipment. Even so Sevastopol (in the Crimea and the scene of the greatest single trial of strength) heroically held out for almost a year.

Its fall in September 1855 opened the way to a possible settlement. The allies were at last in a position from which they could credibly demand the neutralisation of the Black Sea. Yet Palmerston would have preferred to fight on for bigger results. As early as March 1854 he had briefly sketched what he described as his 'beau ideal' – the loss by Russia of Finland, Poland, the Crimea, Circassia and Georgia, not to mention her Black Sea fleet. But victory on this scale would have required the active involvement of at least Austria, Prussia and Sweden. It also had an ominous Napoleonic ring to it. Aberdeen and apparently most of the cabinet sensibly dismissed the scenario as a fantasy. This, however, did not bring ministers any closer to a consensus as to whether this was a war primarily to save and strengthen the Ottoman Empire, or – as Clarendon enigmatically suggested – to establish a 'state of things which will render peace durable' in Europe as a whole, and lead to a review of treaties other than those relating to the Ottoman Empire.

From 1855 Palmerston was prime minister, and he continued to regard the fall of Sevastopol as only a stage in a longer war to create 'a long line of circumvallation' to contain Russia at a safer distance from the heart of Europe and the Near East. He even declared in the House of Commons that 'the kingdom of Poland as at present constituted, and at present occupied, is a standing menace to Germany'. Honesty compelled him to add that it would be for the German powers to decide whether it was in their interest to insist on changes at the expense of Russia. But he left no clue as to how he intended to control the likely ripple effects upon the balance of power of so drastic a revision of Russia's western frontiers. The dangers can be seen from the readiness of many in France, for instance, to support a bigger war provided it led to Polish independence. Shrewd minds in London were bound to ask where it would all end. It was not as if a new version of the 1815 Quadruple Alliance with the same commitment to the status quo was likely to emerge after the defeat of Russia. As it was Britain was to be overshadowed by France at the Congress of Paris, French troops overall having played the larger part in the campaign in the Crimea.

Thus a bigger war might have left Britain in a weaker position – despite her naval and financial resources. France would have demanded major changes to the map of Europe. The German powers would not necessarily have been sufficiently strengthened to preserve the balance in the heart of Europe – or might have been too divided to have done so. Thus Russia (a power which Palmerston himself had sometimes welcomed as a useful partner) might have been seriously weakened primarily to the advantage of France – and Napoleon would surely not have neglected to assert his new-found strength. Palmerston would thus have substituted one challenger for another. The more one looks at his plans, the more probable it seems that they would have had effects far beyond Britain's power to control.

Briefly it appeared as if the new tsar (Alexander II succeeded Nicholas in 1855) would give Palmerston the longer war he desired. Alexander initially argued that concessions were inconsistent with Russian honour. Prussia, however, warned she might have to join the allies unless there was an early peace, while Austria (though still trying to act as a sort of intermediary) threatened to break off relations if the latest terms were refused. The tsar was not without support in St Petersburg, but his leading advisers (including Nesselrode) warned of bankruptcy and the loss of extensive territory to the south and west. Some recalled the fate of Sweden after the death of Charles XII or warned of growing internal disorder. A peace concluded in 1856, they argued, need be no more than a truce; the latest terms gave Russia hope of recovery within a finite period.[32] Alexander reluctantly gave way.

Palmerston, too, was becoming resigned to peace through want of foreign support. The search for a final settlement began in Paris early in 1856. Clarendon represented Britain at the Congress, and if he did not enjoy the eminence of Castlereagh at Vienna, he was able to exploit the fact that he (like Castlereagh before him) was on the spot and better able to evaluate what was and was not possible given the aims, strengths and weaknesses of the other participants. Indeed he claimed to his chief that 'everybody [in Paris] was against us, our motives were suspected, and our policy was denounced'.[33] Palmerston himself admitted to the Queen on 30 March 1856 (the day the Treaty of Paris was signed) that Britain had been obliged to settle for less security against Russia than he had originally envisaged. There was disappointment, too, among those in Britain who had become wildly excited by hopes of a spectacular victory over Russian autocracy and expansionism.

Such people exaggerated British military and diplomatic influence. Clarendon was not alone in his view that 'in the eyes of foreign nations ... our prestige has greatly diminished'. Even Palmerston was learning to be less confident of Britain's ability to dominate the stage. Whereas in February 1855 he may well have been one of the sources of inspiration behind a description of the sort of army that Britain ideally needed if she was to fight as an equal of the other powers, after 1856 he soon acknowledged the unrealism of such an idea. It ran contrary to the nation's priorities and prejudices. He even remarked in the Commons in 1858 that Russia and France, as well as the United States, were 'so far independent of naval warfare that even a naval reverse does not materially affect them'. Technological and economic changes were increasing the security of such states against sea power.[34]

Much more vulnerable was the position of the Habsburg Empire. As Bridge remarks, Austria had bought very temporary security in the east at the price of long-term exposure to danger firstly from Napoleon III and later from Bismarck. Nor could she expect any sympathy from a Russia that was intent on recovering the positions and influence in the Near East which she had lost in the Crimean War.[35] Indeed Russia herself might pose limited or indirect threats to Austrian interests as she looked for ways to re-establish herself as a great power. Yet Austria's gloomy prospects were the product of more than diplomatic miscalculation. In many ways she had been the victim of crises generated by the actions of others. Underlying all was her own vulnerability. Although she could still be ranked above Prussia as a power, she had to sustain more commitments in relation to her basic strength. The Crimea robbed her of any possibility of friendship with Russia until the 1870s, thereby increasing in the interim her vulnerability in Italy and Germany.

Even at the Congress of Paris the Austrian position in northern Italy was being questioned to some extent by Britain as well as France – the two powers with which she was supposedly aligned. There were suggestions that Austria might remain in the Principalities – but only if she gave up her richer possessions in Italy. Although this might have removed France as a potential enemy, there was no guarantee that France (or any other power) would thereafter help Austria to hold the Principalities against a revived Russia – or indeed any of her territory against an attacker. Nor did the Anglo–Austro–French treaty of April 1856 which guaranteed the Ottoman Empire hold out much comfort. Franco–Austrian and Franco–British differences were always probable, while Britain's concern for the Straits could still leave Austria unsupported on the Danube and still more so in Galicia. Thus the Treaty of Paris could never enlist the degree of long-lasting international backing which had been enjoyed by the Vienna Settlement. This had experienced only modest changes due to the self-interest of the four allies. There was no such tendency after 1856 to defend or regulate the status quo. In fact amid the complex manoeuvring of the years down to 1871, it was the revisionist powers, not the defenders of the status quo, which formed the majority. A discontented Russia made it easier for the revisionists (France and Prussia) to assert themselves at the expense of an isolated Austria.

Meanwhile Napoleon III found himself in 1856 (and for a few years thereafter) the ruler of the leading power on the continent. This was the start of what was to prove France's period of greatest influence in Europe between 1815 and 1914. Her army had enhanced its reputation in the recent war; her navy was shortly to cause the British serious if not lasting concern. Paris in 1856 was the scene of the greatest international gathering since Vienna and the biggest French diplomatic triumph since the era of Tilsit, Erfurt and Schoenbrunn (1807–9). Napoleon III could feel that the name of Bonaparte was once more respected (if not trusted). If a revision of the Vienna Settlement did not seem imminent, progress might still be made given the Russian determination to reverse the losses inflicted in Paris. Indeed it was not long before the Russians began to pick up hints that France might be responsive to overtures. Napoleon had already signalled his intent by helping to secure a reduction in Russia's territorial losses in southern Bessarabia.

Despite the fragility of its achievements, the Congress is worthy of some specific attention. The first international meeting to be so categorised for more than 30 years, there were times when the powers acted as if they were moved by feelings of guilt over the recent war, or at the very least as if they felt the need to burnish their images among their peoples by a show of concern for the future peace of Europe. Peace groups (an interesting though not as yet a really powerful force) were urging the Congress to introduce some system of international arbitration. Many references were made to the Concert per se and to the public law of Europe.[36] Briefly – on paper at least – the Congress appeared to be a highwater mark in the history of the European international system. Yet what mattered in the end was the yawning gap between what was professed and what followed in practice.

Article VII, for instance, grandly declared that the Ottoman Empire should 'participate in the advantages of the Public Law and System (*Concert*) of Europe'. Its integrity and independence were guaranteed by all the powers, and any violation would be considered 'a question of general interest'. Article VIII recommended that in the event of any threat to peace involving Turkey and another signatory, there should be no resort to force until the other contracting parties had been given a chance to mediate. Turkey for its part promised reforms under article IX, and affirmed its 'generous intentions' towards its Christian subjects. The European powers recognised the high value of this communication from the sultan, and accepted that they had no right singly or collectively to intervene in the internal affairs of Turkey.

In reality the Turks had secured such ostensibly favourable treatment only after much outside pressure had forced them in February
1856 to promise a comprehensive reform programme. Whether the
Turks could or would deliver such reforms was another matter.
Indeed reforms might merely encourage the various peoples of the
empire in Europe to demand more and so accelerate their progress
to independence. In reality the treaty merely stated how things
should be in the Near East; it was not a solution to its endemic
problems.

Other articles provided for the closure of the Straits to all warships
*in time of peace*, and for the neutralisation of the Black Sea and its
ports. This meant that in time of war foreign navies could mount
an immediate threat to Russia by entering the Black Sea. The semi-
independent Principalities and Serbia also received *collective* guarantees from the powers (though what these would mean in practice
would depend on future circumstances). Indeed the more the unity
and collective responsibilities of the powers were underlined, the
more reason there seemed to be to question their value. The limitations of the Anglo–French–Austrian Treaty of 15 April 1856 have
already been mentioned. In contrast one of the few substantial and
enduring achievements of the Congress was the agreement on the
free navigation of the River Danube. This became part of the 'Public
Law of Europe' with a commission to supervise its implementation.
A second body was set up to improve the navigability of the river.

The Congress also produced a Declaration on Maritime Law
(16 April 1856). This abolished privateering, and stated that for a
naval blockade to be binding it had to be 'effective' – that is it had to
be accompanied by a demonstrable ability to stop ships as they
entered or left a belligerent port. Other concessions were made relating to the treatment of neutral shipping. This could be presented as
an attempt under international law to 'civilise' the conduct of war at
sea. Certainly on paper it heralded a serious weakening of one of the
most important roles of the British navy – namely to injure or destroy
the trade of an enemy. If true, this seemed a surprising concession
for any British government to make (especially in its role as one of
the victors in Paris). In fact ministers reasoned that the agreement
would survive the test of war only as long as it accorded with the national interest. Furthermore much contemporary thinking expected
naval warfare in coastal waters (where an effective blockade might
operate) to take precedence over action on the high seas. Overall

Britain might even gain more than she lost from the declaration. There would, it was assumed, be times when she would be a neutral state. Above all, acceptance was 'prudential', not 'sentimental'.[37]

Finally there was an interesting initiative by Clarendon. This was finally embodied in a protocol despite exceedingly wary responses from Russia and Austria. It urged the powers, 'before appealing to Arms, [to] have recourse, as far as circumstances might allow, to the Good Offices of a friendly Power'. In practice the protocol was ignored in the run-up to each of the wars which was to break out in Europe over the next 15 years. Furthermore not one of the ensuing peace treaties was to be ratified by an international conference. This provides perhaps the best commentary on the efforts to breathe life into the Concert and international law at the Congress of Paris.

# 4

# THE TRANSFORMATION OF EUROPE, 1857–71

'You know where a war begins but you never know where it ends.' (Bismarck)

### Revisionism after the Congress of Paris

Alan Palmer comments on the powers after 1856 that 'for at least 15 years, they were ready again to choose war as an instrument of policy, reverting to the practices of pre-Congress Europe as though there had never been any concept of public law between the nations'. Nesselrode (so often a voice for moderation in St Petersburg) gloomily remarked shortly before his death in 1862 that in 'the future there will be neither diplomacy nor diplomats'.[1] While, as already noted, the strength of the 'consensual' dimension in pre-Crimean diplomacy can easily be exaggerated, it is true that no leader in the previous period had set out to challenge the Vienna Settlement with the same sense of purpose as Napoleon III, Cavor and Bismarck after 1856. Yet, ironically, it had been Nicholas I, the staunchest defender of the status quo, who had helped create conditions which the revisionists were about to exploit to the full.

It is true that the Concert of Europe was not totally eclipsed between 1856 and 1871. Some lesser assemblages met to discuss the Danish duchies, Luxembourg and the Near East. But two such different British foreign secretaries as Palmerston and Lord Stanley agreed that conferences – without considerable prior preparation and agreement – were likely to do more harm than good. Even W. E. Gladstone (who later exceeded even Castlereagh in his support for the Concert) opposed attendance at a congress in 1860 because he expected it to be controlled by the arch-conservatives. Several congress proposals from Napoleon III aroused great suspicion – his aim, it was rightly assumed, being to revise the map of Europe to his advantage.

In short the Concert of Europe was largely irrelevant at a time when the balance among the powers no longer favoured the defenders of the status quo. France, Russia and Prussia were all intent upon change. Not even the challenge presented by subversive forces (notably in Poland and Italy) could persuade the three eastern powers to sink their differences. Indeed Austria aligned herself against Russia at the time of the 1863 Polish revolt. The relations between all the continental powers were therefore highly fluid, and admirably suited to the needs of such skilful opportunists as Napoleon III, Cavor and Bismarck. In the end war could have been averted in 1859 and 1866 only if the common focus of their hostility, the Habsburg Empire, had submitted without a fight. Instead the Austrian leaders were sufficiently confident to choose war, and to do so with some hopes of victory. Both Napoleon III and Bismarck worked assiduously to ensure Austrian isolation, while Napoleon's respect for that empire is highlighted by his expectation of a lengthy Austro–Prussian war in 1866.

The scale of change sought by Bismarck and Napoleon III was inspired in part by the conviction that the existing order at home might be protected and even strengthened by success abroad. This new generation of leaders believed that the obsessive efforts since 1815 to preserve the status quo had failed to create durable defences against revolution as demonstrated by the events of 1848–9. Equally alarming were the programmes put forward by the assorted liberals, nationalists, republicans and socialists in Paris, Frankfurt, Vienna and Rome. Thus if change was inevitable, conservatives and autocrats might find security only by seizing the initiative and showing that they too could win tricks in the new game with nationalism as the most useful suit in the pack. Yet policies of this kind clearly did not lend themselves to adjustment and compromise in the same way as the defensive revisionism of the previous era.

It is true that some restraints on war persisted even after 1856. No power, including France, was strong enough or bold enough to risk conflict with more than one major opponent at a time, and only then if the enemy seemed likely to remain isolated. The attainment of that objective was greatly assisted by Russia's emergence from defeat in the Crimea as a revisionist power. Although Russia herself remained too weak to take major initiatives until the 1870s, her new priorities meant that she welcomed setbacks to Austria and Britain, the main defenders of the Treaty of Paris. Here were animosities which could be put to good use by France (in Italy) and Prussia (in Germany) at the expense of Austria. Furthermore many in Britain (whatever theoretical interest they might have had in Austria as an ally to uphold the Paris treaties) believed that the Habsburgs had no future in Italy. By 1865 Palmerston was again attracted by the idea of a strong Germanic power as the best means of containing Russia and France. If no power wished to destroy the Habsburg Empire outright, several were eager to deprive it (or see it deprived) of certain territories or areas of influence. Above all no powers were willing to fight for Austria provided her losses did not threaten their security. It was only after the unexpected scale of Prussian success in 1866 that the government in Paris realised how much the balance had been altered to the detriment of France. By then it was too late.

In the late-1850s Austrian policy-makers similarly showed little awareness of what was about to befall. They tended to view each problem as self-contained. Francis Joseph was still convinced that Prussia aspired to no more than the second place in Germany. In any case, the empire had to show a bold front to the world: anything less would simply encourage opponents. As Lord Salisbury commented in another context in 1885, 'no state with any life left in it would have allowed a province to be snatched from under its eyes, and stretched out no hand to save it'. Nor, as we shall see, was this brave front by Austria without substance. Finally, if Austrian diplomacy often seemed leaden-footed and uninspired, it has to be remembered that efforts to buy friends would have been a costly and probably unrewarding business in the long run. The only real guarantee for the future lay in other powers reacquiring an interest in the survival of the Habsburg Empire. This did not occur until the 1870s.[2]

The most immediate threat to Austria after 1856 came from Napoleon III.[3] The removal of Habsburg influence from Italy was expected to strengthen France, and was much less likely to provoke a hostile coalition than a bid to extend her north-eastern frontiers.

The aggrieved Russians might be expected to turn a blind eye to a Franco–Austrian dispute over Italy. Although neither Russia nor France could hope for much in the way of assistance from the other, it was enough for Napoleon III to know that Russia would not back Austria. In return he was happy to lend some support to Russian efforts to strengthen the autonomy of the Principalities, Serbia and Montenegro against their Turkish overlords. Indeed increased Russian involvement in the affairs of those peoples might help to keep Russia and Austria apart. As it was, the Franco–Austrian war of 1859 facilitated the early union of the Principalities against the wishes of the Turks, Austrians and British.

With respect to Italy between 1858 and 1860, Napoleon proceeded in such a devious, ambivalent and hesitant fashion that he sometimes drove even that arch-conspirator, Cavor, to anger and desperation. The emperor, whatever he said to Cavor during their conspiratorial meeting of 21 July 1858 at Plombières (only Cavor kept notes), proceeded with considerable caution. He calculated that as many as 200000 French (plus 100000 Italian) soldiers might be needed to defeat Austria.[4] News of some sort of conspiracy soon began to leak out, while Napoleon himself could not resist dropping hints of Franco–Austrian differences. Was this an attempt at psychological pressure on Vienna to yield just enough to make war unnecessary? There were other hints to this effect. But Napoleon's maximum programme was clearly the substitution of French for Austrian influence in northern and central Italy, with an enlarged Piedmont to form part of an Italian version of the German Confederation. A liberal conservative order in Italy should redound to his credit. He also hoped to impress French patriots, reassure Roman Catholics (the pope was to have a leading role in the new federation), and satisfy other interest groups, including some businessmen. Perhaps, too, France might be rewarded by Savoy and Nice. Cavor was in the frustrating position of knowing that he would have to settle for whatever Napoleon chose to deliver.

He could, after all, expect no more than diplomatic and moral support from Britain, and he forfeited even that when a Tory ministry replaced Palmerston in February 1858. The new cabinet wanted stability in Europe, especially at a time when Britain's relations with France were rapidly worsening. The foreign secretary, Malmesbury, was anxious to reduce the risk of an explosion in Italy. He urged the pope and the king of Naples to reform their governments, and offered to mediate between France and Austria. Some leading Frenchmen also opposed war, while the emperor himself remained as ambiguous as ever. A *Moniteur* article of 4 March 1859, for instance, seemed to suggest that he would use force only to defend Piedmont from Austrian aggression.[5]

It was the Austrians who brought matters to a head, partly because they had persuaded themselves that France and Piedmont might not be wholly in agreement and partly because they could not afford to keep their army mobilised indefinitely. They could not compete with Napoleon III in a long game of political manoeuvring – something which clearly suited the French emperor temperamentally as well as in terms of the government's deeper purse. They therefore demanded Italian demobilisation before they would agree to British and Russian proposals for talks. Napoleon responded by acceding first to a Russian proposal for a five-power congress in which the Italians would have only a consultative role, and then to a British plea that he persuade Turin to disarm in return for British support for a Piedmontese role at the conference. Momentarily it seemed as if war might be at least postponed while Napoleon picked up inexpensive gains by diplomacy. Russia, too, seemed to favour peace. It was one thing to encourage divisions among the powers to prepare the way for a revisionist policy in the Near East, but major changes were not wanted in Europe until the reform programme at home had turned Russia into a stronger and more modern power. Thus whatever was said in exchanges between St Petersburg and Paris, cooperation remained haphazard. What mattered was that France could count on Russian neutrality as long as Vienna refused concessions in the Near East, and Napoleon did not become overbold in his revisionist programme.

### The Powers and Italian Unification

The Austrians opted for war in response to the Piedmontese refusal to demobilise. Two Franco–Italian victories followed, though at a heavy cost to all the belligerents. The battle of Solferino (24 June) left Napoleon III willing to make peace on the basis of the addition of Lombardy to Piedmont. The expanded Piedmontese kingdom and Venetia (still under Austrian control) would be members of a new Italian federation presided over by the pope. Such proposals did not impress Palmerston who had returned to power at the head of a Whig–Liberal ministry. His own preference was for a north Italian state which would be 'as independent as possible of foreign dictation, and as likely as possible to consult its own interests, which would lie in commerce and peace', both objectives if attained being very much to the advantage of Britain.

Meanwhile the Prussians had at first seemed uncertain how to react to the war – if at all – especially once it was clear that Austria would make no concessions in Germany. But an upsurge of anti-French feeling in Germany encouraged Berlin to mobilise some troops. While this move helped to induce Napoleon III to make peace, it also reminded the Austrians that they could not ignore Prussian ambitions in Germany. Account, too, had to be taken of possible unrest elsewhere in the empire. But above all the Austrians accepted that they could not defeat the French. Francis Joseph considered it no dishonour to negotiate directly with another emperor and at the same time to shut out Cavor, the Italians and the European 'Areopagus' (or Concert) from the sensitive matter of yielding imperial territory. Even before the war he had described British proposals for a conference as contrary to the honour of himself and his empire. If anything was to be arranged through the Concert it would be done later and on his terms.[6]

The bilateral outline settlement concluded at Villafranca on 11 July was a bitter blow to Cavor. He complained of betrayal by Napoleon. Austria would remain a major power in north-eastern Italy and with friendly rulers again in possession of the central duchies. Piedmont (even with Lombardy) would still find herself overshadowed by conservative regimes in the new Italy. But activists in the duchies asserted themselves and, with the aid of Piedmontese agents, they enlisted popular support to oppose the return of the former rulers. Union with Piedmont became the watchword. Admittedly there were still some anxious moments as the great powers considered their next moves, with the Austrians pushing for a European congress which they hoped to attend, not in the guise of a defeated power but as one which was reasserting its influence in Italy and helping to elevate the power of the papacy. This new Italy (including Austrian retention of Venetia) would be acknowledged by Europe.

A congress, however, required the participation of most, if not all of the powers. Gladstone, a friend of the north Italian cause and also of the Concert, discussed the implications of British attendance at some length. On 3 January 1860 he concluded that the proposed congress was 'a body without definite rights, and one to which each Power is entitled to aim at giving a direction according to its belief of what is just and politic'. In the present instance there was a grave danger that the 'enemy' in Italy – that is, Austria and the pope – might exploit such an assembly to garb themselves 'with authority' and gather round them other powers and states to achieve their purposes, notably to restore the old rulers to the duchies. Therefore, much as he favoured a congress in principle, Britain had to assert herself while there was still a reasonable assurance of French support for the liberal Italian cause and before 'the elements of a powerful conspiracy' drew together to leave Britain in 'a receding minority'. Nor could a French volte-face be discounted, with Britain then able to make no more than a solitary and 'barren protest'. But if no congress were held, Britain might – with a better prospect of French help – demand the exclusion of armed foreign involvement in Italy. Gladstone the moralist could be a shrewd player in international politics.[7]

His worries were finally resolved when Napoleon III decided that the popular will must be allowed to prevail in the central duchies. A congress could clearly no longer serve the purposes of Vienna and Rome. Consequently plebiscites went ahead in the duchies in March 1860, with the people duly voting to join the northern kingdom. There was one sour note. Napoleon III decided that enough had been done on behalf of Italy to justify his claim to Savoy and Nice. This did not much trouble Cavor or Palmerston – after all this seemed a small price to pay for the creation of a substantial northern kingdom. But liberal opinion in Britain saw this as another example of Napoleonic greed and deceit. Palmerston, never one to miss a trick, took the opportunity to speed the expansion of the navy and the fortification of the dockyards in reply to French naval building and completion of the great base at Cherbourg. Over the next few years the British demonstrated that they could more than match any French challenge at sea. Cheap pottery pieces of a British lion standing over a prostrate Louis Napoleon were marketed to take advantage of the patriotic mood.

Further dramatic events were taking place in Italy. The charismatic Garibaldi sailed with an expedition to assist the Sicilians in their revolt against the king of Naples. This intervention by the 'Thousand' necessitated ever more devious politicking by Cavor. Basically he was willing to take advantage of the actions of Garibaldi and other revolutionary forces, while at the same time intriguing to ensure that they did not provoke hostile intervention by the great powers or threaten radical political and social change in Italy herself. From May until October 1860 he carefully analysed the reactions of the powers, probing for signs of sympathy and weighing the limits of their tolerance.

What gradually became apparent was the extent to which the great powers were divided among themselves or were crippled individually by their own inner uncertainties. British policy, for instance, was far from consistent. For a time London was inclined to think that Garibaldi should content himself with Sicily and not cross the Straits of Messina to Naples. But at a crucial moment, the British (not least to ensure that no other power was given an excuse to intervene) decided not to join France in a 'naval blockade' to deny the rebel forces free passage to the mainland. Garibaldi was thus free to complete the overthrow of the Bourbon regime in Naples while the British government was increasingly reassured to find that the unification of the larger part of Italy was being achieved on Italian (or Piedmontese) terms rather than under the influence of France. In these circumstances the British could welcome the formation of a new state which embraced all but Venetia and the Papal States.

In a way the old Vienna Settlement, as understood by the British, was not so much supplanted as updated with a united Italy (no longer 'a geographical expression' famous for its classical ruins, its art and architectural treasures, and the enervating influence of the Roman Church) supplanting Austria as the barrier to French influence in the peninsula – just as Palmerston had proposed in 1848–9. Given so satisfactory an outcome it was easy for the British to persuade themselves that they had given more assistance than was really the case. They had, after all, been fortunate to find in Cavor so able a disciple of Machiavelli – if a much less attractive figure than Garibaldi or Mazzini. Joseph Conrad, in his novel, *Nostromo*, vividly captures the hatred felt for Cavor in the person of a fictional 'member' of 'The Thousand'. Thomas Carlyle thought Mazzini probably came closer to true heroism than any other nineteenth-century figure, especially for his insistence that a patriotic love of one's own country should not demand a hatred of everyone else's.

Cavor, in contrast, had done whatever seemed most likely to max-imise his own control over events. He had also helped to avoid further foreign intervention. He recognised that the radicals could not be allowed to destroy the remnants of the pope's temporal power, a matter of concern to both Austria and Napoleon III. The latter also feared Italian republicanism, while Venetia (still held by Austria) had to be shielded from Garibaldi. Cavor, with the aid of the Piedmontese army and Garibaldi's political naivety, managed to neutralise or master the revolutionary elements. Thus a new Italy emerged in a form which (if flawed internally) did not unduly alarm the other powers.

Just how different things might have been can be deduced from the ideas which had been doing the rounds in other European capi-tals. Austria, for instance, had begun to hint at interest in a revival of the 'Holy Alliance' once the Villafranca settlement began to unravel. It soon became apparent, however, that both Russia and Prussia still expected concessions before this could be considered. Leaders in St Petersburg and even Berlin might join the outcry in Vienna against French and Piedmontese 'piracy', but as matters went no further (thanks to Cavor), both Russia and Prussia soon reverted to their disputes with Austria in the Near East and Germany. Finally, in so far as there existed a mutual interest in Berlin and Vienna in the defence of the Rhine against France, this was overlaid by their in-ability to agree on how power should be distributed between them in Germany.[8]

## The Emergence of Bismarck

If Cavor had been fortunate in the fluidity of great-power relations up to 1860, Bismarck was to be equally if not more so during the rest of the new decade. The meeting of the sovereigns of the three eastern powers in Warsaw in October 1860 had merely underscored the fact that they could not return to the pre-Crimean world. Similarly little life remained in the Franco–Russian entente, while Anglo–French relations were easily strained by mutual distrust. French power in any case had peaked, and Napoleon was soon adding to his problems by embarking upon his rash attempt to found a new monarchy in Mexico. Not only was he to encounter serious local resistance, but this was later followed by the uncompromising hostility of the United States once the North had prevailed in the American Civil War.

The Franco–Russian entente finally expired in 1863 at the time of another Polish insurrection. Much as Napoleon might have wished otherwise, he could not ignore the considerable surge of French popular sympathy for the Poles. The British government also showed sufficient interest for the emperor to feel that something ought to be seen to be done – only to find himself isolated and embarrassed when London backed off in the face of Russian obduracy. His resentment was further inflamed when London curtly rejected his sweeping proposal in November 1863 for a European congress to discuss not only the Polish question but also to 'substitute for the treaties of 1815, now in decay, new stipulations apt to assure the peace of the world'. There was never a chance of British, Russian or Austrian agreement. Prussia alone expressed interest – a token gesture from Bismarck who saw no point in gratuitously offending France. Palmerston doubted if the congress was ever seriously meant: it seemed more likely that Napoleon was bidding for popularity at home.

Historians, however, have cause to be grateful to the French emperor since his proposal prompted Palmerston to set out in a private letter of 15 November 1863 (to the king of the Belgians) his own views on the strengths and weaknesses – especially the latter – of congress diplomacy at this time. The Congress of Vienna, he argued, provided no guide. That gathering had been a necessity following a long period of war and territorial upheaval. The political future of vast areas was at stake. The powers whose armies had overthrown Napoleon's empire were 'the natural and indeed the only arbiters; and they had, by their armies, the means of carrying their decisions into effect'. He might have added that exceptional circumstances had also frightened the allied leaders into a greater sense of mutual dependence than usual.

He believed as matters stood in 1863 that a conference to consider territorial change was more likely to exacerbate than solve problems. He expected Russia to be unmoved by any congress on the subject of Poland. A review of the distribution of territory in Europe as a whole would, he argued, give rise to Russian demands for a revision of the Treaty of Paris, Italian insistence on Rome and Venetia, a French bid for a frontier on the Rhine, and Austrian claims in the Balkans. Lesser states, too, would doubtless make additions to the list. The most likely outcome would find the majority with the choice of either having to use force against the minority, or accepting that it was 'powerless to execute its own decrees'. Europe, he argued, would be spared 'some danger and much embarrassment' if there were no congress. This was sound advice from a man who was by no means satisfied with the current map of Europe, but who was no longer so confident of Britain's influence on the continent. The balance in Europe was no longer so susceptible to British manipulation. He did concede that a lesser dispute between the Germans and the Danes might again be handled by a 'smaller machinery'.[9]

In reality, although this was not evident at the time, the tide was beginning to turn to the advantage of a new and rising figure, Otto von Bismarck. He had been appointed minister-president and foreign minister of Prussia in September 1862 – a desperate last throw by a king who otherwise seemed fated to choose between abdication, a military dictatorship, or capitulation to a chamber of deputies which was bent on thwarting his plans to reorganise the Prussian army. Bismarck had already served in various diplomatic posts, and was famed for his lack of tact, his ruthlessness and bold imagination. Too autocratic and turbulent for normal times (a contemporary commented that he was 'a rough man even in politics'), he was the sort of person to be entrusted with great authority only when the situation bordered on the hopeless.

It cannot be said that Bismarck made a particularly promising start in his first international crisis – the Polish revolt of 1863. His moves were prompted in the main by fears lest the revolt should spread to the Poles under Prussian rule. Indeed his rather heavy-handed overtures were not initially pleasing to the Russians. Second thoughts followed only as France, Britain and Austria became more critical of Russian suppression of the rebels. Russia clearly needed a friend in Berlin, and began to see merits in Bismarck himself (a staunch conservative) once his own days of power appeared to be numbered. For all his faults he was preferable to the alternatives. The men in St Petersburg needed no reminders of how useful Prussia had been for most if not all of the years since 1815. German liberal ambitions in 1848 were not forgotten.

In the end the protests of France, Britain and Austria relating to Poland had not amounted to much, and – better still from

Bismarck's point of view – these powers remained as distant from each other as before. Indeed the British suspected France of new Rhenish plots while Napoleon III was wary of entering into further joint moves with the fickle offshore islanders. Bismarck in the end had earned some credit in St Petersburg, and had gained further insights into the strengths and weaknesses as well as the priorities of the other powers. Both the British and French were distracted to some extent by events in the Americas at this time – the former by the American Civil War and the latter by Mexico. Any action against Russia over Poland would have depended in the first instance on Austria, and she was too weak to take any such initiative.[10]

Bismarck, despite his continuing difficulties at home with liberal critics, was helped by the relatively rapid economic advance of Prussia compared with Austria. The latter's political strength in the German Confederation was balanced by Prussia's position in the *Zollverein*. In short Prussia was fast becoming better equipped to follow a more assertive foreign policy than at any time since Frederick the Great. A British diplomat in 1866 thought Prussia so strong she had become 'the heart and head and lungs of Germany'. These advantages must be borne in mind, even if another minister in Bismarck's place might not have used them to such devastating effect. Above all one must not allow a study of these years to develop into a biography of Bismarck. He had inherited a well-developed power struggle in which the Austrians were 'doing everything possible' to protect and strengthen their political influence in Germany. The only 'appreciable' difference between Bismarck and his predecessors in the view of W. N. Medlicott was the 'fiercely optimistic will' with which he set about his task.[11]

Unlike many Prussian conservatives, Bismarck believed that an aggressive foreign policy might strengthen rather than threaten the existing political order at home. As Lothar Gall comments, Bismarck was increasingly sensitive to the new underlying political trends. He saw that 'the requisite preconditions were lacking [at home] for a revival of a policy of containment and anti-revolutionary bloc-forming along pre-1848 lines, …' Change was unavoidable. The clue was to try to work with rather than against it. Bismarck later remarked: 'a wave carried things along, but it could not be steered'.[12] His task was not to build breakwaters, but to identify those waves most likely to sweep him closest to his intended destinations. The biggest waves and strongest currents were German nationalism, long-established Prussian ambitions, and the favourable co-relation of forces among the other powers.

As the Prussian delegate to the Confederation for much of the 1850s, Bismarck had been ideally placed to study German politics. He had noted in 1853 that the 'cases where in European politics Austria needs or fears us ... [are] the only ones where we can make progress in German politics'. During the Crimean War, while he had agreed with the policy of Prussian neutrality, he had seen that Prussia's future advances were dependent upon retaining the option of friendship with France as well as with Russia. Prussian arch-conservatives in contrast had continued to live in the world of the 'Holy' and 'neo-Holy Alliance' and the struggle to contain France. Bismarck lamented Prussia's failure to exploit either Austria's problems during the Italian crises or the patriotic German emotions which had been aroused at that time. Already the fertility and flexibility which were to distinguish his later policies were becoming evident. Above all he believed that friends should be cultivated wherever Prussia's material (as opposed to 'sentimental') interests led.[13]

The dispute between Denmark and the Germans over the future of Schleswig and Holstein was reopened in November 1863. Prussia was soon in a strong position – though in the first phase rather because of the decisions of the other powers than any moves in Berlin. Napoleon III again aroused widespread suspicion when he proposed a congress to deal not only with the duchies but with Poland and the treaties of 1815. Queen Victoria described this as an 'impertinence', a view supported by Palmerston and Russell. Rejection of the congress suited Bismarck, as did Austria's decision to work with Prussia. The Austrians, not yet having taken the measure of Bismarck, hoped by such means to preserve the Treaty of London of 1852 relating to the duchies, and therefore the status quo. Instead they soon found that Bismarck was dictating policy. By January 1864 both powers had troops in Schleswig, whereas the other states and political forces in Germany with an interest in the duchies had been sidetracked. Danish obduracy also made it easier for Bismarck to use military means while dropping vague hints of territorial gains for Austria (in Italy) and France in regions as yet unspecified.[14]

The British government early in 1864 made a vain attempt to entrust the fate of the two duchies to the five powers in concert as in 1848–52. Napoleon III soon lost interest given fresh signs of divided

opinions in Britain. Prussia and Austria stalled and made conciliatory noises, confident that time was on their side and that the
duchies were not of sufficient interest for any other power to take
strong action. Indeed fears soon developed in London that France
and Russia might use the duchy question to reopen other issues. An
undesirable train of events might result in gains by France on her
eastern borders and by Russia in the Near East. Britain's dependence on other powers was being cruelly exposed, as was the emptiness of the Concert given the current priorities of each power.
Palmerston's warning of 1863 was still valid.

It was only when a Prussian unit crossed into Jutland that Bismarck
briefly seemed in danger of losing control. His own objectives at this
time were modest. He was not taking the first steps towards a new
Germany and a showdown with Austria. Instead he was anxious to
protect his political position and that of the conservative cause from
liberal enemies at home. Abroad he wanted to frustrate liberal hopes
of creating a new north German state under the Duke of
Augustenburg. This would be damaging to a conservative Prussia,
and might even work ultimately to the advantage of Austria and the
German Confederation. But as matters stood, and with the Austrians
in tow, he possessed overwhelming political and military advantages.
Indeed his position was such that he could generously agree to a
five-power conference in London as a consolatory gesture to the
British. Two months of inconclusive talking left him free to force
the surrender of the duchies by Denmark at the end of October by
the threat of overwhelming force.[15]

Despite this success many continued to underrate both Bismarck
and Prussia. Thus France still seemed to be the leading power with
Napoleon III retaining some of the standing of a master diplomat
albeit marred by his reputation as an ambitious and unscrupulous in-
triguer. Napoleon himself shared the popular view that Prussia was
the military inferior of Austria whose troops had, it was thought, per-
formed with more *élan* in the Danish war. The solid development of
the Prussian economy, bureaucracy and army attracted relatively little
notice. Many of Bismarck's liberal critics within Prussia were equally
complacent – although the Austrian foreign minister, Rechberg, was
heard to complain that it was difficult to deal with a man who openly
professed 'political cynicism', who attacked 'German political senti-
mentalism', and who pursued a 'utilitarian policy of expansion'.
Bismarck was another Cavor.[16] A British historian in the 1960s vividly

described his diplomacy as possessing 'a curiously military quality' with 'his use of threats, feints, alliance offers and demonstrations of force to jockey his slightly confused rivals out of one position after another.'[17] Bismarck also knew when to lie low.

### The Displacement of Austria

Austro–Prussian rivalries were by now growing apace. Differences multiplied over matters economic as well as political. Austria was becoming increasingly protectionist, whereas Prussia was better able to introduce tariff reductions and to profit from the growing interconnectedness of the German economy. This also meant that economic interests worked mainly in favour of a *Little* German solution. On the other hand, Austria still seemed much better placed in her political relations with most of the other German states – so much so that Bismarck had to sabotage the congress of princes held at Frankfurt to discuss reform of the Confederation in August 1863. He was unsure at that stage how quickly Prussian economic development and the rise of National Liberalism could be turned to his advantage; hence his suggestions to Austria that she recognise Prussian predominance to the north of the Main. In 1864 Rechberg seemed inclined to consider this (with the annexation of both duchies) in return for Prussian aid to Austria in the defence of Venetia and the recovery of Lombardy. Such ideas, however, failed to impress his emperor, and might not have satisfied Bismarck – at least in the long run.

Austro–Prussian differences deepened over the duchies in 1865, with Bismarck at one point talking of the present being a favourable moment for a war with Austria, a war which could 'scarcely be avoided sooner or later'.[18] Nevertheless he opted for further delay, in part at least because he was not sure that government finances were yet equal to a major conflict. The Habsburgs did not feel strong enough to do other than agree to a compromise at Gastein (August 1865) whereby each power would administer one of the controversial duchies. But few believed that this could be a lasting solution. Bismarck himself used the respite to probe the thinking of Napoleon III and to confirm that the latter's main interest lay in compensation for France if changes took place in Germany. Bismarck said just enough in talks for Napoleon to feel that French neutrality would not go unrewarded in an Austro–Prussian war. The emperor also hoped to cultivate Italy by wresting Venetia from Austria. Bismarck was sympathetic, noting Napoleon's belief that Austria was still the stronger of the Germanic powers and therefore less interested in what Prussia might do in the future.

Meanwhile tensions continued to increase between Berlin and Vienna, so that early in 1866 the Austrians were facing a dilemma. They would either have to abandon the duchy of Holstein to Prussia and thereby yield their claim to primacy in Germany, or stand firm even at the risk of war. The Prussian military, led by Moltke, were anxious not to fight until assured of a significant superiority in Bohemia. They wished to be assured that Italy would tie down 52000 Austrian troops. This alliance was finalised on 8 April 1866. Both Berlin and Vienna continued to court Paris, with the Austrians promising to surrender Venetia to France (which would then be handed over to Italy) even if they won the war. They also traded the creation of an independent Rhineland for Napoleon's assent to Austrian gains in Germany (provided these did not upset the balance of power). Napoleon, it seemed, had reinsured himself against an Austrian victory – the accepted wisdom at the time still being that Prussia had to win quickly if she was to win at all. Many Prussians agreed, and pinned their hopes of success on their ability to mobilise more quickly than their opponent.[19]

A proposal from Napoleon III for a congress was firmly declined by the Austrians unless promised the integrity of their empire in advance. Both move and countermove were predictable, but Napoleon followed this on 6 May 1866 with a surprisingly forceful speech in which he again spoke out against the Vienna treaties and of his desire to see them revised in Central Europe – possibly by war.[20] Such inflammatory talk did his reputation no good in London or St Petersburg. The Russians continued to treat Prussia as a friend whereas the Near East ensured that relations with Austria remained frosty. Indeed Vienna was sufficiently suspicious of Russia to deploy troops in the east which would have been useful in the struggle against Prussia.

Thus by the summer of 1866 Bismarck could feel confident of Austria's isolation. Indeed the last real obstacle was his own monarch who, until very late in the day, remained deeply averse to war. In the end it was the continuing military build-up and mounting tensions on the Austro–Italian border which enabled Bismarck and Moltke to insist on the deployment of forces to threaten the borders of Bohemia and Saxony. The drift to war was accelerated by further disputes over Schleswig–Holstein. Finally the Austrians tried to mobilise the German Confederation on their behalf. A Prussian invasion of Bohemia followed on 21 June. Yet Bismarck still seemed to regard war as a high-risk operation. He melodramatically told the British ambassador that if Prussia were defeated he would die 'in the last charge'. He was also planning to assist nationalist dissidents within the Habsburg Empire. Not surprisingly some writers have suggested that Bismarck would really have preferred to outmanoeuvre the Austrians politically until they bowed to the logic of their position by accepting Prussian dominance north of the Main. In the end, it has been said, he had been driven to a '*va banque* play bordering on self-destruction'.[21]

Thus Prussia's decisive success at the battle of Königgrätz was by no means a foregone conclusion, and some thought even after such a defeat that Austria was far from beaten. The Austrian emperor, however, accepted the verdict of 3 July 1866, and in so doing eased the strain on Prussia's resources. This suited Bismarck. Many have praised him for his subsequent moderation over the peace settlement, yet it was perhaps only a matter of common sense. He seems to have been much swayed by fear of intervention by France and/or Russia. Unlike some in Berlin, he saw how easily others could take fright if the balance of power in Europe were changed too dramatically and quickly in favour of Prussia. Thus he was content with dominance north of the Main, the continued existence of the states of south-west Germany, and no loss of territory by Austria – except Venetia to Italy. His restraint also made it easier to avoid explicit promises of compensation to France. Even so the Russian court felt that things had gone rather too far in the reorganisation of north Germany. This included the dispossession of some princely families.

Thus Alexander II as well as Napoleon raised the question of a European conference to review so sweeping a change to the Vienna Settlement. But a Tory foreign minister in London, Lord Stanley, argued (with good reason) that those who made such a proposal were acting from self-interested reasons. The Prussians, in any case, were masters of the field. It was 'useless to go into Congress without knowing what the basis of negotiations was to be, ... and whether all would accept the award of the Congress whatever it might be'. A conference 'could lead to no practical result'.[22] Thus the future of Germany and Venetia was speedily settled by the former belligerents. Bismarck thoughtfully reminded St Petersburg of his commitment to the conservative cause, and hinted at possible support to revise the Black Sea clauses. The Russians were left to hope that a balance of sorts would survive between Prussia, Austria and the south German states.

Bismarck was also free to make some indirect gains south of the Main. These states had been given a taste of Prussian military power, while secret alliances with Prussia seemed a small price to pay for the retention of most of their territory. Nor were they sorry to be given additional security against the unpredictable French. Finally Austria's defeat enabled the Magyars to secure considerable autonomy in 1867. This was to have an impact on future imperial foreign policy.[23]

### From Luxembourg to Sedan

The Luxembourg question developed out of the French anxiety for compensation to offset Prussia's gains from the war of 1866. Adolphe Thiers, in an attack on recent French foreign policy, went so far (in March 1867) as to argue that the balance of power, not nationalism, should be the basis of French foreign policy. There could be no balance if one power were allowed to make unilateral territorial gains. The government instead of acting decisively had dithered and now found itself isolated. Bismarck's revelation four days later of his treaties with the south German states (a response to criticism from the National Liberals on the continuing division of Germany) left Napoleon III even more exposed to attack at home.[24] He was, however, constrained by the evident lack of popular enthusiasm for a high risk foreign policy (not least after the setbacks in Mexico).

The future of Luxembourg had first been raised with Bismarck by the French on 26 July 1866. A complicated diplomatic game followed in which the French made various suggestions as to how their frontier might be pushed eastwards. French proposals, however, encountered a confusing mixture of Bismarckian outrage, objections, vague expressions of interest or – as in the case of Belgium and Luxembourg – of disinterest. Bismarck played with the French much as a cat might play with its victim – though probably as yet with no more in mind than the consolidation of the new status quo at home and abroad. Even so he was being supplied with incriminating evidence of France's territorial ambitions which he was later to use to good effect – notably at the start of the Franco–Prussian war in 1870 when it helped to discredit the French in the eyes of such non-belligerents as Britain. This and other information could also be used to stir up patriotic feeling in Germany.

In fact by the spring of 1867 German opinion had become rather more excited on the subject of Luxembourg than suited Bismarck's purpose at that particular time. He was anxious therefore both to disarm his critics at home and to avoid a crisis with France. Here perhaps was a suitable matter for the Concert. His solution was to insist on a European guarantee of the neutralisation of Luxembourg to allow Prussia to disengage gracefully from the grand duchy (a Prussian garrison having been stationed there since 1816) without appearing to yield to France. The British were finally persuaded with some difficulty to agree not only to a conference in London in May 1867 but to a collective guarantee of Luxembourg. Lord Derby (the prime minister) later told the House of Lords that a collective guarantee imposed no 'special and separate duty of enforcing its provisions'. This was carrying Britain's growing detachment from Europe rather too far. A somewhat embarrassed foreign secretary (his own son, Lord Stanley) agreed that 'the amount of obligation really incurred' was unclear, but added that he would not have signed anything that was 'purely illusory'.

A few months earlier Stanley himself had suggested a use for the Concert. He thought that the sultan, confronted by Serbian discontent, might welcome 'pressure put on him by the [united] Powers'. Such pressure might allow him to make concessions without loss of face.[25] Bismarck's own use of troubles within the Ottoman Empire was rather more positive. A number of incidents had tempted the Russian foreign minister, Gorchakov, to reopen the question of a major revision of the 1856 treaties. Britain, France and Austria had been unhelpful, but Bismarck seized the opportunity to express some sympathy with the Russian case. As usual he was careful to commit himself to no more than was absolutely necessary. But it was a further step towards the verbal understanding of March 1868 whereby each state promised to support the other if it was threatened by two powers. Bismark could expect Russian neutrality in the event of a Franco–German war, and it was possible that Russian forces would again be placed on the Austrian border.

There was much to keep Russia and Austria apart in the Near East. Apart from the Austrian commitment to the Treaty of Paris, Austria's own commercial and strategic interests in the Danubian region were steadily growing. Indeed some in Vienna were coming to see the Balkans as the only remaining area where the empire might be able to expand. If the Austrians were not yet fully resigned to eclipse in Germany, they were ill-placed to contemplate another war with Prussia 'for a long time'. Indeed the increasingly influential Hungarians had no interest in such a war: their prime minister, Julius Andrássy, was more troubled by Russia. If he shared Beust's hope in 1870 that France would triumph in a war with Prussia and so effect a general improvement in the balance of power to the advantage of the Dual Monarchy, he still saw the Monarchy as above all a 'bulwark against Russia'. As long as it was a European 'necessity', other powers would have a vested interest in its survival.

Any disposition in Vienna to listen to French overtures was also constrained by the empire's obvious need for a long period to recuperate from the defeat of 1866. War was not something it could enter into unless or until success was assured. Yet ministers in Paris became strangely confident of Austrian (and Italian) support in the event of war. It was only as events unfolded in the summer of 1870 that they realised that no solid backing from others would be forthcoming until France had won decisive victories on her own account. Even then the Austrians might have found it necessary to keep a wary eye on Russia – the power that Bismarck discreetly continued to cultivate – as well as on their Hungarian partners in the Dual Monarchy.

Bismarck's strategy and tactics in the period leading up to the war with France in July 1870 have excited much curiosity and controversy centring in particular on the question of how far its outbreak was masterminded to complete the unification of Germany. Many historians (such as Otto Pflanze, Lothar Gall, W. N. Medlicott) all insist that one must understand his general approach to foreign affairs and simultaneously try to make sense of the contradictory evidence which surrounds his actions in 1870. All are impressed by his desire to explore and preserve as many options as possible. W. Carr outlines three different theories: namely that war was forced on Bismarck by an aggressive France; that he truly did seek war to obtain unification for domestic and international reasons; and lastly that he was engaged in a diplomatic manoeuvre which happened to result in war.[26]

Before these possibilities are explored, it may be useful to set out what seems to be reasonably well established. Initially, after 1866, Bismarck needed time to consolidate in north Germany. Internationally he also had cause to let the dust settle and persuade other powers that he was not looking for further territorial gains. France could not be expected to tolerate more changes in Germany without war, and it was desirable that no war should break out unless and until Bismarck wished it. Within Germany, particularism and fear of Prussian domination and authoritarianism remained strong in the south-western states. Catholicism in the south was a major barrier to union with the essentially Protestant north. On the other hand Bismarck, as we have seen, had concluded military alliances with three of the four south German states which were required to model their armies on that of Prussia. The renewal of the customs union cemented economic connections. Yet strong opposition persisted against political links. Bismarck reminded himself that 'for a calculating politician the essential precedes the desirable'.

Nevertheless as time passed he became more disturbed by the state of politics in the south. Dissension was increasing between conservatives and progressives, not to mention the assertiveness of the extreme Catholics. William Carr concludes that 'on the eve of the Franco–Prussian War anti-Prussian sentiment in the south was, in fact, growing stronger, not weaker'.[27] The chancellor also faced political difficulties north of the Main and with France. There was still much talk in Paris of France's need for compensation, and even more of the damaging implications of the new balance in Germany. Considerable (if not immediately effective) efforts were being made to improve the French army. The situation in general was deemed sufficiently menacing for Lord Clarendon, foreign secretary in Gladstone's Liberal government of 1868, to urge both powers to reduce their annual intakes of recruits. Bismarck retorted that Germany's position between three great military powers made this impossible. Clarendon then suggested that military rivalry between states was being replaced by economic, political and other non-military forms of competition. Franco–Prussian rivalry, however, was too serious to be tempered by appeals of this kind.[28]

Clarendon also took note that a revolution in Spain in 1868 (which led to the search for a new monarch among the royal houses of Europe) was breeding unease and suspicion – particularly in France. He took some steps (though not perhaps all he might have done) to discourage candidatures which would alarm Napoleon III and his ministers. The French for their part continued to show too little insight into the thinking of other powers. Official interest in 1869 in the extension of French railway influence into Belgium (a move finally thwarted by new Belgian legislation) inevitably excited alarm in Britain. Misplaced French optimism concerning the thinking of the Austrians and Italians has already been noted.[29]

Thus Bismarck by 1870 was well placed to opt for war or peace as he saw fit. The army was ready, but it was essential that Prussia should not appear to be the aggressor or to be threatening the European balance of power. In any crisis he wanted the south Germans to feel that it was their quarrel so that they would voluntarily follow a Prussian lead. Bismarck warned against 'arbitrary interventions in the evolution of history'. Such advice, however, did not stop him from giving history a nudge (if not a shove) when from February 1870 he pressed the Hohenzollern family (against the wishes of his own king) to respond to Spanish overtures on the subject of the empty throne. Bismarck was well aware of French touchiness concerning Spain's dynastic politics – a German candidate could not fail to cause a furore. He also noted that war might be more likely following the appointment on 15 May of a new French foreign minister, the touchy Duc de Gramont.

Even so the virulence of the response from Paris when news of the candidature leaked out early in July 1870 might well have exceeded even his expectations. Indeed it was so strong that many throughout Europe at first held Napoleon III and his advisers mainly responsible for the ensuing war. French prestige, it was said, was given precedence ahead of a responsible and diplomatic search for a solution. Some French ministers seemed to accept that something had gone wrong on their side when they later tried to claim that public opinion (admittedly a bigger factor in French politics following the introduction of a more liberal constitution) had left them no choice. In fact it seems that a truly formidable war fever developed among the public only after ministers themselves had taken crucial and ill-considered decisions.[30] Voices in favour of caution were weakened by the widespread (and misplaced) faith in the strength of the French army and in Austro–Italian sympathy.

Diplomacy, however, was given a final chance. Talks between the Prussian king and French ambassador were constructive, and Thiers for one was persuaded that France had secured 'a victory: Sadowa is almost avenged.'[31] It is true that some critics of the government were less impressed, but it was Gramont who was mainly responsible for the demand for further Prussian assurances which led to the fatal exchanges of 13 July between the king and ambassador. Meanwhile Bismarck – reassured by reports that he had nothing to fear from Austria, Britain or Russia – had been looking for ways to step up the excitement. His editing of the Ems Telegram was another firebomb thrown on the blaze. In Paris last minute interest in the possibility of a congress to discuss ways to guarantee the non-renewal of the Hohenzollern candidature soon gave way to the feeling that war was unavoidable. Both in France and Prussia it was widely felt that their countries had been intolerably insulted. Indeed, for Prussia one should begin to read Germany. This was a war between nations as well as governments. Each side was confident of victory, but it was Bismarck who had the better understanding of the correlation of forces.

He had also grasped the importance of ensuring that this was seemingly a war about national honour. Neither in Germany nor among the non-belligerents was this initially regarded as a war of Prussian aggrandisement.[32] There was little international sympathy for France until the scale of German success (and the desire for Alsace and Lorraine) became apparent. Only then were there serious complaints of German ruthlessness and talk of a threat to the balance of power. The war remained localised, although the Russians became sufficiently nervous of the effect of Germanic 'Napoleonic' successes (including possible reactions among the Poles) for them to take some soundings in Vienna. The Austrians, however, were resolved on peace once it was apparent that France could not win.[33] The British showed some initial nervousness concerning Belgium but were soon reassured by the two belligerents. If Bismarck had been dealt a good hand he had played it shrewdly as well as ruthlessly in the early summer of 1870.

# 5

## *REALPOLITIK* AND MILITARISM, 1871–90

'All politics reduces itself to this formula: try to be one of three, as long as the world is governed by the unstable equilibrium of five great powers.' (Bismarck)

### A New International Setting

The map of Europe and the distribution of power in 1871 was very different from that devised at Vienna in 1814–15. It was also a map which, except for south-east Europe, was to remain unchanged until the First World War. Germany had clearly displaced France as the most formidable continental power, the latter having no foreseeable prospect of reversing the verdict of the 1870–1 war except with the help of a powerful land ally. Russia was still largely on the defensive despite the repeal of the Black Sea clauses at a conference in London (March 1871). She had huge potential, but was a long way from realising it. Austria–Hungary could look realistically only to parts of south-east Europe for additional influence or territory. Yet even in this region there existed both internal and external reasons why she too might find it difficult to take the initiative. The future of Italy, the weakest of the powers, was largely dependent on the opportunities presented to her by the needs and setbacks of other powers. Finally the British, despite some initial fears of the new Germany, were fairly quickly persuaded that Bismarck was content with the new frontiers. A British diplomat confidently predicted that Europe would enjoy greater peace and stability with the 'rooting up, once and for all, of the pretension of France to a privileged and exceptional position in Europe'. Germany was thus well placed – at least for the time being – to maintain her new ascendancy in the heart of Europe.

On the other hand it was understandable that the other continental powers should strive – in so far as their internal political and economic circumstances allowed – to emulate Prussia's military institutions and methods from its much-admired general staff downwards. Wars had become a thoroughly professional and scientific matter. Given the emphasis on speedy mobilisation and deployment, strategy was very much a matter (as an American general insisted in a later age) of getting there 'fustest with the mostest'. Although war in Europe was avoided by the powers after 1871 for an unprecedented period of 43 years, this was without doubt an era of 'armed peace'. Furthermore it was punctuated by several major crises whose repercussions could affect even the insular and imperially-minded British. Indeed, once the imperial dimension was added, Britain and Russia (not Germany) were frequently regarded as the powers most likely to trigger the next great war.

The maintenance of 'peace' for so many years raises interesting questions concerning the character of international statecraft and diplomacy in this era. It may be that by examining why war was avoided for so long some insights can be acquired into why war broke out in 1914. It is also important to establish the degree of continuity or discontinuity in thought patterns among the policy-makers. One cannot fail to be struck, for instance, by the similarities between some of the doom-laden and bellicose utterances in Berlin in 1887–9 and those more often cited from the years between 1912 and 1914. If readers of such statements were unaware of the dates in each instance, they could be forgiven their surprise when told that the two warlike outbursts were separated by no less than a generation.

There was occasional and not wholly unsuccessful recourse to the Concert in these years, while two so-called peace conferences met in 1899 and 1907. More significant still, however, were the several agreements and treaties which the powers individually negotiated with the primary aim of either defending the status quo or providing for limited orderly change. Bismarck was deeply involved in such activities – at least after 1875 – even if his methods did not always seem best calculated to soothe the nerves or win the trust of others. The post-1871 period also experienced rapid economic growth and change, the spread of mass politics and new social tensions, all of which had profound domestic implications which often spilled over to affect the conduct of foreign affairs.

Technological advances throughout the period helped to compound the firepower of armies, notably at the turn of the century, and accelerated the evolution of steam-powered, armoured and big-gunned warships – not to mention new and increasingly lethal smaller craft. Defence costs were burdensome even in time of peace, and many feared that modern societies might collapse under the strain of anything other than a short war. Indeed some hoped that the more fearsome the preparations, the greater would be the reluctance to resort to war. The effect might be so damaging as to threaten the established order. Defeat had caused the downfall of Napoleon III in 1870, while the newly established Third Republic had been challenged by the Paris Commune of 1871. Revolution was also to follow Russia's defeat at the hands of Japan in 1905. Yet fear of the consequences of war seemed only to stimulate the search by governments and general staffs for ways to win short wars whose political and economic effects – it was hoped – could be controlled. Safety lay not in defence but in the ability to launch massive offensives at short notice.

Industrialisation was also accompanied by a revival of protectionism save in Britain, and both were among the several causes of the intensification of the scramble for territory and influence in Asia and Africa. Germany and Italy joined Britain, France and Russia in the imperial struggle. Such rivalry could disturb the relations of the powers inside as well as outside Europe. There were, for instance, European and Asiatic dimensions to the Near Eastern crisis of 1875–8 (not to mention the fears that it might extend right along the northern fringe of Africa to Morocco and the Atlantic). The alignment of France and Russia from the 1890s, although ostensibly directed against Germany, was often more relevant to the global rivalries of those two powers with Britain. Disputes of this kind began to feature more and more in the calculations of many European leaders – particularly from the 1880s. The belief was spreading that no power could be truly great without a major presence in the wider world. A global balance of power seemed to be in the making.

Meanwhile within Europe nationalism was becoming an ever more potent force. Many Austrians by July 1914 saw war as perhaps the only way to save the empire from the centrifugal ethnic forces at work within it as well as the enemies without. Indeed nationalist forces were becoming so formidable in the Balkans that all the interested powers were finding it ever more difficult to restrain and control such peoples as the Serbs and Bulgars. Nationalism was also doing much to sharpen and intensify the ambitions of the great powers themselves. These took their most explosive forms in Germany and Russia.

In this world of rapid change it is not difficult to find evidence of the concern of many of the key policy-makers over the difficulties of managing home and foreign affairs – not to mention the degree to which the two were becoming ever more intertwined. Bismarck before 1870 had stressed that leaders could only try to identify and take advantage of the great currents of history. In the years after 1871 there seemed more reason to question the possibility of riding the crests of ever larger and more turbulent waves. Lord Salisbury observed in 1895, 'Governments can do so little and prevent so little nowadays. Power has passed from the hands of the statesman, but I should be very much puzzled to say into whose hands it has passed.' If he was more influential in the conduct of foreign policy than he sometimes pretended, he did have cause to feel that the world was becoming a more volatile and therefore a more dangerous place. In Germany and Russia conservative leaders were apprehensively watching the rise of socialism and other 'dark' forces even as they tried to ensure that their empires would be among the select handful that would dominate the approaching century. Not surprisingly they also looked to foreign triumphs to help temper domestic discontents and divisiveness.

Even so there were still times when fears of internal unrest could stimulate at least a partial revival of the pre-1854 sense of solidarity and common interest among the monarchs and other strongly conservative elements. After the wars of unification – and given the experience of the Paris Commune and sundry lesser warnings ranging from radical republican experiments in Spain in the early 1870s to the assorted revolutionary and terrorist groups in Russia – some conservatives were disposed to tread more warily in foreign affairs.

One of the most immediate challenges confronting policy-makers in Berlin as well as in the other leading capitals was that of coming to terms with Germany's sudden emergence as the strongest military and economic power on the continent. Bismarck himself, while content with the frontiers of the new Reich, had difficulty in deciding what balance should be struck between the imperious, bullying tactics which had served him so well in the 1860s and the new requirements of painstaking consensus-building. If at first he was too inclined to threaten and wave the big stick when tactful diplomacy might have been more profitable, the later Bismarck (despite his phobias) often showed a greater sense of proportion than some of the other leading figures in Berlin. At times he was thoroughly exasperated by the refusal of Russia and Austria–Hungary to see that logic and self-interest pointed to a division of the troublesome Balkans between them. But he was the first to agree that politics lacked logic.

> Politics is less a science than an art. It is not a subject which can be taught. One must have a talent for it. Even the best advice is of no avail if improperly carried out. Politics is not in itself an exact logical science, but the capacity to choose in each fleeting moment of the situation that which is least harmful or most opportune.[1]

The words 'least harmful' are particularly revealing.

Central to all his manoeuvring was the continued isolation of France. Like Metternich and Palmerston before him, Bismarck was most fearful of the creation of a Franco–Russian alliance. At the very least Germany had to form part of any majority grouping of the powers. France, through the loss of Alsace and Lorraine, had been more harshly treated than in 1814–15. The terms had also been imposed unilaterally by Germany, no attempt being made to temper or dignify the treaty with references to the well-being of Europe as a whole. French isolation, however, suggested that no war of revenge could be waged in the foreseeable future – especially given the ideological divide between a French republic (however moderate) and tsarist Russia. Bismarck for this and other reasons was soon playing on Alexander II's fears of radicals and revolutionaries – although this did not prevent some Russians from asking where the 'Minotaur in Berlin' might strike next. A French republic could also be expected to be less sympathetic than a restored Bourbon monarchy to Ultramontanism when Bismarck became involved in a far-reaching dispute with the Catholic Church.

On Germany's southern flank Bismarck could draw some comfort from the growing realisation in Vienna that the new German empire had come to stay. Beust even spoke of an Austro–German alliance as the 'central bulwark of European peace'. Bismarck and many of the Prussian elite had no wish to add ten million Austrian Catholics to the new Germany and thereby tilt the balance against the northern Protestants. In 1871 the historian Treitschke was among those to argue that all who worked for the fall of Austria–Hungary were enemies of the German Reich. Successive conservative German leaders agreed that the survival of Austria–Hungary fitted in well with their domestic as well as their international needs. This empire was one of the great stabilising factors in European affairs after 1871. In return Bismarck required the Habsburgs to act with restraint in the Balkans and towards Russia.

The Franco–Prussian war of 1870–1 had brought mixed blessings to Russia. Freed from the Black Sea clauses, she felt less secure on her western borders given the unification of Germany. Russia had also become more deeply involved in Asia since 1856, and any Anglo–Russian collision – wherever it began – could easily spread to the Near East and perhaps draw Austria into the arms of Britain. Finally there was still much rebuilding and modernising to be done at home. All these considerations meant that her leaders had good cause for the time being to cultivate their connections with Bismarck, and to try to put an end to their quarrel with Vienna. Austrian friendship (or neutrality) might be useful in Russian dealings whether with Britain or Germany.

Britain, meanwhile, remained a somewhat uncertain quantity, not least because of the thinking of the current prime minister, Gladstone. Quite apart from his enthusiasm for international goodwill and the public law of Europe, his government was insufficiently assertive, and too intent on defence economies to count for much in Europe at this time. Similarly those in Britain (such as Disraeli) who had initially talked of the destruction of the balance of power in 1870–1, were soon moving on to other issues. Even a Bismarckian and highly militarised Germany might prove sufficiently temperate to uphold the balance in Europe to Britain's advantage. The new Germany had further appeal as primarily a Protestant if not a liberal power. Above all British ministers were happy to settle for a Europe which left them free to act elsewhere.[2]

Bismarck and Germany were thus clearly the key players in the European power game, yet the chancellor was ever on his guard against some sudden movement of the pieces on the board to his disadvantage. He outlined his basic thinking in the important Kissingen note of June 1877. Germany would be best placed when 'all the powers except France had need of us, and would thus be deterred as far as possible from coalitions against us by their relations with each other'. He also hoped that Anglo–Russian rivalries could be pushed as far as possible into the remoter parts of Asia – thereby minimising the threat to peace in any of the regions of direct or indirect interest to Germany. It was important, too, to ensure that Austria and Russia should not come into conflict with each other, and that each should accept its need of German friendship. Here was a classic statement of defensive *realpolitik*.[3]

## The *Dreikaiserbund* and the Near Eastern Question, 1872–8

A meeting at Ischl in August 1871 between the leaders of the three eastern powers was the first of several which over time brought about a revival of the old conservative alliance system. Not all differences were resolved – or even discussed. The Austrians, for instance, were divided on the subject of how they should pursue their interests in the Balkans. Advocates of a defensive policy were being challenged by Francis Joseph and groups with commercial and strategic aims in Bosnia and Herzegovina. Nevertheless the three powers continued to converge, a Russo–German military agreement of 6 May 1873 being followed by the Austro–Russian Schönbrunn Convention of 6 June 1873. Interestingly enough this spoke not only of cooperation in the Near East, but also of an Austro–Russian interest in 'the maintenance of peace in Europe against all attempts to destroy it, from whatever quarter they come'. Here was a clear hint of a degree of concern in both St Petersburg and Vienna at the sheer strength of Germany, and the desire for some element of reinsurance against her. It was also natural that the two foreign ministers (Gorchakov and Andrássy) should wish to avoid being unduly eclipsed by Bismarck. Gorchakov had proved himself a worthy if more egotistical successor to Nesselrode, and had skilfully defended Russian interests during the Polish revolt. But his vanity and sensitivity increased with age, and his personal relationship with Bismarck became increasingly difficult as the 1870s wore on.

The three emperors league (*Dreikaiserbund*) as constituted in October 1873 was initially centred on Austria and Russia rather than Germany. But Bismarck was soon intent upon using it to his advantage. He had a healthy respect for Russia's long-term potential, and welcomed any arrangement which might give him greater influence in St Petersburg. The league also had obvious relevance in his dealings with Austria and France. The martial side of his personality, however, was by no means fully under control, and this reached a climax in April–May 1875 when (with the 'War-in-Sight' crisis) he succeeded in arousing considerable alarm in St Petersburg, Vienna and London as well as Paris. The crisis was in part an offshoot from Bismarck's pre-existing quarrel with Ultramontane Catholicism (with its hostility to the modern secular state), a quarrel which was soon being waged abroad (notably in Belgium, Spain and France) as well as inside Germany. Bismarck's fears included a Bourbon monarchical restoration in France and a serious strengthening of the extreme Catholic cause. The year 1874 found him meddling as far afield as a civil war in Spain not only to ensure the defeat of the Ultramontane claimant to that throne but also, it seemed, to embarrass France.

Such activities and the attendant rumours naturally caused many ministers and diplomats around Europe to wonder if something more sinister was afoot than Bismarck's quarrel with Rome. Was he looking for an excuse to attack France before she had fully recovered from the defeat of 1870–1? The French foreign minister both in 1874 and 1875 naturally did his best to enlist the sympathy of the other powers. The British were particularly active in helping to defuse the tension in 1874.[4] Fears in 1875 that Bismarck might be trying to provoke a war with France (the 'War-in-Sight' crisis) led both the British and still more the Russians to intervene in Berlin. Gorchakov also saw this as a chance to win French gratitude. Bismarck hastily backed off once he saw that he was isolating Germany, not France. Pflanze describes this as the biggest diplomatic defeat in his career. Dismayed and depressed, Bismarck retreated to his estate at Varzin to brood at length on the future.[5]

A new crisis in the Near East did much to assist his reappraisal. This spanned the years 1875–8 and included in its several facets an ominous warning that, while the leading chancelleries might propose, other lesser forces might dispose to a much greater degree than in the past. The implications proved particularly damaging to the *Dreikaiserbund*. Yet at the start Bismarck, Gorchakov and Andrássy were seemingly well in control and working sensibly together. The only wild card among the powers was Britain where Benjamin Disraeli (heading a new Tory government) was intent on making good the damage which he held that the previous Gladstone ministry had done to Britain's standing in Europe.

Alexander II had inherited from his father a policy of limited encouragement to the semi-independent states of Serbia and Montenegro. For the first 20 years of his reign, however, problems at home and Russian distractions in Central Asia meant that his government was forced to proceed with considerable discretion in the Near East. Despite some moments of difficulty, the region had remained relatively quiet, with the Turks apparently making intermittent progress with their reform programmes. The abrogation of the Black Sea clauses by international agreement in March 1871 boosted Gorchakov's hopes that Russian interests might continue to be advanced by diplomacy and international conferences. His cooperation with Austria and Germany in the early 1870s was a move to that end. But some Russians were more impatient. They were eager to reduce Turkey to a dependency and to unite the Balkan Christians to build a barrier against Austria–Hungary.

Gorchakov and his school at first responded warily to the unrest in Bosnia–Herzegovina in 1875. Even so Slavophile groups were able to send aid to the rebels against their Turkish overlords. Although Bismarck preferred the maintenance of the status quo in the Ottoman Empire, he was ready – if necessary – to condemn Turkey to the fate which had befallen Poland in the late-eighteenth century. Unfortunately neither Russia nor Austria believed that a Balkan partition would work to their long-term advantage. Gorchakov preferred to give great-power diplomacy another opportunity. Perhaps a European conference would force Turkey to make concessions to its Christian subjects. The reforms would be supervised by an international commission and by military occupation where appropriate.[6] Andrássy, too, hoped that Turkish concessions might restore stability and avoid difficult – even painful – choices.

Bismarck was disposed to be helpful, and together they produced the Berlin Memorandum of 13 May 1876. This contained a hint that the Turks might be coerced unless they were amenable. Here, it might seem, was the basis for constructive action by all the powers. This was well received by the British foreign secretary, Lord Derby (formerly Lord Stanley). The prime minister (Disraeli), in contrast, drew up a long list of objections which included not least (and quite fairly) the difficulties which would attend any great-power intervention. He was, however, also intent on showing that the *Dreikaiserbund* could not draw up proposals without prior consultation with Britain. Although he was able to stall the Berlin initiative, he found it impossible to put anything in its place. He tried in vain, for instance, to work with Russia to secure limited Turkish concessions to the Bosnian insurgents.[7]

All the powers, in fact, seemed to be underestimating the ease with which peace could be restored in the Balkans. News reached London at the end of June of Turkish massacres of Bulgarian rebels following an abortive rising. Disraeli's cabinet was soon paralysed by its own divisions, and by a popular outcry (with Gladstone in the vanguard) against the massacres. Even Disraeli at times began to question if the Turkish empire could be saved if reports of the atrocities were true. Despite his readiness to consider a variety of solutions (provided they were compatible with British prestige and interests), he could make no real progress either with cabinet colleagues at home or through overtures to foreign leaders. Not until 1878 did Russophobia outweigh Turkophobia in Britain and provide a basis upon which to build a policy.

Meanwhile in 1876 Gorchakov and the tsar were doing their best to avoid the errors which had contributed to the Crimean War. They were well aware that Russia's reform programmes needed more time. Peace in Europe was vital while government finances and the armed forces were fortified. The Russians anxiously tried to keep in step with Vienna, firstly during the Serbo–Turk war in 1876 and later when they began to look for ways to put direct physical pressure on the Turks. Suggestions to this effect in September 1876, however, brought so frigid a response from the Austrians that the tsar ominously remarked that if they were not prepared to act as partners they might have to be treated as enemies. Gorchakov even asked Bismarck to summon a congress to settle the Near Eastern Question for all time, a step which Bismarck very reasonably refused. It was more likely to make Germany the focus of the ill will of every interested party once it became apparent how little could be achieved.

At least the Russians were able to exercise some influence in Constantinople on behalf of the Serbs who, having gone to war with the Turks, were soon being badly beaten. A ceasefire was arranged at the end of October 1876. On the other hand there was a growing feeling even among the moderates in St Petersburg that strong action would have to be taken sooner or later.[8] But the Russians now tended to look to the Bulgarians rather than to the recently defeated Serbs. The main line of the Russian offensive in 1877 was in fact to be directed through Sofia.

The growing risk of a Russo–Turk war was not at all to Bismarck's liking. Germany in his view had no direct interest in the Near East. But the situation was becoming more unpredictable, and who could tell where serious trouble once started would end? Such was his nervousness that he even tried to ingratiate himself with the British.

The winter months (no season for campaigning in the Balkans) found all the interested powers dedicating themselves to a review of their political options and to manoeuvring for advantage. The Russians above all needed to prepare the ground diplomatically (in Berlin as well as Vienna) in case war proved unavoidable with the Turks. Bismarck's great concerns were to give offence to neither of his partners in the *Dreikaiserbund*, and to ensure that the Near East did not cause an Austro–Russian rift. Convinced that self-interest ruled everywhere, Bismarck strove to turn the self-interest of others to his advantage. He aimed to exploit 'conflicting interests (within a largely closed system) for the creation of balanced options, which reserved to himself (and the interest he served) the freedom to choose, even while denying it to others'. Every assurance he offered to Russia or Austria was therefore qualified by emphasis on the need for restraint.[9] In addition he hoped that the British would do enough to deter Russia from advancing too far at the expense of Austria.

While Bismarck intrigued from Berlin, an international conference was held in Constantinople at the end of 1876. This, too, failed to find solutions to the Bulgarian and Bosnian problems, while the Turks unfortunately decided that the powers were too divided to exert real influence. The tsar, however, had already threatened to act 'independently' if no progress was made. Russia had to fulfil her 'sacred mission'. Nevertheless further efforts were made to convince Vienna that there would be no Pan-Slav crusade and that no large Slav state would be created in the event of war. The Austrians in return promised their benevolent neutrality.

Suspicion of Russian intentions continued to increase in Berlin where the general staff began to make precautionary plans for a two-front war against Russia and France. Bismarck, too, voiced his worries concerning both powers, and put out feelers to Britain – firstly hoping for her benevolent neutrality if a Franco–German war developed and then raising the question of an alliance. In February, however, the Russian ambassador described him as favouring a Russo–Turkish war – provided it was short and Russia distanced herself from France. Bismarck was probably seeing war as inevitable, and was hoping to minimise its scale and consequences. As for Germany and a Near Eastern war – this would not be worth 'the healthy bones of a single Pomeranian musketeer'. He still toyed with ideas for a great-power partition of Turkey, above all one which would ensure that all the powers would be left sufficiently in competition with each other so that none would be able to risk a quarrel with Germany. 'Every war, even a successful one', he insisted, 'is a misfortune'.[10] One measure of relief came from an unexpected quarter. A fortuitous improvement in relations with France developed later in 1877 with the electoral advance of the Republican 'Left'. This produced a ministry which (much to Bismarck's satisfaction) was less interested in foreign affairs.

Meanwhile the Russo–Turkish war had duly begun in April 1877. It soon highlighted Russia's continuing military deficiencies even against the Turks, her army being held up for six months by a stout Turkish defence of the fortress at Plevna which stood south of the Danube and guarded the route to Sofia. Serious in itself, this setback also had the unfortunate effect of strengthening Slavophile emotions and influences at home, with Alexander II himself becoming more receptive to the ambitious ideas of Ignatiev (his ambassador in Constantinople).[11] Turkish resistance crumbled rapidly after the fall of Plevna, and an armistice followed in January 1878 with Russian troops once again lying within striking distance of Constantinople.

Success on this scale bred Russian overconfidence. It also generated widespread alarm in Britain. Serious defence preparations were begun in February, but these came too late to influence the Russo–Turk negotiations which produced the Treaty of San Stefano of 3 March 1878. Its most important provision was the creation of a big Bulgaria (contrary to earlier Russian promises to Vienna) which stretched south to the Aegean and south-west into Macedonia. Whatever the regional merits of this plan, the Russians could not escape the ire of both Austria and Britain. The new state seemed designed and destined to become a Russian satellite. The Germans agreed that San Stefano was a treaty too far.

In London a new foreign secretary, Lord Salisbury, decided that his detestation of the Turk must now take second place to his fear of Russia. In his famous circular of 1 April 1878 he argued that Russian conduct was posing a threat to 'every country having interests in the east of the Mediterranean Sea'. He also contended that Russian influence in Turkey in Asia would threaten British interests all the way to India. The danger of war between Russia on one side and Britain and Austria–Hungary on the other for a time seemed very real. Fortunately the tsar was soon persuaded by Gorchakov and his war minister that Russia could not yet risk a repeat of the Crimean War. The minister of finance issued the usual reminders of the precarious state of the financial reform programme. Even the victorious generals encamped near Constantinople feared for their own forces if Britain came to the support of the Turks.

Complex negotiations duly made it possible for the powers to meet in congress in Berlin in June 1878, the chair being taken by a reluctant Bismarck who was required to act as an 'Honest Broker'.[12] He had been forced to agree, so convinced was he that German interests demanded the avoidance of war. The proceedings were brusquely opened with the frank comment, 'We are not here to consider the happiness of the Bulgarians but to secure the peace of Europe.' Basically he hoped that any necessary changes to San Stefano would still allow Russia to retreat without too much loss of face so that the all-important *Dreikaiserbund* could be reconstituted. He often proved as subtle behind the scenes as he was cavalier in some of the plenary sessions. Yet in many ways the affair was a piece of theatre, a stage on which the great could strut and show their political skills, the professionals having completed much of the crucial business in advance.

The Congress of Berlin ensured that the 'big Bulgaria' of San Stefano was split into three to limit Russian influence in the southern Balkans – as required by the British and the Austrians. The British also insisted on assured passage through the Aegean and the Straits into the Black Sea. Here again the question of Indian security impinged in that strategists believed that the interruption of Russian lines of communication with Central Asia would lessen the need to fight in remote and inhospitable places such as Afghanistan. To this end Salisbury added a rider to a new international agreement on the Straits. Britain would agree to respect their closure only if she believed that the sultan was acting as a free agent. Bosnia–Herzegovina was occupied by Austria–Hungary, a return to Turkish rule being considered unthinkable. This seemed a not unreasonable decision at the time, yet it was fraught with future perils.[13] Finally not even Bismarck could persuade the Russians that he had behaved with total disinterest at the congress. Relations would become a lot worse before there was a turn for the better.

## The 'Bismarckian' States System, 1879–84

Bismarck remarked to a Russian diplomat in 1880: 'All politics reduces itself to this formula: try to be one of three, as long as the world is governed by the unstable equilibrium of five great powers.' To the charge in a French newspaper in 1877 that he suffered from a 'coalition nightmare', he commented that 'this kind of nightmare will long (and perhaps always will) be a legitimate one for a German minister'. At other times he talked of politics among states as a struggle for power which transcended material interests and ideological commitments. Security, whether sought by alliances, concessions or war, should have priority over other interests. In practice Bismarck himself occasionally discovered that political and economic affairs could not be separated so easily, and certainly he was to make some crude mistakes in 1887 when the two became intertwined in dealings with Russia.[14] In general, however, he was able to concentrate for the most part on high politics and the alignments of the powers – actual and potential.

The British historian, W. N. Medlicott, subsequently described his thinking in this realm as both narrow and uncreative. Through his reliance on balanced antagonisms Bismarck 'had made a deadlock and called it peace'. Germany, he argued, was protected above all by her own power, military and economic. 'Alliances or not, she was formidable; foreigners must take notice of her.' Better behaviour would have done much to win goodwill. Bismarck exaggerated the dangers to which Germany was exposed, and by his heavy-handed and (at times) belligerent search for security he helped to turn some of his nightmares into realities. Diplomatic methods which had served him so well in the unification of Germany subsequently did more harm than good. He was too insecure, too cynical and too pessimistic to do otherwise.[15]

In contrast a German scholar, Otto Pflanze, defends Bismarck's methods as not unreasonable in the context of his times. Thus on the subject of the chancellor's obsessive search from 1879 for security by treaty, he argues that Bismarck believed that great-power relationships had become so volatile and unpredictable that detailed arrangements were imperative in time of peace as well as in war. Whatever their limitations the treaties concluded during his last 11 years in office offered a degree of reassurance or, at the very least, might buy time in a crisis – a precious commodity for a diplomat when speedy mobilisation obsessed the generals.[16] As will be seen, Medlicott and Pflanze each has a strong case. Bismarck helped both to increase and control tensions. Thus in 1887 he thwarted with one hand German advocates of preventive war against Russia but with the other encouraged an increase in tension with France to facilitate the passage of a new army bill.

The initiation of more detailed agreements in time of peace coincided with the sharp deterioration in Russo–German relations after the Congress of Berlin. Personal animosities as well as Russian dismay over the outcome at the congress all played their part. Bismarck did not help matters by his clumsy efforts to promote the claims of Peter Shuvalov to succeed the aged Gorchakov as foreign minister. Bismarck thought Shuvalov a man with whom he could do business. Indeed Shuvalov had made a brave but vain attempt to persuade Alexander II that Bismarck had not led 'a coalition of Europe against Russia'.[17] Relations were also injured by increased tariffs as Russia sought to protect infant industries while Germany tried to defend agrarian interests from cheaper Russian produce. In addition Bismarck, anxious to strengthen the government in the Reichstag, used higher tariffs in his search for more support in domestic politics from the agrarian right.[18]

A great deal of scholarly controversy surrounds Bismarck's alliance of 7 October 1879 with Austria–Hungary, both as to his precise motives, and as to whether in the long run it did more harm than good to the interests of Germany and Europe. Bismarck himself does not help the historian by his own twists and turns along the way. Britain and even France were included in his preliminary search for security. Yet there is a strong case for arguing that he was always hoping to revive the *Dreikaiserbund* in some form or another. It was the worsening relations with Russia in 1879 which seem to have persuaded him that he had first to make sure of Austria, if only as a temporary expedient until Russia could be persuaded to return to the earlier triple understanding.

The Austrians themselves made difficulties. Andrássy was determined to keep the Habsburg Empire free from any engagement to assist Germany against France, and he was equally firm when Bismarck in the final stage of the talks raised the possibility of a three-power arrangement to include Russia. But Bismarck was not to be put off. Once he found that the Russian ambassador was responsive to the idea of a new tripartite agreement between the eastern powers, he promptly ended his exploratory talks in London. He still had to wait until 1881 before the desired alignment was completed, but he was driven on by the conviction that Germany would be best served by ties with Russia and Austria. To this end Bismarck was careful to minimise his commitments to Austria–Hungary. The latter was offered no more than protection against Russian aggression; there was no wish to advance Austrian interests in the Near East; there were no military talks until 1882, while German tariffs were damaging to Austrian (as well as Russian) economic interests.[19]

Bismarck also faced an uphill task in St Petersburg. Many educated Russians, plus some of the military, were vehemently hostile to the Central Powers. It did not require much imagination to see that such animosity (if unchecked) could easily lead to talk of a French alliance – something which began as early as 1882. Even Peter Shuvalov was among the early critics of Bismarck's overtures, fearing that Russia would be no better than a clerk within the proposed league. The tsar himself was open to a range of suggestions. Increasingly influential was N. K. Giers. Of Swedish–German–Lutheran stock, he later became a partisan of the German connection and proved in many respects the inheritor of the mantle of Nesselrode. But initially he refused to be hurried to a conclusion, examining for instance the pros and cons of a deal with the new Liberal government in Britain. Conscious of Russia's economic and military limitations, he argued that if Britain could be reassured on the subject of India, Russia might be left to pursue her other Asian interests at less risk and cost to herself. He also suggested that Britain and Russia might cooperate within the Concert to their mutual advantage in Europe and the Near East. In particular Russia might be able to end the fifty-year-old use of the Concert to defend Turkey against Russia. This last point was not entirely true – as Giers surely realised – but it was a good argument when dealing with a prickly tsar.[20] For a time the tsar and Gorchakov were persuaded to wait and see if a Gladstonian concert had anything to offer Russia.

In the end it was the realities of power which prevailed. The men in St Petersburg could not ignore the greater damage which Germany and Austria united (as opposed to Britain alone) could inflict on Russia, and similarly the greater assistance which they could offer as friends. Given that a collision in Central Asia seemed all too likely, the British would then seek entry to the Black Sea in order to harass Russian lines of communication as well as to tie down as many Russian forces as possible in that theatre. But with German and Austrian support the Straits might be closed to the British navy. A triple agreement with the Central Powers should also ensure Austrian restraint and cooperativeness in the Balkans. Thus the more the matter was examined, the more the scales were tilted towards the Central Powers. Above all 'it made far more sense in a world of *realpolitik* to work with those [the Central Powers] who could inflict the greatest injury [on Russia] as enemies'.[21] It soon became apparent that Gladstone's version of the Concert would do little to assist Russia in the Near East. Although Giers did not immediately despair of Britain, there was general agreement by 1881 that Russia's most pressing need was German benevolent neutrality and active support – especially at the Straits.

Much Bismarckian pressure and persuasive skill were still required to bring the Austrians into line. They gave way only in June 1881. The new Three Emperors Alliance (18 June 1881) provided for the benevolent neutrality of the others if one of the trio was at war with a fourth power (primarily, that is, Germany with France or Russia with Britain). This clause did not apply in the case of the Ottoman Empire – unless prior agreement had been reached concerning its future. Clearly there should be no more San Stefanos. But the Russians were pleased by clauses which allowed for the enlargement of Bulgaria and underlined the closure of the Straits in time of war. For their part they admitted Austria's future right to annex Bosnia–Herzegovina – but not the Sanjak of Novibazar since this would have opened a route for Austria between Serbia and Montenegro into the rump of the Ottoman Empire. Bismarck also declined an Austrian request to guarantee Romania against Russia.

The expressions of monarchical solidarity against the various forces of revolution proved no mere formalities (Alexander II was, after all, assassinated in 1881), while Bismarck had good cause to try to exploit anything which might distance his partners from republican France. Admittedly the three powers would, for numerous reasons, have to interact carefully (like porcupines making love). Yet for Bismarck the rewards from even limited success would be the isolation of France and the greater prospect of peace in Europe. Even the British might find it difficult to extend a Central Asian quarrel with Russia to the Near East, and thus raise the danger of Austrian and finally German involvement. While the tripartite bonds lasted, the treaty with Austria could be effectively shelved. Marvellous to relate, in 1883 Russia and Austria managed to cooperate in response to radical unrest in the Balkans.

Nevertheless it was not long before General Skobelev and many Russian nationalists raised the question of an alliance with France, while the foreign ministry became the target of those newspapers which considered it too subservient to Bismarck. More serious still was the continuing growth of Balkan nationalism. The *Dreikaiserbund* was clearly a weak craft unequal to any but the smoothest of waters. Bismarck felt it necessary in 1882 to add Italy to his alliance system, a state which attracted his interest when the agitation for a Franco–Russian alliance was further stimulated by Skobelev on a visit to Paris. The Triple Alliance of 20 May 1882 provided for German–Italian cooperation against France – Italy and France being rivals in the Mediterranean. Austria for her part needed Italian neutrality in the event of a war with Russia. The alliance included no military agreements, but the three governments showed genuine signs of nervousness concerning possible revolutionary activity and even of a French-led republican confederation embracing Italy and Iberia. The *Dreikaiserbund,* however, remained the keystone for Bismarck (it was renewed in 1884), the other alliances being held in reserve.

These Bismarckian activities coincided with a radically different attempt to influence the management of great-power relations. Gladstone had returned as prime minister of a Liberal government in Britain in 1880. Earlier, in his famous Midlothian campaign, he had promised to re-establish the Concert of Europe under British guidance and in accordance with high ideals. He entertained exaggerated hopes relating to the public law of Europe and a non-violent advance of the Liberal cause. He even spoke of the creation of 'a tribunal of paramount authority, the general judgement of civilised mankind'. Yet he once admitted that his 'great faith' in the impact of moral forces on European politics had been 'possibly ... sometimes a misleading one'.[22] Bismarck himself had never had any doubts. He bluntly stated, 'I do not recognise the concept of "Europe's solidarity".' He likened the Concert to six old maids shut up on an island with one man. The burning question was, who was to get the man? 'I fear it would not be settled by a conference.' For him the Concert usually had more mundane uses. He once suggested that it consider the current tensions over the future of Egypt, but he did so only in the expectation that it would accentuate the differences among the powers to his advantage. 'Our task would be easier', he commented on another occasion, 'if in England that race of great statesmen of earlier times, who had an understanding of European politics, had not completely died out.' The British, especially under Gladstone, could be too quixotic and unpredictable to contribute to the counterbalancing tensions which he wished to cultivate and exploit among the powers. He was, however, able to profit from the ending of Anglo–French cooperation in Egypt in 1882.

### The Breakdown of the 'Bismarckian' System

In 1882 British and French interests in Egypt were at risk from increasing political turmoil. Gladstone at first hoped to deal with the matter through the Concert, and secondly by cooperation with France. When neither proved possible, he reluctantly agreed to unilateral British intervention. Despite ostensible military success, the British soon found themselves not only unable to disengage from Egypt, but dependent on the agreement of the other powers for the management of Egyptian affairs. Bismarck naturally exploited this liability to the full (though for motives which have been much debated by historians down the years). Certainly he picked up a number of colonies along the way, and used the quarrels with a British Liberal government both to embarrass his constitutionally-minded opponents at home and to woo support from other interest groups. But equally interesting is the fact that the international environment as a whole (and particularly his satisfactory relations with Russia and Austria) allowed him the luxury of engaging in some colonial activities in the knowledge that Germany was secure in

Europe. As he himself once illustrated by a wave of the arm to Germany's position in Europe between France and Russia, 'This is my map of Africa.'

Africa, as it happened, gave rise to one of the more successful interventions by the Concert of Europe. The Berlin conference of 1884–5 is described by Alan Palmer as 'a model of anticipatory diplomacy'.[23] Useful work was certainly done to regulate the growing 'scramble for Africa'. Yet such issues were obviously much more tractable than those relating, say, to the future of south-eastern Europe, the Straits and Constantinople. Indeed the British claim to a right of passage into the Black Sea erupted as a live issue in 1885 as Britain and Russia disputed the course of the Afghan border at Penjdeh. War briefly seemed possible – even under a Gladstone government – with British strategists looking to fight key battles in the Black Sea. This scare vindicated Bismarck's policy towards Russia and Austria since he was able to put the Straits out of bounds as far as British forces were concerned. A German military mission was sent to advise the Turks on their defence against the British. France, too, supported the neutrality of the Straits, so that when Salisbury returned to office in 1885, he ironically noted that Gladstone had succeeded in one of his prime aims. He had indeed united Europe, but unfortunately he had united it against Britain. Salisbury sensibly (if vainly) put out feelers in Berlin.

A different sort of trouble was soon brewing in the Near East. Eastern Rumelia revolted against the Turks in favour of union with Bulgaria. The tsar, already angered by the Bulgarians' lack of gratitude and cooperativeness despite Russia's part in the creation of their state, opposed the union. Germany and Austria gladly took the same line, each anxious to preserve the status quo and to earn cheap credit with Russia. Bismarck suggested an ambassadorial conference in Constantinople (though only to 'drown the question in ink'). The ambassadors, however, were soon busier than expected. The Serbs, fearful of Bulgarian enlargement, attacked their neighbour in November 1885 only to be emphatically defeated. They had to be rescued by Austria from further humiliation. For the time being the three eastern powers were able to maintain their unity, prompted by their mutual desire to avoid any further disruption of what remained of Turkey in Europe. A timely proposal from Lord Salisbury that the Rumelian question be settled by a 'personal union' under Alexander of Battenberg (the ruling prince in Sofia) was approved by the other powers. British naval power also helped to deter a restless Greek government from causing trouble further south.

So far the powers had handled matters well, but Bismarck still believed that a durable solution depended upon a division of the Balkans between Russia and Austria. He calculated that even if Russian influence reached the Dardanelles, this would leave Russia with a highly exposed right flank to Austria in the west.[24] The Austrians, however, remained convinced that in the long run the Russians must emerge as the stronger force, helped by their Slav and Orthodox affiliations. Not surprisingly they were soon dismayed to find that the status quo was under threat as Alexander III lost patience with the obstreperous Bulgars.

Russian efforts to regain the initiative in Sofia triggered off a chain of events straight out of a Ruritanian novel. Prince Alexander was kidnapped by Russian supporters in Bulgaria; released by the Russians; and finally forced to abdicate by his own ministers when he sent an excessively polite telegram to the tsar. The Russians broke off diplomatic relations in November 1886 and an invasion seemed possible. International controversy and mutual suspicion surrounded the search for a successor to Prince Alexander. In St Petersburg Pan-Slav feeling threatened to make Giers's position untenable. As if there was not trouble enough in the east, Franco–German relations were also taking a turn for the worse in the west. This was due in part to Bismarck himself – a degree of tension with France being stirred up for political and electoral purposes at home, and to facilitate the passage of a new army bill through the Reichstag.[25] But he was less happy to find French and Russian chauvinists pushing for an alliance between their countries. Militant French nationalism was further strengthened by the threat from the Boulangist movement to the political stability of the Third Republic.

Meanwhile the Bulgarian crisis rumbled on, and for a time it seemed as if Bismarck would be forced to take a higher profile in southern Europe much against his better judgement. The Triple Alliance was due for renewal in 1887, and Rome was able to procure assurances from Berlin of more diplomatic backing in the Mediterranean. Fortunately for Bismarck, Britain was no longer confident that her fleet could deal with both France and Russia in the Mediterranean. Salisbury therefore negotiated the so-called Mediterranean Agreements with Italy and Austria–Hungary. Although these fell short of an alliance, all parties expressed their interest in the maintenance of the status quo from the western Mediterranean and its shores to the Near East. For Bismarck this meant that Britain was at last beginning to act in ways which he thought appropriate (namely by helping to deter Russia), even if she was doing so on her own terms under the shrewd direction of Salisbury. Italy and Spain further reinforced the status quo with an exchange of notes on 4 May 1887. These included a promise to defend the monarchical cause against the danger of a 'Latin republican brotherhood'.

If the Austrians had some reason to feel reassured, this had been gained partly at the expense of conceding that Italy was entitled to some say in the affairs of the western Balkans. In addition they still correctly feared that Bismarck was engaged in some backdoor exchanges with Russia. By now their own relations with Russia over the future of Bulgaria had deteriorated to such a degree that there could be no question of renewing the *Dreikaiserbund*. The Austrian foreign minister, Kálnoky, insisted that the choice of a new prince for Bulgaria could not be left to Russia alone. This was a European matter.

Bismarck, however, could hope that the new Mediterranean Agreements, if they meant anything, should reduce the need for open German backing of Austria against Russia, thus leaving him with the possibility of retaining some links with St Petersburg. Earlier he had insisted that the *Dreikaiserbund* should be spun out 'as long as a strand of it remains'. Now he had to find an alternative. Again he was fortunate in that Alexander III was open to reason despite his anger towards the Bulgarians and the Central Powers. He was resisting Slavophile pressures and began to listen to the temperate advice of Giers as early as March 1887. Alexander agreed that Russia's rising national debt and the dangers of isolation meant that he could not afford a high risk policy. Nor was he yet ready to turn to republican France.

Bismarck therefore began to gain the hearing in St Petersburg which he so strongly desired. He shrewdly underlined his personal commitment to the maintenance of an equilibrium among the powers. Even if current Franco–German tensions led to war, the chancellor insisted that it would not be in the interest of Germany to cripple her opponent as a great power. The French navy, for instance, was required to help offset British naval supremacy (a major interest of the Russians). Bismarck thus rarely missed an opportunity to show how the security of each power was bound up with the preservation of the current balance between them. His diplomacy doubtless had some effect, but he was able to attract the attention of the tsar and his advisers above all because of their awareness of the current weaknesses and special needs of Russia. The negotiations produced the Reinsurance Treaty of 18 June 1887. This defined the conduct of each party if the other should find itself at war with a third great power. Benevolent neutrality, however, would not apply if Russia attacked Austria, or Germany attacked France. Russia's preponderant influence was recognised in Bulgaria, but another proviso forbade any change to the territorial status quo without the prior agreement of the two signatories. Bismarck was also happy to support the continued closure of the Straits – much to the relief of Russia.

This treaty has been much debated. Was it, for instance, compatible with Germany's obligations to Austria–Hungary? How could Bismarck with one hand support Russia over the Straits while giving discreet encouragement to the signatories of the Mediterranean Agreements with the other? Was it all a house of cards? On behalf of Bismarck it might be said that the peculiar circumstances of the time defy critics who apply too rigid or logical a test. Although he excited distrust in Vienna and still more in St Petersburg, it was no secret that Germany's interests required the survival of the Habsburg monarchy or that Russia could not be indifferent to the destruction of France. Furthermore, as matters then stood, neither Austria nor Russia was strong enough nor confident enough by itself to start a war (save in desperation or in a moment of irrationality). In effect Bismarck could follow a policy whose apparent contradictions did not seriously conflict with the realities of the moment. To the argument that the treaty was superfluous if this was indeed the case, Bismarck could retort that any deal was better than none if it helped to strengthen and reassure the more level-headed and peacefully minded groups in Russia. He could in any case and in all honesty signal his deep desire for peace in the Near East – including restraint by Austria.

What he could not do was save Russia from obvious and conclusive defeat in Bulgaria. Here he was bound by the limits imposed by his own game plan and his interpretation of German national interest. The Bulgarians were therefore able to elect Ferdinand of Coburg in the summer of 1887 as their new prince, and to fend off Russian demands for his expulsion with the moral support of the signatories to the Mediterranean Agreements. This meant, however, that many Russians continued to see Bismarck as an evil genius who was intent on frustrating their legitimate ambitions. In fact the chancellor was as good a 'friend' as they were likely to find in Berlin at that time. In contrast Friedrich von Holstein, a rising force in the foreign ministry, had been hoping as early as March 1887 that 'the inevitable war in the Near East ... [would start] as soon as possible with Britain and Austria aligned against Russia'. He would have welcomed outright Bulgarian defiance of the Russians, and he was later to condemn the Reinsurance Treaty as 'political bigamy'.[26] Bismarck might have admitted to being less than honest and faithful, but would have denied that he had entered into commitments that could be compared to the spirit and letter of nineteenth-century marriage vows.

Even so he still faced serious problems. The Russian armies in Poland were being reinforced and by December 1887 the German military were becoming decidedly jittery. Moltke was arguing that Germany should join with Austria in a pre-emptive war against Russia. The vice-chief of the General Staff, Count Waldersee, was even more insistent. Reports from France added to the fears of the military. In fact the Russians were sceptical of their chances of victory at this time even in partnership with France. Yet the German generals continued to press the case for war, arguing its necessity not merely because of current Russian military preparations, but more seriously because time was not on the side of Germany – she was caught between two great and expansionist powers whose combined resources would ultimately outweigh her own. Such arguments were doggedly resisted by Wilhelm I and Bismarck, the latter stating that even if one accepted the assumption that war was probable in the future that was no reason for fighting now.

Bismarck also spoke out forcefully in the Reichstag in February 1888, arguing that 'Bulgaria ... is not sufficiently important to plunge Europe from Moscow to the Pyrenees, from the North Sea to Palermo, into a war the outcome of which nobody can foresee; and after the war people would not even remember why they had fought.'[27] The extent of his geographical references was deliberate. He was issuing coded warnings to hotheads at home and all round Europe. Holstein, in contrast, continued to back those who argued that Germany was never likely to enjoy so favourable a position again. Indeed he thought it so strong that Russia might well back down if faced by an 'ultimatum'. He did not, however, consider how this would affect Germany's eastern prospects in the long run.

In Vienna the German military attaché was similarly urging Francis Joseph to seize the initiative against Russia. The Archduke Rudolf was a leading figure in the war party in Vienna, while some Hungarians were among the militants. The emperor, however, agreed with his favourite general, Beck, that the army was not ready. There were doubts, too, over public support for war. Kálnoky recommended caution despite his own gloomy view of the future. Russia, he feared, could not accommodate herself in the long run to the rise of Germany and the existence of the Dual Alliance. She had, it seemed, to be regarded as a permanent enemy. Ultimately only war would decide whether 'Slavic Russia will dominate Europe or not'. Thus the crucial questions were whether time was on the side of Russia or Austria, and whether Slav propaganda would soon begin to undermine the Habsburg Empire. He finally considered it wiser to buy time than engage in a preventive war. A majority of advisers in Vienna also favoured delay. Priority should be given to the search for allies and friends.

Advocates of this course were encouraged by a further strengthening of the Mediterranean Agreements in December 1887 (an alignment still very much in accord with Bismarck's needs). Austrian distrust of Bismarck was another reason for caution in Vienna. Even if Austria were at war with Russia she might have to suffer major defeats before Germany came to the rescue. It was also noted that, despite reports that the German military regarded Russia, not France, as their main potential enemy, no Austro–German staff talks were taking place. In short, the Austrians could look with no great confidence to Berlin – which was exactly what Bismarck himself intended.[28]

It is, of course, important not to make Bismarck appear cleverer or more far-sighted than he actually was. Much was decided in other European capitals. Yet he can be credited on this occasion with trying to stop matters getting worse – or at least with trying to postpone the evil hour even if, like death, it could not be avoided for ever. Bismarck's own assessment of the military situation is also revealing. He agreed that, while Germany at that time might well prove victorious over Russia, total victory would be another matter. He did not see how Germany could succeed where Napoleon had failed.[29] The

German general staff itself subsequently began to take the same view, so much so that their war plans relating to Russia and France were turned on their heads. Once a quick and decisive victory seemed unlikely in the east, the search began for ways to achieve a decisive blow in the west. Russia could then be forced to come to terms due to her isolation (as in 1855–6). From 1892 Schlieffen was the guiding force in German war planning – the main force to attack France while a smaller army stood on the defensive in the east.

Meanwhile Bismarck had been preoccupied with political questions. In February 1888, with Austrian assent, he decided to publish the terms of their alliance – both to demonstrate its defensive character and to warn the Russians not to play with fire. In various ways he tried to show that Germany, while she did not fear war, loved peace. Basically he believed that a waiting game was best for Germany. At the same time he could not help but fear that others might be playing the same game. He suspected that the British might be particularly adept in such matters.

Nor was he wholly conciliatory in his dealings with the Russians. It seems he hoped to remind them of their financial vulnerability when, in November 1887, he forbade the Reichsbank to accept Russian securities as collateral for loans. Perhaps, too, there was a reluctance in Berlin to do anything that might ease Russia's financial problems and so increase her capacity to wage war. But panicky German businessmen began to unload Russian securities which were then bought up by the French. This was an important step towards the later alliance between the two powers, with French loans serving as a major political as well as a financial lubricant. Russo–German relations were further damaged in 1887 by a ukase which adversely affected the interests of German landowners in western Russia. Indeed Giers, a diplomat of the old school, voiced his fears to Herbert Bismarck in June 1888 that 'the stepped up economic struggle of our times influences the political attitudes of peoples'.[30]

Although the years 1887–8 finally passed off without a war, there was no reason to suppose that anything had been resolved in the longer run. Apart from crises arising out of Balkan politics, many Russians were as determined as ever to secure the Straits once the time was ripe. In Germany there was further talk in 1888 of an ultimate war. Holstein insisted that Russia was intent on the destruction of Austria–Hungary, an event which would leave Germany without a real friend in Europe. Again he argued that time was not on

Germany's side. General Waldersee was increasingly critical of Bismarck's eastern policy, claiming that military intelligence suggested that Russia was intent on war in the long run. Diplomacy, perhaps, might usefully buy a little more time to perfect Germany's military preparations, but the moment of decision might come as early as the spring of 1890. Waldersee professed himself ready to confront Bismarck himself if the latter tried to be obstructive.[31]

The chancellor thus faced many problems at home and abroad. He had to try to come to terms with a new kaiser, the excitable and erratic Wilhelm II. France as well as Russia continued to seem threatening. Franco–Italian commercial and colonial disputes were particularly worrying. Matters were so serious that Bismarck even began to talk of Britain as 'the decisive factor in the European situation'. If only her firm attachment to the Triple Alliance could be obtained, the balance would be tilted decisively against France and Russia. From August 1888 until March 1889 he was seriously exploring the possibility of a deal with London, hoping that the current Franco–Italian tensions would make the British more amenable. In January 1889 he even suggested that an Anglo–German alliance should be concluded for up to three years. Salisbury, however, was fearful of controversy at home and wary of entering into anything more binding than the current Mediterranean Agreements. He had stated in 1888 that (as matters then stood) Britain would probably assist Italy in the event of a gratuitous attack by France at sea.[32] But he also conceded that the British navy at that time did not seem strong enough to uphold British interests from Gibraltar to Constantinople. His admirals argued that the fleet could not operate in the east as long as it was threatened by the French fleet at Toulon.

Everything therefore pointed to a major expansion of the Royal Navy rather than a deal with Bismarck with all that this would entail in binding commitments. Britain could afford the extra cost. The Two Power Standard (with special reference to Russia and France in the Mediterranean) was therefore announced in 1889, although nearly ten years elapsed before the admirals were persuaded that the navy could deal simultaneously with two enemies. In contrast Salisbury seemed reasonably confident in March 1889 that Russia would not risk an aggressive move in the Near East until something akin to the *Dreikaiserbund* had been revived. Even in the middle of 1892, despite the pessimism of and warnings from the Admiralty, he doubted if a crisis was imminent. Russia was not equal to 'a general war', her fleet was 'incomplete', her land forces 'very imperfect', and her finances were in 'disorder'. This was an accurate assessment.[33]

As for Bismarck, W. N. Medlicott sees the overtures to Britain as proof that by 1889 he feared that his policies had failed or were on the brink of doing so.[34] What one can say for certain is that the men who replaced him in 1890 promptly reached this conclusion, and decided not to renew the Reinsurance Treaty despite the disposition of the tsar and Giers to do so. The latter were not acting out of any love for Germany but in the belief that Russia was still not strong enough to break its line to Berlin. In contrast the new German chancellor, Count Caprivi, and others such as Holstein, believed that Bismarck's policy had become too contradictory and complex. They feared that a continuing attempt to square so many circles might end in the ruin of Germany's relations with existing friends.

Caprivi was in any case anxious to build on Bismarck's efforts to woo Britain. In July 1890 large parts of Germany's East African colonial claims were given up in return for Heligoland. The Mediterranean Agreements and the Two Power Standard fitted in with this new German approach. Reciprocal tariff cuts were also being made with friends, whereas a commercial war with Russia dragged on until 1894. Wilhelm II was pro-Austrian at this stage, while Vienna was relieved by the departure of the devious Bismarck. If Italian *irredentism* caused some tension, the Austrians for once had money to spare to improve their army. In any case the Central Powers seemed well placed in the Balkans. Thus the new men in Berlin for the time being felt confident that they had been right to abandon Bismarck's elaborate checks and balances. Yet paradoxically within a very few years the latter was seemingly vindicated by a revival of tolerably satisfactory relations between Russia and the Central Powers.

# 6

## IMPERIAL RIVALRIES AND EUROPEAN DIPLOMACY, 1890–1907

'The partition of the greater part of the globe among such powers is ... now only a question of time.' (George Bernard Shaw)

### Crises Deferred: Europe in the Early 1890s

The years between 1890 and 1907 do not provide a neat progression to the more obvious and immediate origins of the First World War. It is true that France and Russia concluded a military convention against Germany in 1894, but in practice each found itself mainly preoccupied with imperial rivalries with Britain. This distraction in the case of Russia even facilitated a significant improvement in relations with Germany and Austria–Hungary during the second half of the 1890s. Most surprising and therefore revealing was the fact that yet another Near Eastern crisis reinforced rather than weakened these trends. Consequently for some years (and in striking contrast to the late 1880s), it seemed quite possible that the next great war would see Britain ranged against either Russia or France – or both of those powers – and with Germany and Austria (at least in the opening phase) in the role of interested by-standers.

In such circumstances it is hardly surprising that, while Britain's relations with Germany were by no means untroubled in these years, her policy-makers tended to regard Germany (as well as Austria–Hungary) as a defender of the status quo in Europe.

Whatever the differences between Berlin and London, a serious and lasting rift was not confirmed until 1905–6. In view of Britain's other concerns, the launch of German *weltpolitik* in 1896 and the great Tirpitz naval building programme from 1898 at first had a relatively limited impact on British policies. Indeed in 1901 the cabinet instructed the Admiralty to place Germany among the naval powers which were assumed to be friendly or neutral. There was interest, too, in an Anglo–German alliance.

No study of Germany's increasing activity outside Europe can be complete without some reference to the activities of the other leading powers as well as to the ambitions of certain groups within Germany herself. Given the strength of interest in navalism and imperialism in the later nineteenth century (even some Americans caught the infection), it would have been surprising if a proud people with such vast resources and energy had not entered the competition. They also found it easy to do so when Russia's prime concerns lay with industrial development at home and expansion in Asia rather than in Europe. Naturally the German ability to wage a two-front war against France and Russia was carefully nurtured, but such matters caused fewer headaches than in the late 1880s.

German policy-makers in the later 1890s and early 1900s therefore had less need to follow Bismarck in pointing to Germany's location between Russia and France as their 'map of Africa'. Far from it. Many felt that their position in Europe and the existing strength of their army left them free to take up new overseas and naval policies. At the same time some felt that this should be done by discreet rather than by blatantly aggressive methods. Germany should exploit the difficulties which the other powers created for themselves rather than necessarily take the initiative herself. This was not always possible given the impatience and love of histrionics by the kaiser and his entourage. Yet study of this period may help to explain why Germany resorted to much more aggressive tactics only from 1905–9. At the same time it might encourage a degree of scepticism concerning the claims of some scholars that the rise of *weltpolitik* and the new navy were from the very outset prime causes of the formation of the ententes of 1904 and 1907, and similarly that they made the outbreak of the 'world war almost inevitable' in 1914.[1]

To see all this in context, one must first note the difficulties and delays which attended the creation of the Franco–Russian alignment in the early 1890s. The conclusion of the Russian military convention with France (4 January 1894) might seem a natural response to the Dual Alliance and to the tensions of the late 1880s. Yet the process was a slow one, and occasioned much debate – especially in Russia. Skobelev had led those who favoured the French agreement, whereas Giers represented those who tried to maintain some sort of connection with Germany. The French for their part had obvious reasons why they should try to end their virtual isolation, but they could not expect Russia to be willing to risk war on their behalf to recover Alsace and Lorraine. Although French investments in and loans to Russia from the end of the 1880s became a useful basis for other connections, the ideological divide between the republic and the tsarist empire was not easily bridged. The Boulanger political drama in France added to the reservations of Russian conservatives and those who believed that the imperial interest demanded the avoidance of war in Europe. Giers (and to a lesser extent the tsar himself) continued to believe that it was too risky to cast Russia totally adrift from Germany – hence the abortive attempt to renew the Reinsurance Treaty in 1890.

There was one point, however, on which most key figures in St Petersburg could unite – namely that Russia's own limitations as a power meant that her security was tied up with the survival of France. Together they might hope to deny Germany hegemony in Europe. Thus Alexander III as early as March 1892 had insisted that if Germany attacked either France or Russia, the other must immediately throw her forces into the fray to maintain the balance of power. Given, too, the speed with which the German army could be mobilised, some advance military consultations were obviously needed irrespective of the actual state of their relations (good or bad) with Germany at any one time. A Franco–Russian military convention followed in 1894. By then the Germans were undoubtedly planning to defeat France as quickly as possible in the event of a crisis. On the other hand no less an authority than Moltke had warned the Reichstag in May 1890 that the great powers were now in such a state of preparation that no war could be settled in one or two campaigns. He feared that another seven or even a 30 years war might ensue.[2] Yet any suggestion of lengthy conflicts – with all their economic and political dangers – seemed only to intensify the resolve of every major continental capital to improve the offensive capabilities of its armies.

Such planning and preparation, however, did not mean that war was imminent, or that Russia was concerned only with possible conflict with the Central Powers. A demonstration of Franco–Russian intimacy in October 1893 by the visit of a Russian naval squadron to Toulon could also be seen as a warning to Britain, Toulon being the base of the powerful French fleet which was easily the most important single problem facing the British Admiralty. Improved Russian relations with France also made it easier to raise the resources needed for accelerated industrialisation in Russia and railway building in Asia, while Russia's own fleets were being expanded against Britain. Indeed all such objectives strengthened the case for better Russian relations with Germany and Austria.

The German response to the developing Franco–Russian alignment is also revealing. Rather than returning to the pre-emptive military thinking of the late 1880s, Berlin chose to try diplomacy in the first instance. Austria and Britain became uncomfortably aware that they could not expect overt German backing when (from about 1892) they again began to feel vulnerable to Russia in the Near East. Salisbury on handing over the Foreign Office in August 1892 to Lord Rosebery (on the formation of Gladstone's last ministry) gave simple but emphatic advice to treat the limited alignment with Italy as the key to the defence of British interests in Europe, Italy was a member of the Triple Alliance which ensured the maintenance of an equilibrium which admirably suited Britain. Salisbury feared, however, that Italy, if denied a firm expression of British interest, might feel obliged to come to terms with France, a step which might persuade the Central Powers to turn to Russia. If they became sufficiently intimate, this might result in agreement on a great-power partition of the Ottoman Empire with Constantinople falling to Russia. Britain, Salisbury argued, should try to prevent this through her link with Italy.[3] He was clearly looking for maximum security at minimum cost and commitment by Britain, and recommending his own version of Bismarck's pursuit of an equilibrium by means which required other powers to do much or most of the work.

Britain's Italian connection, however, could not prevent Germany from edging towards Russia – primarily to weaken or neutralise the emerging Franco–Russian partnership. Austrian confidence also suffered as contacts with Berlin lessened. Vienna was even warned that Berlin was ready to tolerate Russian control of the eastern Balkans and Constantinople itself. Britain and Austria could no longer count on German support to try to localise any war in which they (as signatories to the Mediterranean Agreements) might become involved. Indeed limited Russian advances in the Near East might even prove advantageous to Germany since this would thrust Britain into the front line in any Near Eastern crisis. Caprivi as chancellor had commented in the early 1890s, 'for us the best beginning of the next great war would be for the first shot to be fired from an English ship.' The Triple would then become the Quadruple Alliance.[4] This would have turned Salisbury's strategy on its head.

This new German gambit was soon forcing the Austrians to review their position. Relations with Italy, Romania and Serbia were becoming less satisfactory, and the tie with Britain was precarious. Kálnoky as early as 1894 began to show some interest in talks with the Russians, and detected some encouraging reactions in St Petersburg.[5] The sudden death of Alexander III in 1894 increased German hopes of a friendly hearing, and encouraged those in Berlin who hoped that foreign policy might be based on a 'free hand' rather than on detailed arrangements of the kind previously sought by Bismarck and Caprivi. Meanwhile the fiercer the imperial rivalries between Russia, France and Britain, the more Germany's security improved in the heart of Europe. These same rivalries also seemed likely to improve Germany's bargaining power overseas. Diplomacy might succeed without direct recourse to the sword.

Thus the new Franco–Russian alignment, though important, did not lead to the formation of two hostile camps in Europe. Instead it induced the Germans to work more assiduously for a better relationship with Russia. This is not to say that there existed a complete consensus among those who directed or influenced German policy. Wilhelm II was given to bouts of impetuosity, grand postures and even grander rhetoric interspersed with spells of anxiety and caution. His views of other countries and their leaders changed almost as often as he changed his uniforms. Political imperatives at home could also affect foreign policy. Nevertheless this was an era (1894–1904) when German thinking and conduct provide fewer direct clues to the events of July–August 1914 than might be assumed if hindsight is allowed too much play. This latest approach smacks of variations on Bismarckian and even earlier policies with its emphasis on a working if not a detailed relationship with Russia as well as Austria. Holstein was one of its strongest supporters.

## The 'New Imperialism' and the Near Eastern Question in the mid-1890s

A crucial test of the strength of the new diplomatic trends, a Near Eastern crisis in the mid-1890s, passed off with surprisingly few difficulties between the three eastern powers. Indeed, with the help of other developments, it tended to push them closer together. Vienna discovered further reasons why it should follow Berlin on the road to St Petersburg, while the Russians – intent upon other interests – had reason to reciprocate. Military planning and preparations naturally continued along well-worn lines in Europe as a whole, but there could be no doubt that for many the future of Asia and Africa was of most pressing importance.[6]

This greater interest in the wider world had many roots. The search for profitable trade and investments by businessmen often became entangled with questions of imperial security and national pride. Between 1870 and 1883 British writers such as Ruskin, Froude and above all Seeley declared that the world's largest empire was not yet strong enough to guarantee Britain's future as a world power. On the continent scholars and writers joined politicians, bureaucrats, soldiers, businessmen and adventurers in arguing that no European power could remain truly great without extensive territory and influence in the wider world. A French professor, Leroy Beaulieu, argued in 1874 that France would sink to the level of a secondary power without a great African empire. Gustav Schmoller, a German economist, wrote in 1890 that 'the course of world history in the twentieth century will be determined by the competition between the Russian, English, American, and perhaps the Chinese world empires, and by their aspirations to reduce all other, smaller states to dependence upon them'. Max Weber (1895) and Professor Delbrück (1896) argued that Germany could never be truly great and help to 'coin the human spirit' unless she engaged in '*weltmachtpolitik*'. If a global balance of power had not yet superseded the European balance, it was readily believed that the future would be dominated by a few truly great world powers or empires. George Bernard Shaw in 1900 thought 'the partition of the greater part of the globe ... now only a question of time'.

Even the British, despite their huge possessions, were not certain of their capacity to compete at this level in the long run unless they found ways to increase the efficiency, cohesion and sheer economic and military power of the empire. Many Russians similarly felt an urgent need to push on with their advances in Asia, not least because of the strategic interconnections involving the Near East, Central Asia and British India. Some Frenchmen after 1871, resigned to their inability for the time being to wage a war of revenge against Germany, sought compensation in more intensive empire-building. Italy, too, was looking outward, although the practical importance of her ventures tended to lie mainly in the difficulties which they generated with others – notably with France, and thereby increasing Italian dependence on other powers. Germany was only one player in an already contested field.

*Weltpolitik* was not officially proclaimed until January 1896. Yet as early as the 1870s one finds Albrecht von Stosch, for instance, insisting that German unification was but a step to a greater world role. It was fitting that he should have served as chief of the Imperial German Navy from 1872 to 1883, and in so doing have anticipated some of the thinking associated with Admiral Tirpitz. He became increasingly preoccupied with trade and colonial rivalry with Britain. War was an ultimate possibility. 'Only in battle can Germany become great.' Earlier in April 1870 he had written, 'I cannot stop thinking that we are called to be a Great Power! The House of Hohenzollern is the representative of godly order in Europe.' Germany should become a European and then a world power.[7] Wilhem II, shortly after his accession, declared that Germany would have bled in vain in 1866 and 1870–1 unless she became fully involved in the great decisions of the world. Only warring nations progressed. The Social Democrats, with their less belligerent view of the world, were enemies of the Fatherland and did not deserve the name of Germans.

By the mid-1890s enough of the German leadership had become convinced that for a variety of reasons they could and should embark upon *weltpolitik*. Admittedly the counter-argument was still to be heard in some quarters that Germany had first to secure her position against France and Russia in Europe. It is also evident that in the early days there was often as much noise and bluster as substance in the new policy, especially when it was related to domestic political needs. The patriotic card was a useful weapon in the ongoing struggle to create and nurture centre-right coalitions in the Reichstag and in the battle to combat the rise of the left among the electorate. *Weltpolitik* had a special appeal among the lower middle classes and skilled artisans who felt squeezed between the rise of big business and mass trade unions. In so far as the policy had substance for them, it included the dream of German settlement colonies as an alternative to migration to the Americas with the threatened loss of national and cultural identity. Big business was less interested in colonies as such. It thought in terms of the spread of German trade and investments outside Europe supported as necessary by state power.[8]

Holstein tried to strike a balance between Germany's European and global interests. He argued that all powers should feel obliged to cultivate German friendship so that each in return would be compelled to pay generously for that privilege. He opposed unduly assertive policies in any direction, but especially an unrestrained pursuit of *weltpolitik* against Britain. Germany might forfeit her central position, and be more likely to find herself a belligerent at the very start of any war. In practice his words of caution often went unheeded as fears of Russia in Europe lessened and opportunities beckoned abroad. There was, for instance, the embarrassing telegram which the kaiser insisted on sending to congratulate the president of the Boer Republic on the defeat of the ill-conceived Jameson Raid. But Japan's victory over China in the war of 1894–5 caused Russia to welcome German (as well as French) assistance to force revision of a treaty which was thought too favourable to Japan. For the Germans (including the kaiser) this was encouraging evidence of Russian preoccupation with areas outside Europe and the Near East. As the tsar and other key figures became more excited by dreams of empire and influence from Samarkand to Peking, Witte and his allies found it easier to plead for caution and restraint even in the Near East. Berlin was pushing at an open door when it encouraged Russia to look eastward.[9]

As Russo–German relations improved, so Germany had less interest in the Mediterranean Agreements. She declined a British request to put pressure on France to remain neutral in the event of a war in the Near East. Austria for her part began to doubt Britain's firmness (as well as that of Germany) at the Straits not least because of British respect for the French fleet in Toulon. Some policy-makers in Vienna began to ask if it was not time to bow to the inevitable and see what terms could be made with the Russians. Perhaps even Constantinople might be treated as expendable. But this was not yet the view of Goluchowski (foreign minister from 1895). He did not think that the Habsburg Empire could be adequately protected by any deal, nor did he wish to add to Austrian territory or responsibilities in the Balkans.[10]

It was the change in British policy between 1895–7 (in parallel with Germany's growing detente with Russia) which finally forced Goluchowski to review his position. Salisbury on his return to office in June 1895 had inherited a crisis following an Armenian revolt against the Turks. Reports of Turkish savagery against the rebels so inflamed feeling in Britain as to rule out the option of a pro-Turkish policy. Salisbury also discovered that the admirals were still unsure of Britain's ability to command the Straits and the Mediterranean. Since 1892 Arthur Balfour (Salisbury's able and influential nephew) had been arguing that only with extensive pre-war preparations (including troops at Malta) could the British hope to win a race against the Russians for control of the Straits. Salisbury pronounced himself 'no bigot' on the subject of British interests there, though he warned that the empire's influence and prestige from the Mediterranean to India might suffer if Britain retreated from the Straits. She might also injure her standing with other powers.

In his anxiety to find a satisfactory solution, he was understood by the German ambassador in July–August 1895 to suggest that he might not be averse to a partition of the Ottoman Empire in cooperation with Russia or Germany. Salisbury, it has been said, was sometimes inclined to think aloud even to foreign diplomats, and Hatzfeldt might have taken him too literally, especially since he knew with what keen interest such news would be received in Berlin. For his part, Salisbury was aware that he might soon have to rewrite British policy in the Near East, and he wished to avoid as far as possible any impression of British weakness. This might be avoided if Britain could conduct a dignified retreat behind the cover provided by some great international negotiation and perhaps even a comprehensive settlement of the future of the Ottoman Empire. He was later to become rather more explicit on this subject.

Unfortunately Anglo–Russian differences from China to the Near East meant that there was little early prospect of any meeting of minds. Pan-Slav opinion was naturally anti-British. Nor did the fact that the Russians had potentially rebellious Armenian subjects of their own help matters. Berlin was unlikely to do anything which would threaten its line to St Petersburg, while German relations with Britain in the winter of 1895–6 were still suffering from the effects of the Kruger telegram. Only the Austrians had reason to be interested. Ever conscious of Austrian weaknesses both at home and in the Balkans, the last thing Goluchowski wanted was a great-power collision. Resort to the Concert might, even if it achieved little or nothing, keep the powers talking rather than quarreling.[11]

Neither Salisbury nor the tsar was in a particularly strong position when they met at Balmoral in September 1896. The British minister thought Nicholas II 'purely Russian in his views', yet also conciliatory, honest and eager to preserve the territorial status quo. The tsar feared it would be all too easy to trigger a European war. Personally he wanted no more territory. The Straits, however, 'were the door to the room in which he lived, and he insisted he must have the key to that door'. Salisbury thought this would be strongly resisted by other powers as long as the Turks controlled Constantinople. He did, however, try to interest the tsar in another scenario which linked the issue of the Straits to the future of the Ottoman Empire and the interests of the other powers. A total Turkish collapse, he suggested, might create conditions in which other states would be able to satisfy their own needs under some comprehensive settlement. Consequently if they were prepared to allow Russia control of the Straits, Britain would 'seek some arrangement by which it could be met'. Nicholas agreed that this would be the best outcome. Salisbury then added the important caveat that he had been speaking personally, and that due regard had to be paid to the British cabinet, Britain's allies and 'past traditions'.[12]

These talks, though revealing, understandably did little to improve matters in the short run. Some in St Petersburg argued that the moment was ripe to take advantage of Turkish vulnerability. Nelidov, the Russian ambassador in Constantinople, was particularly insistent. In October 1896 the British director of naval intelligence thought such an operation was eminently practicable – 'no doubt their plans are made!' Given the 'established friendship of France and Russia', Britain would find that war with either must mean war with both at a time when the balance of power in the Near East and Mediterranean was tilted against her.[13] In fact the question of a surprise Russian descent on Constantinople was discussed by a Russian Crown Council on 5 December 1896. But Witte led critics who persuasively argued that this would be a reckless and extravagant diversion of resources at a time when other programmes needed absolute priority if Russia was to be assured of her proper place among the greatest of the great powers in the future. It was finally agreed that the survival of a weak Turkey was preferable to all the unpredictable consequences of a costly international struggle over the spoils.[14]

Russia's opponents were, as we have seen, equally cautious. In Britain both the navy and army were already looking to Egypt (with Alexandria as a new base) to serve as the key to their strategy in the eastern Mediterranean. Thus when the Austrians tested British views on the future of the Straits in January 1897, they received only a tepid response from Salisbury. He stressed the popular antipathy in Britain towards the Turks, the sultan's aversion to help from the western powers, and the difficulty of forcing the Straits. Although he did not rule out British intervention in all circumstances, he warned that Britain must reserve her freedom of action. Nevertheless he was still anxious to avoid giving any impression that Britain was retreating. He said that Ottoman integrity had been established by the Concert of Europe, 'the only authority competent to create law for Europe'. Balfour, who had spoken in most dismissive terms of the Concert in 1879, agreed. In contrast Gladstone feared that the Concert had become the agency of the conservative powers (as in 1860) rather than a means to promote progress. Salisbury and Balfour were more interested in drawing a veil over any British retreat once they began to accept that imperial interests would have to be defended from Egypt rather than at the Straits.[15] Vienna, meanwhile, unsurprisingly decided that Britain was a broken reed, and turned to see what arrangement could be reached with Russia.

The Austrians were encouraged in February 1897 by Russian conduct at the time of a Cretan revolt against Turkish rule. This was followed by a Greeko–Turkish war in April. Russia – with no reason to fear Britain at this time but still anxious to avoid a major crisis in the Ottoman Empire – warned the Serbs and Bulgarians not to become involved. Early Turkish military success against the Greeks suggested that talk of the empire's dissolution had perhaps been premature. This made recourse to the Concert more appealing, and in 1898 it was finally agreed that Crete should enjoy autonomy under Prince George of Greece as high commissioner. Meanwhile Goluchowski was so impressed by Russia's restraint that for the time being she (not Britain) seemed the most reliable partner with which to defend the status quo in the Balkans. The time had come to return to the policies of the early 1880s.[16]

An Austro–Russian understanding was reached as early as April–May 1897. Although there was no written protocol, the two powers basically agreed to uphold the status quo in the Near East for as long as possible; not to interfere in the development of the Balkan states; to cooperate so that other powers would be unable to play Russia and Austria off against each other; to renounce con-quests for themselves if a threat to the status quo developed; and jointly to devise a future configuration of the Balkans which they might hope to impose on other powers.[17]

Unfortunately this entente, as Roy Bridge argues, was always a 'fragile' affair, and one which was unlikely to survive any significant challenge to the status quo. In the long run Russia's interest in the future of the Straits and the eastern Balkans, coupled with the pressures from Russian Slavophiles, was bound to threaten Austria–Hungary whatever the current disposition in St Petersburg. Goluchowski treated the arrangement as a second-best solution from the start. Its durability was heavily dependent upon Russian distrac-tions elsewhere. Fortunately for the Austrians these were to be pro-vided over the next ten years by the activities of the Japanese in the Far East and the British in India and the Persian Gulf.

## The Powers at the Turn of the Century

Holstein noted that Japan's surprise victory in 1895 caused the idea of China's disintegration to spread like an 'epidemic throughout Europe'. From 1895–6 even Austria–Hungary tried to maintain a small naval presence in Far Eastern waters. In January 1896 *weltpolitik* became official policy in Germany, though not all took it up with quite so much gusto as Wilhelm II. Among the professional German diplomats, Holstein in Berlin and Hatzfeldt, the long-serving ambas-sador in Britain, favoured patience and discretion. Hatzfeldt in 1901, for instance, argued that time was on the side of Germany with her powerful economy and many other assets. If only her people would but sit still, 'the time would soon come when we can all have oysters and champagne for dinner'. He also disagreed with those of his countrymen who feared that Britain wished to stir up trouble in Europe and the Near East. The ever suspicious Holstein, however, was more sceptical of Britain's commitment to the status quo, and protested at one point that 'every [British] proposal ... is a trap designed to set us at odds with Russia'.[18] Yet his tendency to distrust all the leading powers only reinforced his aversion to risk-taking at this time.

Where he had formerly criticised Bismarck for his caution, Holstein now complained that the great man had found it a 'psychological necessity ... to make his power felt by tormenting, harrying, and ill-treating people'. Bismarck had had a pessimistic view of life, scorning both truth and mankind.[19] It was not until 1906 that Holstein was shaken from his belief that Germany would fare best by standing apart from the intense competition of the other powers. Earlier he had welcomed the Anglo–French crisis on the Nile of 1898, and similarly the Anglo–Japanese alliance of 1902 which underlined Britain's rivalry with Russia. He had his own fears of Russia, not least because of his anxiety over the long-term future of Austria. Berlin should be neither too close to nor distant from St Petersburg. This might be done through the cultivation of a 'community of interests'.[20]

On the subject of Britain, he oscillated between hopes of friendship and fear of her power and intentions. Above all it was vital that she should not displace Germany at the centre of the balance of power. In retirement he continued to reflect (very much in Bismarckian terms) on the ways in which the interests and resources of all the powers might interact to maintain the equilibrium. He even welcomed British naval superiority since this could act as a useful curb on the unpredictable Wilhelm and the obsessions of Tirpitz. Bülow himself had commented in 1898 on German interest in Britain's survival as a power while Admiral Müller, despite his insistence that 'world history is now dominated by the economic struggle', did not rule out the possibility that Britain and Germany would finally learn to coexist as satiated world empires.[21]

Several Anglo–German exchanges actually took place between 1898 and 1901 on the subject of an understanding or alliance, prompted in particular on the British side by fears of Russia in Asia. Salisbury, however, remained sceptical. He thought the fears exaggerated, and disliked the thought of paying 'blackmail' to the Germans for their friendship. Furthermore, as the talks proceeded, they highlighted the lack of scope for bargaining and cooperation rather than the existence of profound differences in Anglo–German relations. Unlike Britain's subsequent (and finally successful) talks with France and Russia, the imperial rivalry between Britain and Germany was not serious enough in itself to give London and Berlin compelling reasons to compromise.

It is true that Holstein noted that if the governments did decide to come to an understanding, the actual process of negotiation would have been hampered by commercial competition and mutual popular hostility. As it happened, the talks foundered on the fact that at bottom Germany had no desire to assist Britain in her extra-European disputes with France and Russia, whereas the British were determined to make no advance commitments on the defence of Germany in Europe. Berlin could also be forgiven for recalling that Britain had gained much more than Prussia from the Seven Years War, and for hoping that the opposite might be the case this time round. The Germans could also expect to have more bargaining power once their new navy was completed. On the British side, Salisbury delicately summed up the situation to Bülow as he saw it in 1898. There was, he thought, no current need for an alliance: meanwhile 'we will try to avoid everything which could hinder' its possible conclusion at a later date.

As matters then stood Holstein seemed to have good reason for his belief that Britain would in due course need German friendship, and would have to pay dearly for it.[22] British policy on the future of Egypt, the Sudan, the Nile valley, the Boers and South Africa excited growing hostility throughout Europe. Salisbury was finding it increasingly difficult to curb assertive colleagues such as Joseph Chamberlain. He would have liked, for instance, to have treated France more generously in West Africa. It is true that Salisbury himself could speculate uneasily concerning the probable vulnerability of the British Empire in the next century, but at that particular time he failed to see anything in the then state of international affairs to warrant radical changes of policy, and certainly not a departure from the 'free hand'. Relations between all the powers remained relatively fluid, while the Royal Navy was stronger than for many years.

He was thus unmoved by those colleagues during the Boer War who warned that a continental coalition might be formed against Britain. The French were indeed drawing up plans for an invasion of Britain – an exercise which spanned the years between 1897 and 1908.[23] Yet Salisbury was vindicated by the view from Berlin where the Germans calculated that successful pressure on Britain by a European combination was more likely to benefit France and Russia than themselves between 1899 and 1902.

## From the Hague Peace Conference to the Anglo–French Entente

Salisbury had struck an almost Gladstonian note in his Guildhall speech of 1897 when he commented upon the dangers arising from the international rivalries of the time, and especially from the continuing growth of armaments. These could have disastrous consequences for Christian civilisation (more prosaically he also privately feared for the future of the British aristocracy if its families were exposed to crippling war taxes). The only hope was for the powers to work together. Ultimately they might create an 'international constitution' and initiate a 'long spell' of peace and prosperity. Salisbury was perhaps doing no more than think aloud or publicise his desire to see a relaxation in current international tensions. But he spoke at a time when others were more than usually interested – or at least were eager to be seen to be interested – in progress in this direction.

Professor Westlake, holder of the Cambridge chair of international law founded in 1854 when some hoped that a start might be made to the creation of an international tribunal, was among those to take seriously suggestions of this kind. In 1894 he had been struck both by the advance of international law and by the influence of those who argued that the nation must be permitted to triumph at any cost. He later speculated in his book (*International Law*, 1904) that what began to take shape in an uncertain political form and environment might perhaps develop into a 'settled custom, ... We are in the presence of the first stages of a process which in the course of ages may lead to organised government among states'. Meanwhile T. J. Lawrence, another jurist, was pinning his hopes on the primacy of the European powers, 'their regulative authority', and the tacit acceptance of their authority and right to 'speak for the whole body of European states'.[24]

Interest in the prevention and regulation of war was growing in other quarters. The Interparliamentary Union had been formed in Paris in 1889 and was holding yearly congresses for parliamentarians who wished to discuss such matters. Individual European parliaments debated peace resolutions. Although such activity did little to shake the prevailing belief that war was an unavoidable, legitimate, moral and creative force, even believers in *realpolitik* could be troubled by the sheer cost of peacetime arms budgets, quite apart from the horrendous implications of an actual conflict. By the later 1890s the Russian minister of war (as well as Witte with his financial responsibilities) was sufficiently disturbed by defence costs to favour a diplomatic initiative of some kind to ease the strain. The tsar also met and was impressed by the Polish banker, Jan Bloch, the author of a six volume study (*The Future of War*) in which he argued that a great-power conflict might well prove suicidal to all concerned. The arms race alone might so overburden economies as to cause social revolution. Such was the background to the Russian 'peace manifesto' of 24 August 1898.

The idea was well received by many in Britain and the United States, but faith in war as an instrument of policy as well as scepticism over the feasibility of any worthwhile steps remained stronger.[25] No government, however, (not even that in Berlin) wished to be held responsible for wrecking the proposal. The conference opened in May 1899 and interestingly included both the United States and Japan – the Japanese having recently earned their place with a conclusive victory over China. The range of discussion was limited, the Russians in particular being fearful of saying too much in case they drew attention to their many weaknesses. German participation was far from enthusiastic, with one of their delegation speaking privately of the difficulty of finding a decent cloak to 'cover up the inevitable fiasco'. Holstein thought disinterested arbitration was an illusion, except when the most powerful were dealing with weak states. The state had no higher purpose than its own interest – and this was not necessarily promoted by peace. Treitschke wrote of the supremacy of the state with the army as its visible embodiment.[26] Other Germans feared that arbitration would nullify the advantage they drew from their ability to mobilise faster than any other power.

German agreement to the creation of the Permanent Court of Arbitration was given to please the tsar. Arbitration in any case could not be made compulsory – though Salisbury thought it might prove useful in minor matters. An American at the conference grimly concluded that no such body had ever assembled with so much 'hopeless skepticism as to any good result'. In the light of the horrors of war in the following century this verdict might seem a little too cynical, but it is true that in the end many were relieved that so little had been accomplished.[27]

Germany's tough stance at The Hague had not been particularly disturbing to the British. Balfour provided an interesting sketch of Britain's strategic needs in December 1901 shortly before he succeeded Salisbury as prime minister. He started from the premise of a possible war with Russia and France in the Far East. This could soon spread to the Channel and the Mediterranean. It was therefore, he argued:

> ... a matter of supreme moment to us that Italy should not be crushed, that Austria should not be dismembered, and, as I think, that Germany should not be squeezed to death between the hammer of Russia and the anvil of France.[28]

For their part the British army chiefs (in 1902) at first welcomed the projected German Berlin–Baghdad Railway as a useful obstacle to Russia's Near Eastern ambitions and therefore a likely cause of dissension between the latter and Germany. The Admiralty's concern over French and Russian naval strength explains its enthusiasm for an Anglo–Japanese alliance in 1901–2. Admittedly it was beginning to take some note of the German navy, with the first lord of the Admiralty himself observing on 10 October 1902 that it must be 'designed for a possible conflict with Britain'. He argued that one could not 'safely ignore the malignant hatred of the German people or the manifest design of the Germany Navy', yet he still had the impression that the German government itself was not 'really unfriendly'. It was, however, thought prudent to take out a little insurance with a small addition to the naval estimates over and above the Two Power Standard.

In contrast Tirpitz was much tortured at this time by fears of a sudden onslaught by the British to try to destroy the new German navy in its infancy. This seemed eminently logical to him given the ultimate purpose of the fleet. Along with the kaiser, he regarded Germany as an incomplete power (especially on the global stage) without a powerful navy. The programmes from 1898, while unequivocally directed against Britain, were also based on the assumption that the Russian and French navies would remain the prime concern of the British Admiralty. Tirpitz estimated that if Germany could achieve a ratio of 2:3 against the Royal Navy, this would enable the new fleet to exploit Britain's vulnerability after the expected war with her long-standing enemies. 'Then, perhaps, even a partnership based on equality would be possible, with the Reich's new ally tolerating or even actively supporting German colonial aspirations.'[29] The United States was already (in the early 1900s) beginning to win concessions in the Americas from Britain. Indeed the Admiralty secretly admitted that the United States could grab the trident from the Royal Navy if it so chose. It was, however, to take a very different view of German naval building when this accelerated over the next few years.

Not all Germans agreed with the Tirpitz programme. General Waldersee from the outset queried whether his country's fate in a future war would be settled by any battles fought at sea. In Bismarckian tones he asked, 'But what will the [German] navy do if the Army should be defeated, be it in the East or in the West?'[30] This argument gained more weight once rivalries lessened between Britain, France and Russia (after 1903–7), and when it became evident that the German navy would be too small to wring the ex-pected concessions from Britain. At the turn of the century, however, there was nothing to suggest that a diplomatic revolution on this scale could take place. Russia and France had duly played their assigned parts by trying to exploit Britain's embarrassments during the Boer War. A French loan was helping to construct the Orenburg–Tashkent railway to increase the Russian threat to India. Joint military talks envisaged the dispatch of 100 000 French troops to the Channel coast in the event of an Anglo–Russian crisis, while the French continued with their invasion plans. The men in Berlin might not have known all the details, but there was enough to suggest that everything was steadily working in their favour.

At this time the French did not wholly trust Russia – there were too many contacts between St Petersburg and Berlin for comfort – while Russia had given France no support during the Fashoda crisis in 1898. The looseness of the relations between the powers is further highlighted by the comparative lack of Austro–German contacts at this time. The Austrians were dismayed by German economic activi-ties in the Balkans, whereas their entente with Russia was being used by both partners to uphold the political status quo for fear of some-thing worse. This entente, however, depended heavily on the belief of key groups in St Petersburg that Russia was in no fit state to handle a major European crisis given the numerous other calls on limited resources. Contingency plans to seize the Straits were essentially precautionary.[31]

The next major catalyst was the growing political instability in Morocco and the consequent belief among the French that this would soon require (or enable) them to intervene in territory which bordered on their great colony in Algeria. The French government, while determined to secure the dominant position, accepted that some astute diplomacy would be needed to prepare the way. Given the choice of a deal with Germany or Britain, it was soon decided that the British would prove less demanding. Delcassé, the foreign minister, finally agreed that an already touted exchange deal with Britain (in effect, a free hand for the latter in Egypt in return for French dominance in Morocco) offered the best way forward. The entente which resulted in April 1904 was essentially a settlement of a number of imperial disputes. It is true that some of the policymakers in London also welcomed it as a possible stepping stone to the bigger prize of a compromise with Russia for the greater security of India. In addition a few agreed with Joseph Chamberlain that the entente would strengthen Britain against Germany. Finally, fear of a Russo–Japanese war gave Paris and London good reason to hasten the completion of the treaty as neither wished to be dragged into a conflict by its ally.

Doubtless the Germans would – in due time – have disputed French claims in Morocco, and similarly would have looked for ways to disrupt the British entente. But Russia's major setbacks in the war with Japan encouraged them as early as 1905 to pursue both objectives more blatantly than they might otherwise have done. The war also tempted the kaiser to try to establish closer bonds with St Petersburg. He persuaded the tsar (dismayed by unrest at home and the lack of French support against Japan) to sign a draft agreement at Björkö on 11 July under which each power was to aid the other if attacked by a third European power. Russian ministers, once aware of the agreement, insisted that nothing should be done to strengthen Germany. Russia must retain her links with France if there was to be any sort of balance. Nicholas pleaded for a compromise, but Björkö was buried when the French early in 1906 insisted that Russia – dependent on French loans – back them against Germany in the conference called to discuss the Moroccan question.[32]

In the interval Germany had left no one in any doubt of her readiness to exploit her current military ascendancy in Europe. The civilian leaders were tempted to pressurise Paris given the assurances from Schlieffen that the German army was more than equal to war. Indeed so menacing was their tone in the early summer of 1905 that Delcassé's colleagues speedily agreed to his sacrifice. Berlin, however, took this as a signal of weakness, and continued to exert pressure. It was then that London became seriously alarmed: for the first time the defence departments embarked on serious studies of the implications of war with Germany. Suddenly it no longer seemed almost inconceivable that a British army would have to fight on the continent. Nevertheless the foreign secretary, while firmly behind France, still hoped to avoid a permanent rift with Germany.

It was only with the appointment of Sir Edward Grey to the Foreign Office (under a new Liberal government) at the end of the year that military talks were begun with the French, and when Grey (unlike his predecessor) strongly sided with the increasingly influential anti-German elements among his own professional advisers. He was profoundly disturbed by the lack of balance in Europe as a result of Japan's victory and the revolution in Russia. It was difficult to see how Germany could be constrained on the continent until Russia had recovered as a military power. Meanwhile there was the little matter of the conference on which Berlin had insisted to discuss the Moroccan question.

This duly met at Algeciras early in 1906. The American president, Theodore Roosevelt, rightly suspected that more than the future of Morocco was at stake. The conference became a test of nerves and loyalties by the leading powers, all of which had serious implications for the European balance of power. To their dismay the Germans found themselves almost isolated on certain key issues – even Austria–Hungary was a reluctant rather than a 'brilliant second'. Paris was strongly backed by Britain, and was well placed to exploit Russia's need of French loans. The United States also opposed Germany on major points.

Just how seriously the outcome was viewed in Berlin can be gathered from some of the contemporary correspondence. Talk of the inevitability of war began to resurface. Germany, it was said, was encircled by hostile powers, and was in danger of being excluded from future shares of the 'wide open spaces' in the world. She had, it seemed, lost her position as the power best able to benefit from the rivalries of the other leading states. The simple movement of the right hand towards the hilt of Germany's sheathed sword might no longer suffice. The policy of the 'free hand', too, had seemingly out-lived its usefulness.

Yet Germany herself was not solely to blame for her changed prospects. She had not been the prime cause of the formation of the Anglo–French entente of 1904 – however much she subsequently strengthened it by her conduct in 1905–6. Similarly her actions in 1905–6 were to be only a part cause of another entente, that between Britain and Russia. This owed more to Russia's defeat at the hands of Japan in 1904–5 and the resulting revolution in Russia. The men in St Petersburg, very much against their own inclinations, were forced to come to terms with Britain.[33] Similarly the initial breakdown of the Austro–Russian entente in the Near East in 1908 was to owe nothing to Germany, the latter's relations with Russia not being seriously injured until Berlin's heavy-handed intervention in 1909 to persuade the Russians that the issue had to be settled in favour of Austria. Scholars of whatever school who concentrate on Germany's role in the origins of the First World War have often and too readily assumed that Germany was shaping events as much before 1909 as she was thereafter.

# 7
## FROM THE ANGLO–RUSSIAN ENTENTE TO THE BALKAN WARS

'… if we once allow Germany to defeat France, our expeditionary force would be valueless and the duration of our naval predominance could be measured in years.' (British General Staff memorandum, 13 August 1911)

### The Bosnian Crisis and the Growing German Problem

It might have seemed a source of hope and encouragement when delegates assembled for the second Hague Peace Conference in 1907 that the European powers should have avoided war among themselves for no less than 36 years. The main participants, however, were interested at best in marginal additions to such constraints on war as already existed. Even the visiting Americans were anxious to give no impression of weakness. The British feared German plots to reverse their ententes with France and Russia, while the Austrians believed that Britain was bent on causing Germany the maximum of embarrassment. The Germans objected to anything that threatened their naval or military freedom of action. As for the moves which led to the Declaration of London (1909) on neutral rights and contraband, key British policy-makers saw the 'agreements … as mere words to be interpreted in the light of circumstances if Britain found herself a belligerent'.[1] This was confirmed in the first year of the war when such restraint as accompanied the British blockade was

142

inspired by the need to avoid giving offence to the Americans. The Germans were taken aback by the speed with which the British broke the Hague Convention on private property.

August 1907 saw the completion of the Anglo–Russian entente. This would have been welcomed by the British (given their worries over the North-West Frontier of India) irrespective of the state of their relations with Germany. But they were now also seriously alarmed by the current power imbalance in Europe, something which could be redressed only by a speedy Russian military recovery. The view from St Petersburg was very different. As a result of defeat by Japan and revolution at home, Izvolsky (the new foreign minister) stated bluntly that Russia had to be on good terms with 'everybody'. She had to adjust her foreign policy to accord with 'the real powers of the country', and seek peace from 'Kamchatka to Gibraltar' over the next ten years. Stolypin (the prime minister) doubled the peace period to '20 years'. From Kokovtsov as minister of finance came reminders, if reminders were necessary, of the emptiness of the treasury. Yet it was only with regret and from dire necessity that the tsar and some other advisers acceded to the entente. Britain, not Germany and Austria, was the main rival.[2] It was only liberal groups, with their dislike of Germany as the embodiment of autocracy, who took a more positive view of Britain. The same was true of some businessmen who feared German competition, and naturally of those who favoured a more active role in the Balkans.

The fact that a crisis occurred with Austria and Germany as early as 1908–9 was due on the Russian side primarily to the personal ambition and impatience of Izvolsky when, contrary to his earlier calls for restraint, he attempted to pull off an old-fashioned diplomatic coup. Ironically he was encouraged to do so because Russia seemed to be on relatively good terms with *all* the great powers in 1907. In such circumstances Stolypin's strict warning to attempt nothing in foreign affairs that might endanger recovery at home did not apply. It seemed possible that the British might prove flexible over the question of the Straits. But above all he hoped to use the entente with Austria to strike a deal with her foreign minister, Aehrenthal, a man who was equally anxious to pull off a Balkan coup.

Aehrenthal wished to prove that Austria could still assert herself as an independent power. As matters stood, he was assured of German support only if the future of the Habsburg Empire itself was under threat. Its collapse, in the view of the German chancellor (Bülow), would have internal as well international implications for Germany. Following in the footsteps of Bismarck, he claimed that the addition of some 15 million (Austro–German) Catholics to Germany would overwhelm the Protestant majority. The ratio between the faiths, he claimed, would resemble 'that which ... led to the Thirty Years War' in the seventeenth century. German security at home and abroad depended upon the avoidance of such 'a horrible position'.[3] On the other hand German interests in south-eastern Europe were often pursued at the expense of her ally. As early as the 1880s German financiers had developed an interest in railways, oil and harbours in Romania. The origins of the Berlin–Baghdad Railway project can be dated back to 1889, while Wilhelm II had ostentatiously posed as the friend and protector of the Turks since 1898. By 1907 Austria had good reason to look askance at her ally's attitudes and behaviour, and to seek ways to remind others that she was still a great power in the Near East.

The Austro–Russian entente of 1897 had been relatively successful in dealing with the awkward problems posed by Macedonian unrest against the Turks between 1902 and 1906. Yet success had rested on the conviction in each government that it was more likely to suffer than benefit from a serious crisis in the Ottoman Empire at that time. As it was some strains had developed and Russia (weakened by the events of 1904–6) looked to and received some assistance from Britain to limit Austrian influence in Macedonia. Aehrenthal, sensing that the days of the entente with Russia might be numbered and worried by worsening relations with Serbia, favoured early action to strengthen the Habsburg Empire by the annexation of Bosnia and Herzegovina (these had been administered by Austria since 1878). In so doing, he failed to take sufficient note of the recent popular outcry in Russia over plans for an Austrian railway in the Sanjak of Novibazar – a sensitive area which lay between Serbia and Montenegro. Izvolsky similarly (and despite his awareness of the need to work with moderate liberals in the Duma) believed that he could carry off a deal with Austria provided it was accompanied by a revision to Russia's advantage of the treaties governing the use of the Straits.

Superficially it seemed as if the Russian and Austrian ministers had worked out a mutually advantageous modus operandi at Buchlau in September 1908, though each man was not entirely honest with the other. In practice it was the Austrian who struck first with the sudden annexation of Bosnia. This inevitably provoked an outcry in Russia. Izvolsky's reputation was irreparably damaged while Stolypin was so shaken by the mood in the Duma that he declared that Russia could not accept the annexation of any Slav territory by Austria.[4] The two foreign ministers had doubtless done no more than hasten the demise of the 1897 entente – already coming under threat from the intensification of nationalist feeling in Russia and the Balkans. As for Izvolsky, he was further discredited once it became clear that there could be no question of a revision of the Straits treaties.

In the prolonged epilogue which followed, the Serbs demanded compensation for Austria's gains, and did so with the full backing of Russian Slavophiles. Russian ministers, however, knew that the means were lacking to handle a major crisis. In contrast the Austrians, sure in this instance of German backing, refused to yield an inch to the Serbs. The British, anxious to impress the Russians with the utility of the entente, vainly tried to save a little face for Serbia and Russia. The crunch came in March 1909 when the Russians, looking to Berlin for help to devise a golden bridge over which they might gracefully retreat, were sent a blunt and imperious demand (a 'veiled ultimatum') to abandon the Serbs.

Although more finesse might not have earned Berlin much credit, a more discreet intervention would not have aroused such widespread suspicion over German intentions. The 'ultimatum' also weakened those Russian conservatives (such as Witte and Durnovo) who, while not uncritical of Germany, believed that the two empires still had much in common. The Bosnian crisis had thus effectively put an end to a period of more than ten years during which the three eastern powers had managed to rub along without too much difficulty in contrast to the tensions in the years immediately before and after Bismarck's resignation in 1890.

The behaviour of the German leadership in March 1909 (following their conduct over Morocco in 1905–6) shows just how much a combination of ambition – coupled with growing anxiety concerning the future – was beginning to take hold. Even historians who give special weight to the influence of *weltpolitik* in German foreign policy (and hence to the naval race with Britain) in the first 11–12 years of the twentieth century note that worries over German isolation and encirclement had resurfaced before *weltpolitik* was seriously questioned in Berlin. Talk soon followed of a German war with France before Russia was once again a real force. Schlieffen, echoing Waldersee, warned that the outcome of any great conflict would turn on the campaign in France – not on the war at sea. In 1909 General Moltke (the younger) stated that this was probably the most 'propitious' time to fight a continental European war. As matters then stood the Central Powers could blast 'any ring' around them.[5] His civilian colleagues, however, chose to use this strength merely to insult Russia, thereby compounding the error made over Morocco in 1905–6. Germany could not afford to antagonise too many powers at the same time.

The British, by now, were deeply committed to the naval race with Germany. In addition to the huge new construction programme, the Admiralty was planning in the event of war to recall any capital ships stationed in the Mediterranean. It reckoned that Britain needed a 60 per cent battlefleet superiority over Germany. In reality the Royal Navy was still well placed to prevail in the North Sea – given no serious worries elsewhere in the world. Work also continued on a small expeditionary force which could, if it was so decided, be sent to fight Germany on the continent. The hope was that some 150 000 troops might prove just large enough to prevent a speedy defeat of France by Germany. Its size, however, was primarily determined by what the government was prepared to spend and the number of volunteers who could be recruited. It was not determined by detailed strategic calculations.

Preparations to fight in Europe must not be confused with a firm commitment to France. Thus at the time of the outbreak of a second crisis involving Germany and Morocco (Agadir) in the summer of 1911 the Committee of Imperial Defence on 23 August 1911 rather diffidently agreed 'in principle' that the expeditionary force – if it was to be used at all – should be sent to support France or Belgium. Once again great care was taken to remind Paris (in November 1911) that Britain was not bound to fight in the event of war. In contrast the General Staff, in a memorandum of 13 August 1911, had already argued that strategic logic would force Britain to intervene. If Britain held aloof, this would probably entail the annexation of the Low Countries by Germany and the defeat of France. Were this to happen 'the duration of our naval predominance could be measured in years'.[6]

Even so some influential figures continued to criticise the extent to which Germany was being allowed to absorb the attention and resources of the armed services. Similar warnings emanated from the Foreign Office, despite the strength of anti-German feeling in that department. How for instance, the critics asked, could British interests in other parts of the world be adequately protected given the navy's new priorities? Churchill's response was that, following a victory in the North Sea (the 'decisive theatre'), all else could be put straight in due course. Yet while the service chiefs devoted most of their attention to Germany, those entrusted with foreign and imperial affairs continued to see Germany as only one (if for the time being the most pressing and potent) among several major threats. Consequently the alliance with Japan (renewed in 1911) and the ententes with France and Russia were all designed to help reinsure Britain and her empire against avowed partners as well as against the well-publicised rival across the North Sea.

Eyre Crowe, for instance, in his well-known discussion of the German threat (his memorandum of 1 January 1907) had included a warning that Britain's interests would not be served by a weakened Germany since this could lead to a 'Franco–Russian predominance equally, if not more formidable to the British Empire'. In April 1912 Nicolson, the permanent under-secretary in the Foreign Office, was yet more emphatic, writing that 'it would be far more dangerous to have an unfriendly France and Russia than an unfriendly Germany'. The old fears of Russia 'in the Mid-East and on our Indian frontier' easily resurfaced. Balfour around the same time – while sharing many of the current fears of Germany – thought it amazing that one could talk of conflict as 'inevitable' when there was 'no quarrel ... We live in strange times.' He personally doubted in any case if Berlin would risk war until Tirpitz's fleet was much stronger.[7]

In short it would not be too much of a simplification to claim that as long as Britain was able to maintain her naval supremacy in the North Sea, and as long as her new rival had not achieved a position of hegemony in Central and Western Europe, neither the home islands nor the empire stood in serious peril from Germany. There were, however, attendant fears that Japan might feel free to exploit British distractions in Europe to advance her interests in China. More serious still would be a Russia which was able and chose to resume her forward policies from the Near East to Afghanistan. Indeed what British policy-makers most desired was as total an acceptance as possible by all the powers of the current balance and status quo – both in Europe and beyond. A major war would mean vast expenses, uncertainty and change. If Bismarck has been criticised for working for a deadlock in Europe in the 1880s, the British were following much the same course before 1914.

In many ways Germany was unintentionally assisting Britain when she compelled France and Russia to devote so much of their energy and attention to Europe. Unfortunately, as we shall see, Germany was ultimately prepared to risk war on the continent because the existing balance was no longer acceptable to her. Indeed it has been argued that British naval and imperial policies (by their very success) made an important contribution to the outbreak of the First World War because they forced Germany from 1912 to back away from *weltpolitik* and to concentrate on expansion in Europe with such fatal results in 1914. A growing number of people undoubtedly came 'to realise that *Weltpolitik à la* Tirpitz was an impossibility'.[8] Yet British success only assisted other forces which were already at work in Berlin and demanding a return to a German foreign policy based primarily on the army. As has already been argued, a land-based strategy had been put in the shadows by special circumstances – notably the temporary rapprochement between the three eastern powers from the mid-1890s to 1908–9. *Weltpolitik* could flourish only as long as Germany felt secure in Europe and the Near East. This was ceasing to be the case from 1909.

Indeed some historians have gone so far as to argue that there was often more bravado than substance to *weltpolitik* – even at its height. Unlike the systematic (if still inadequate) naval programme, *weltpolitik* itself was not consistently the centre of attention. It owed more to opportunism and improvisation than careful planning. At times it could be driven primarily by domestic politics rather than clearly defined aims abroad. In any case Germany's formidable economic growth continued with little help from *weltpolitik*, one striking feature of her economy being the scale of investment at home, and the consequential shortage of capital for investment overseas compared with the huge funds at the disposal of the British and French. Finally it should be noted that some of the most important rivalries involving German businessmen and financiers occurred among themselves rather than with foreigners.[9]

This said, it must be conceded that long-term speculation concerning the future distribution of power across the world was one of the most significant causes of Anglo–German tensions. Despite the reappraisal of German priorities in 1911–12, many politicians, navalists, academics, and businessmen contended that their country could not fulfil her destiny unless she built a comprehensive world presence which would include extensive gains at the expense of Britain. Indeed the German craving for 'a place in the sun', and the British fear of Germany's aims to that end, had as much (and probably more) to do with the world of the future than of the 1900s. The British feared that Germany might ultimately prove too strong for them to retain their imperial pre-eminence. Yet in 1909–12 this was largely academic compared with the question of the balance of power in Europe. Realistic Germans saw that domination in Europe had to come first while their British counterparts saw obvious links between a satisfactory balance of power in Europe and the safety of their empire.

Some interesting examples of how contemporaries viewed the state of international affairs around 1909 can be found in the final volume of the magisterial *Cambridge Modern History* (published in 1910). Stanley Leathers, while agreeing that the years since 1871 had taken the form of an 'armed peace', drew comfort from the belief that the piling up of such vast and expensive military forces had done much to prevent war. With others he was impressed by the potential destructiveness and unpredictability of modern conflicts – these had a salutary calming influence on sensible leaders. He argued that, in contrast to the impulses and traditions which had fired Napoleon III to action, the 'nations appear to desire peace, and if they desire it, they may perhaps retain it'. Although Germany had at times posed problems, her responsible leaders were not seeking warlike expansion as advocated by Treitschke.

Two other contributors were less optimistic. The German historian, Hermann Oncken, emphasised the degree of opposition which his country faced abroad, her geographical position at the heart of Europe making her the most vulnerable of the leading powers. Even if she followed peaceful policies as hitherto, 'she will learn the truth of that moral law of the existence of nations, that life means struggle'. Sir Frederick Pollock commented perceptively that recent events in the Balkans (1908–9) had put an end to the Concert whose history (despite its relative success over Greece and Crete in 1897) had been full of animosities and irregularities. He believed that only a reversal of the current tendency towards exaggerated 'national and racial differences' held out any prospect of a new international 'system'. There were, he warned, strict limits to the amount of tension which any system could bear.[10]

### Russia and the Central Powers in South-eastern Europe

The Russo–German tensions of 1909 did not prevent some subsequent short-term and mutually advantageous arrangements between the two powers. Nevertheless the underlying trends augured ill for the future. The two governments were so ambitious in their objectives – and were in any case subject to such pressure from strong-minded groups at home – that major collisions of interest could hardly be postponed for long. Their relations were decidedly more volatile than in the late 1890s and early 1900s.

Given the huge needs of the Russian civilian economy, it might have seemed sensible for the government to have pursued a more selective policy. The tsar and his ministers, however, were determined to restore Russia to the ranks of the first-rate great powers as soon as possible. This required a major naval construction programme as well as rebuilt and modernised armies. In the short term she needed forces which, with France, would ensure the containment of Germany. Unfortunately the more the Russians tried to attain that objective, the more determined the Germans became to fight to preserve and increase their advantage while time was still on their side. The Russians were also intent upon returning to more than the status quo as it was before 1904. There was the future of the Straits and the Balkans to consider, and it was not long before renewed efforts were made to extend Russian influence in Persia – notwithstanding the entente with Britain. In the meanwhile Russia, as the weaker party, had to suffer further setbacks at the hands of the Central Powers in south-east Europe, humiliations which made the leaders in St Petersburg all the more determined to be better placed to handle future crises. Defeats and humiliations also added to the influence of the Russian nationalist groups – although these never became so formidable as their counterparts in Germany.

In these years the advocates of patience and selectivity in Berlin were undoubtedly losing ground even if with respect to south-east Europe Germany's role remained fairly intermittent and erratic until the First Balkan War in 1912.[11] Most inflammatory at this time was Balkan nationalism, with all the sympathy or alarm which this could excite in Russia and Austria–Hungary respectively. Balkan nationalism made it ever more likely that these two powers would collide at some time or other over the successor states to the Ottoman Empire. At best in the past they had been able to agree to no more than the most modest forms of cooperation, the more ambitious efforts of 1876–7 and 1908 to regulate difficulties breaking down once serious changes took place. Finally there had been sharp reminders since 1875 of the growing difficulty of controlling the peoples of that region as they achieved or made bids for independence.

The Austrians had suffered a sudden and worrying departure of the Serbs from their orbit in 1903. Relations had continued to deteriorate, while Vienna was ever mindful of the Russian ability to appeal to the common brotherhood of Slavs and Orthodox Christians. In contrast the Dual Monarchy suffered from the growing restlessness of Slavs (and others) within the multinational empire. If the empire was not so close to dissolution as some claimed or feared, efforts to lessen discontents from Bohemia to Bosnia still seemed likely to create as many problems as they solved. The dominant Germans and Magyars would not readily make sacrifices to try to appease the other ethnic groups. In no other power were foreign and domestic politics so intimately linked. In the last resort Austrian security rested on Russian preoccupation with other problems (at home or in Asia) and upon German support.

It is true that the policy-makers in St Petersburg were sometimes less purposeful and aggressive than they appeared in Vienna. Indeed had it not been for the strength of nationalist feeling both in south-eastern Europe and Russia, the situation might have lent itself – at least in theory – to a degree of management by responsible diplomats. The prime concern of the tsar (as well as of many of his advisers) was centred on the future of the Straits rather than on the Balkan Slavs. Yet even when relations had been most relaxed with the Central Powers from 1897, the Russian minister of war (Kuropatkin) had felt compelled to remind his colleagues that disputes could still arise in the future. Russia, in the best of times, needed credible military forces on her western and south-western frontiers if her diplomats were to be taken seriously by Austria and Germany. The train of events as early as 1908 confirmed Kuropatkin's worst fears.

Such was the outcry in the Duma (and elsewhere) over the Bosnian humiliation that Stolypin was driven to promise a review of his government's priorities in foreign policy as soon as circumstances allowed. Izvolsky's successor (Sazonov), though sensitive to Russia's current limitations as a power, was a strong believer in her right to the prime role in the Near East.[12] The Russian leadership from the

tsar downwards was understandably swayed by proud imperial, aristocratic and military traditions. Issues of honour and public reputation
mattered as well as material influences. War was an acceptable and
legitimate instrument of policy: it was still thought of in heroic terms.
On the specific subject of the Near East, although Russia's rulers were
not following a 'conscious messianic course of foreign policy inspired
by a holy cause' on behalf of their Orthodox and Slav brethren,
statesmen and diplomats could not fail to be susceptible to the 'cultural context' within which they were operating. Russian state interests came first, but intangible influences could not be excluded.[13]

In such an atmosphere and environment the alternative policies
proposed by Witte seem far from practicable. These were based in
part on the widespread fear that war in the near future might well
result in defeat and another revolution. In addition Witte advocated
a continental coalition whose objectives would include the preservation of the Habsburg Empire as well as the protection of continental
Europe's interests against the predatory British, Americans and
Japanese. He believed that any German differences with Russia were
dwarfed by those with Britain – and with whom Russia had major differences of her own.[14] Nicholas II, if deeply hostile to the Habsburgs,
still attached some importance to his family ties in Germany. Yet any
attempt to return to the relationships of 1895–1907 would surely
have required something akin to an autocratic government in
Russia, and would have been very much to the advantage of the
Central Powers – especially Germany.

The obstacles to lasting peace with Germany and Austria are also
highlighted by the interesting ideas put forward by Prince G. N.
Trubetskoy, one of the most intelligent advocates of the alignment
with France and Britain and of the advance of Russian (and perhaps
Slav) interests in the Near East. Trubetskoy was head of the foreign
ministry's Near Eastern department in 1912–14, and he enjoyed considerable influence with both Nicholas II and Sazonov. He accurately
perceived that some Balkan regimes were as likely to precipitate
crises as the men in Berlin or Vienna. He was as conscious as Witte
of Russia's need for many years of peace, and hoped that ways could
be found (such as through mutually profitable trade) to enable
Russia and Germany to coexist in the long run. He was a great believer in the restraining influence of the balance of power – provided there was a real balance. For this to succeed, however, he
appreciated that reforms were needed in Austria–Hungary to reduce

ethnic divisions and generate a genuine sense of '*Austrian*' national-ism. Such an empire might even act as a restraint on its German ally, whereas its disintegration could only result in a great Russo–German war. Trubetskoy was more perceptive than Witte, but those in Russia and elsewhere who dimly perceived the underlying dangers and who tried to work within the best traditions of nineteenth-century state-craft, were able to exercise only a diminishing influence over events.[15]

In fact there were those who, having at first been influenced by the head rather than the heart, were beginning to favour a stronger line on foreign affairs. In Russia fears of defeat and revolution were receding as the empire regained its strength. Furthermore, both inside and outside the government it was strongly held that Russia must not be reduced to second-class status. The time would surely come when she would have both the need and the strength to make a stand against the Central Powers. Each humiliation fuelled the belief that concessions merely encouraged Germany and Austria–Hungary to be more demanding. Nor were the Russians re-assured by Aehrenthal's assertion that the Habsburg Empire was ter-ritorially satiated after the annexation of Bosnia. A power could do much to extend its influence by means other than conquest.[16]

Thus Sazonov insisted that Russia needed half a million 'bayonets to guard the Balkans' against a German or Austrian assault. Kuropatkin described control of the Straits as 'Russia's main task in the twentieth century'. In the circumstances it is not surprising that Russia's defence spending outstripped that of Germany in most years between 1907 and 1914. Although the sums allocated to the army in 1914 were three times larger than those spent on the navy, the latter's budget had still risen by nearly 300 per cent – six times as much as that of the army – and exceeded that of Germany by 1914. The need to maintain what were virtually three separate fleets ac-counts in part for this exceptional effort. The Baltic fleet was dir-ected against Germany; the Black Sea fleet against the Turks; and there were even hopes that Tsushima might ultimately be avenged in a war with Japan. Thus long-term plans in the Baltic appear to have been based on more than thoughts of defence against Germany. In 1911 the navy minister was calling for a battlefleet of no less than 28 capital ships within 20 years.[17]

Russia faced special problems in the Black Sea. Shipbuilding facili-ties had to be improved. Turkey appeared to be developing into a

more serious threat even if its efforts at modernisation were spas-
modic and relied heavily on purchases from other states. The
Russians were decidedly nervous, and believed that here, as with the
arms programmes as a whole, their forces were unlikely to be equal
to the tasks expected of them before 1917–18. Three or four dread-
noughts were thought essential, though the earliest were not deliv-
ered until 1915. Meanwhile the importance of the Straits to Russian
trade continued to grow. By 1912, despite annual variations, the
traffic from the Black Sea had become of greater importance than
that from the Baltic. Grain exports were of particular value as a
foreign currency earner. Just how much damage might be done to
the economy was highlighted by the Italian and Balkan League wars
with the Turks in 1911–13. Closures for even brief periods injured
exports. Nowhere was the intertwining of strategy, politics, econom-
ics and national feeling more complete than on the future of the
Straits. Indeed war might occur on that question alone.[18]

German involvement in the Near East was also rapidly increasing.
By 1912 the kaiser was talking of the need for a Balkan grouping of
states which would act as 'a seventh great power and be closely con-
nected with Austria and the Triple Alliance'.[19] Germany's interests in
the Turkish Empire continued to grow. Her line of advance was
cutting directly across that of Russia. Thus any Russo–German
Middle Eastern agreement in August 1911 could be at best a modus
vivendi. It even suited the British that Germany should help to serve
as an obstacle to Russia in that region.

### Crises in the Balkans, 1912–13

This awesome potential for conflict must not be allowed to disguise
the fact that Russia was still far from certain as to how best to
proceed in the Near East. An offer was made, for instance, in 1911 to
guarantee Turkish integrity if Russian warships were allowed to use
the Straits, and if the Turks agreed to form part of a defensive
Balkan wall against Austria–Hungary. This was unrealistic. A Balkan
League was, however, negotiated by Bulgaria and Serbia (March
1912), and was joined by Greece two months later. Although this was
directed against Turkey, the Russians hoped that no war would start

without their approval. With France they tried to make this less likely by urging the Turks to make reforms in their remaining European territories. The Russians followed this in September by bluntly warning the League against war, while some preliminary thought was given to concerted action with other powers. The League members, however, took matters into their own hands and began the First Balkan War in October, an action described by a French diplomat as the first instance in the history of the Eastern Question when the small states had felt able to act in complete independence of the great powers, and 'indeed to carry them along with them'.[20] More than that, the League began to win decisive victories over the Turks.

The tsar and Sazonov, who had been tentatively proceeding in full knowledge of Russia's unpreparedness for a major crisis, soon discovered that they had unintentionally helped to bring about the destruction of most of what remained of Turkey in Europe.[21] Indeed the Russians at one point feared that Bulgaria might jeopardise their own preference that – for the time being – the Turks should continue to control the Straits and Constantinople. The Austrians had even more reason to be dismayed by the great expansion of Serbia. They could not, however, be certain of German support, and were in no condition to act on their own. Vienna thus contented itself with limited military precautions (including the reappointment of the fire-eating General Conrad von Hötzendorff) to serve as warning signals to Belgrade. Above all the Austrians were hoping that the Concert of Europe – or some other form of great-power diplomatic cooperation – might come to their aid once the members of the Balkan League fell out among themselves over the spoils of victory. Perhaps, too, a new Albanian state might limit Serbia's gains.

Meanwhile the First Balkan War had generated sufficient tension for the Russian war minister early in November 1912 to consider partial mobilisation. Although this was promptly vetoed by other ministers, Sazonov and Kokovtsev had to send out further reminders that the military force and public support were lacking for Russia to risk a general war.[22] There was alarm, too, in Berlin, with Vienna being assured on 2 December that German support would be forthcoming in the event of a Russian attack. The military in both capitals favoured war against Serbia even though it was acknowledged that this might lead to a wider, even a general European conflict. Wilhelm II talked theatrically of a 'life and death' struggle – originating with the Slavs, but in which Russia would have the support of France and Britain.

At the so-called 'War Council' in Berlin of 8 December 1912 the kaiser called for a strong Austrian stand against Serbia for her own internal security. Moltke argued that a wider war was inevitable: it was now a case of 'the sooner the better'. When Tirpitz asked for an 18-month delay to strengthen the navy, the general retorted that the navy would still not be ready by 1914 whereas the army would be relatively weaker. It seems, however, that Moltke did not press his case any further. The council also took note of the unpreparedness of the German public for a war originating over an Austro–Serb dispute. The result of the council, according to one participant, was 'pretty much nil'.

The meeting was an odd affair, especially given the absence of the chancellor. Bethmann Hollweg himself was still claiming that time was on Germany's side militarily and diplomatically. He thought that German influence might be extended by non-military means into parts of south-eastern Europe. But he too gave a public promise on 2 December 1912 that Germany would support Austria–Hungary against a third party which threatened her existence. London now began to share in the alarm. Britain, it was stated, could not be indifferent to a threat to France. Bethmann Hollweg, however, clung to the hope that German naval strength might soon make Britain more amenable. At home he was looking to improve the position of the government in the Reichstag, and to win approval for a major increase to the army. The kaiser, mercurial as ever, was soon talking of new Balkan alliances (perhaps including Turkey). These would make Austria the preponderant power in the Balkans, and would break up 'the dreadful wave of Pan-Slavism'.[23]

The conclusion of an armistice between the League and the Turks in December 1912 encouraged the powers to see what could be achieved by diplomacy – notably by a conference of ambassadors in London. Briefly at the start of 1913 the powers seemed as interested in the utility of the Concert as at any time since 1897, even if their preliminary contacts suggested more eagerness to demonstrate loyalty to friends and allies than the finding of solutions to the problems of the Near East. Thus the French assured the Russians of their resolve to honour their treaty obligations against Germany. On the other hand the Austrian foreign minister, Berchtold, continued to look to the Concert to assist Habsburg interests. Aehrenthal's earlier assertiveness had had mixed results, and there were the usual worries over the state of Austria's armed forces and the reliance to be placed on the Germans. In Berlin they were still trying to work out a Balkan strategy and to woo Britain away from the ententes.

In London the Foreign Office gradually gained sufficient confidence (albeit strictly within the limits imposed by the ententes) to take up the role of a conciliator. Britain, after all, had no wish to be drawn into a general European war precipitated by obscure disputes in a region in which she no longer had a major direct interest. The British ambassador in Berlin in November 1912 spoke for many as he considered the damaging implications of a Balkan war whatever course his country chose to follow. 'What friends should we have left? And what figure should we cut?' if Britain stood aside.[24] In practice (although the British took careful account of Russia's claims on behalf of Serbia) some progress proved possible. Most of the ambassadors knew the chairman (Grey) and each other well. Basically, however, the conference was driven by the desire in each major capital to avoid war, while only a strong show of unity was likely to make any impression on the Balkan victors. Even so the outcome was still a great disappointment for Austria, Serbia having doubled her territory. The other powers did not, of course, have the Serbs as neighbours, and Austria was left to act alone to recover Scutari from the Montenegrins and so deny Serbia access to the Adriatic.

Although the Germans took note that south-eastern Europe had been forced higher up the agenda, in the middle of 1913 no consensus existed either in Berlin or between Berlin and Vienna. Wilhelm II opposed Austrian desires to weaken Serbia – this, he said, would drive 'all Slavs into the arms of Russia'. The two governments could only agree that the sooner the Balkan League disintegrated the better. Unfortunately when this duly occurred, the Second Balkan War (July 1913) resulted in a stunning defeat for an isolated Bulgaria, while yet more territory fell to the Serbs by the Treaty of Bucharest (August 1913). Once again Austria felt the limitations of concert diplomacy.

In October 1913 the Austrians did manage to force the Serbs from disputed Albanian territory, and even received some moral support from Berlin. The new state of Albania and the denial of Serbian access to the Adriatic, however, offered little in the way of reassurance to ministers in Vienna. Desperate measures now seemed necessary if the empire was to survive. Austro–Russian relations were at least as bad as in the late 1880s and early 1890s. Vienna, however, could still not act against Serbia without a sure sign of German backing. At least the Triple Alliance benefited from a deterioration in Italy's relations with France, while Austria's naval programme (directed initially against Italy from 1909) began to impress even the British.[25]

# 8

---

# To August 1914
## and the End of an Era

'... in a certain sense it was a preventive war'. (Bethmann Hollweg)

### Preliminary Observations

The last seven months of peace before August 1914 have been among the most intensely studied and hotly debated in the history of Europe. Explanations of the origins of the First World War have ranged from the absurdly simple to others of such complexity as to threaten to drive all but the most assiduous reader to despair. It has been attributed in particular to German ambition and militarism, or more generally to imperialism (variously defined), monopoly capitalism, the arms race, secret diplomacy, unbridled nationalism, the use of foreign policy to ease domestic problems, not to mention sundry combinations of these and other factors. The war has been described both as inevitable and avoidable. Alistair Horne suggests that a 'sort of impassioned triviality' prevailed in 1914, while James Joll argues that the 'rhetoric' of imperialism contributed 'even more than the reality' to the widespread mood in Europe which made war possible, acceptable, and – in some cases – welcome.[*]

[*] See A. Horne in *The Times*, 8 September 1994, and J. Joll, *The Origins of the First World War* (1984), pp. 167–8. See also John Lowe, *The Great Powers, Imperialism and the German Problem* (1994); H. W. Koch, ed., *The Origins of the First World War* (1984); R. J. W. Evans and H. P. von Strandmann, eds., *The Coming of the First World War* (1988); J. W. Langdon, *July 1914: the long debate, 1918–90* (1991); and K. Wilson, *Decisions for War, 1914* (1995), passim.

Outbreaks of war are not to be explained solely by the motives of the contending parties. Account has also to be taken of the particular circumstances prevailing at the time. For instance, if Russia had been stronger or had felt less isolated, a major war might possibly have broken out in the Near East in 1829, 1878, or on more than one occasion between 1887 and 1913. Germany, in contrast, was strong enough to have started a war in 1887–8, but Bismarck and Wilhelm I adamantly opposed those who favoured this course. It is also evident that lengthy periods of serious rivalry and tension could occur without leading to bloodshed – such was the case with respect to Britain and France in the middle decades of the century. Finally the Crimean War stands as a classic warning as to how easily the powers could slide into a conflict they did not really want. In this instance, however, each government not only felt that the issues warranted a strong stand, but they also believed that they were in a position to test the resolve and unity of their opponents – that is, until it proved impossible to draw back.

In the light of the above it is reasonable in the context of July 1914 to consider not only the aggressive mood and actual decision-making in Berlin and Vienna, but also the growing belief in St Petersburg that Russia was sufficiently strong (and assured of French backing) to resist what were seen as the aggressive intentions of the Central Powers. Another capitulation was regarded as too dishonourable and damaging to Russia's international credibility and the government's standing at home to permit – regardless of the issues of substance which were at stake.

As for Germany, it must be reiterated that after 1871 the war option was most seriously discussed when policy-makers feared (or claimed) that their country was in danger of losing its advantageous military position – that is, its ability to defeat or protect itself (and Austria) against Russia and France. Such fears became most acute in the years immediately before 1914. At other times Berlin (when convinced that time was on its side) had been content to seek advantages with the help of no more than the shadow cast by its military power.[1] There are, in consequence, grounds for arguing that a prime (though obviously not the sole) cause of the long peace from 1871 was not so much the existence of a true balance of power from the Pyrenees to the Urals as of an imbalance (economic, diplomatic and military) which normally operated in favour of Germany, and one that was reinforced by such elements as Russia's Asiatic and domestic distractions. Germany, in short, did not opt for war when she was best placed to fight. Furthermore even in 1914 her leaders took careful note of public opinion at home, and were reassured to find that so many Germans should have begun (or had been easily persuaded) to believe in encirclement and a very specific threat from Russia.

This chapter will concentrate upon the key policy-makers in Europe in the last months of peace as they tried to peer into the future and to review their apparent options in the light of the most pressing of a host of external and domestic pressures and considerations. Nor should one forget the influence of past experiences (and how these were recalled and interpreted) together with the general mood and outlook of the time. Relevant too was the extent to which coherent decision-making was or was not possible given the character of the governmental systems and the societies within which this took place.

Above all it is evident that (setting aside German angst and ambition) the most serious threat to peace in Europe lay in the Balkans and Near East where nationalist turbulence ensured that the three eastern powers could not re-establish one or other of the varied forms of coexistence which had so often tempered their relations since 1815. These same agreements had done much to preserve the peace of Europe as a whole. It was particularly ominous that Germany was by now developing so many direct interests of her own in south-eastern Europe, and just at a time when Russia was less distracted by domestic or Asiatic preoccupations. It is again pertinent to ask if Germany's leaders (for all their great ambitions) would have been so fatalistic and aggressive in 1914 had it not been for Russia's lengthening shadow from the Baltic to the Balkans.

Indeed Russia's revival was arousing the concern by 1914 of a few key figures even in London – despite the existence of an entente. The British wanted a true balance in Europe (one that would maintain the status quo and keep the peace), not a war to defeat Germany. Fear of Russia and the more nebulous 'Slav' threat was also infecting German Social Democrats and those businessmen who, without necessarily believing that war was necessary to fulfil their commercial strategies, feared that it might be essential for German security. Bethmann Hollweg was much influenced by the belief in the summer of 1914 that the nation would (or could be made to) rally behind its leaders as long as Russia was seen to be the aggressor. In Russia the leadership was becoming less fearful of war as a powder trail to revolution, and more apprehensive of a popular nationalist backlash if the government failed to make a stand in a Balkan crisis. Sazonov told Nicholas II in July 1914 that Russia would not 'forgive' another capitulation.[2] War was coming to be seen as an option and even a necessary risk in St Petersburg as well as in Berlin.

The stakes were also being raised. In Vienna the conviction was growing that the very existence of the empire would be at risk until the Serb threat had been neutralised or eradicated. For St Petersburg the Slav issue was inseparably bound up with Russia's overall interests in the Near East where she felt endangered by Germany as well as Austria–Hungary. In Berlin, among those best able to exert a direct influence over policy, both defensive and aggressive considerations could lead to the same conclusion – namely that Germany could not sit idly by while Russian and Slav power and influence undermined the Habsburg Empire. Hence the repeated claims that 1914 was the last satisfactory time to wage a war whether for maximum or minimalist objectives. In contrast no sensible Russian could regard 1914 as the best time to fight – only that Russia could and must fight if seriously challenged. Thus in all three capitals in the east the earlier deterrents and objections to war had been seriously weakened – and in some cases erased entirely. Even a Bismarck would have been hard put to have thwarted this lemming-like preference for suicide out of fear of death.

Ministers in Paris were also affected by this new atmosphere and environment, even if they did not directly share the sense of insecurity induced in the east by the absence of natural frontiers on the north European plain, and were not tormented by the belief in an inevitable clash between Teutons and Slavs. At its simplest many felt that France could and must stand by Russia if Germany set out to upset the balance of power. The recent adoption of an offensive strategy by the French war department is also highly instructive, based as it was on a renewed confidence in both their own and the Russian armies. Only in London was there less unity and alarm at the top. Many ministers had only a sketchy or selective interest in and grasp of the details and possible implications of continental rivalries and the frightening emotions which were abroad. The British military and diplomats in contrast believed that the national interest demanded unequivocal support for France – and perhaps Russia as well – in the interest both of the homeland and the empire.

With these general points in mind one can now outline the main events and moments of decision leading up to August 1914. Particular attention will be paid to Russia, Germany and Austria–Hungary, with France and Britain receiving attention in so far as it seems appropriate. Although both Russia and Germany took due account of the attitudes and reactions in Paris and London, the immediate causes of the war (whatever its later pattern, character or implications) lay primarily in the east.

## To Sarajevo

A seemingly trivial incident in the winter of 1913–14 – the extent to which a German general, Liman von Sanders, should be involved in the command of the Turkish army – led to a crisis between Germany and Russia. Britain and France lent some support to Russian protests. St Petersburg correctly inferred that the Germans were seeking to extend still further their influence in the east. Indeed Wilhelm II was talking of the Germanisation of the Turkish army and its development as 'a counterweight to the aggressive designs of Russia'. Although a compromise was devised in January 1914, the outcome was widely viewed in Germany as a defeat. The German press was now discussing the future in terms similar to those used by Moltke and Conrad: namely that the longer the collision with Russia (and France) was delayed, the poorer would be the chances of victory by the Central Powers. Moltke insisted that 'it will basically be a war between Germandom and Slavdom'. It was a prospect, however, which he viewed fatalistically – not with any enthusiasm.

German nervousness over the Near East and Balkans was increased by the shortage of capital available for investment in competition with the British and French. France, for instance, remained dominant in Greece, while insufficient German funds were available to bind Romania securely to the Central Powers. This shortage of capital (as well as political considerations) helps to explain the belated compromise with Britain over the Berlin–Baghdad Railway. Again one might ask if German policy in the Near East in general would have been so aggressive if Berlin had been better able to compete financially with Paris and London and buy political support. As it was, more credence was being given to those who doubted if a *Mitteleuropa* could be created by peaceful means. Relations seemed precarious between even the Turks and Germans.

The tsar himself was by no means in a pessimistic mood at the start of the new year. He was not expecting war. If he did not think that the Habsburg Empire could long outlive the aged Emperor Francis Joseph, he naively thought it might be possible to partition Austria–Hungary between Germany and the Balkan states. Given his hope that Russia and Germany might learn to live together on tolerable terms, he innocently suggested that the extinction of Austria might remove a major source of dissension.[3] Yet the fact that the fate of Austria could be discussed in such casual terms shows how far doubts had developed concerning the solidity of the current status quo. Doubtless the tsar hoped that serious changes could be postponed until the completion of Russia's great defence programmes. He needed to be in a stronger bargaining position, especially with regard to the future of the Straits.

There was even a brief revival of the hopes of pro-German conservatives in Russia that the tsar could be persuaded to drop Sazonov with his pro-British leanings. Germany was still viewed as a natural ally against democracy and British liberalism and imperialism. The tsar, however, was soon fearful of a German plot to secure Constantinople and so bottle up Russia within the Black Sea. This would have to be resisted – if necessary by war. In the same month a French diplomat commented on the 'surprising' deterioration in Russo–German relations in the last two years, notably in the Balkans. Sazonov for his part was hoping to turn the Triple Entente into an alliance.[4] Others in Russia shared his belief that a war with Germany might be inevitable and wanted solid military promises from Britain. The divide between the two camps was becoming too deep to be closed by the most imaginative diplomacy. Reservations as to the use of force were becoming less frequent.

Just how quickly the international environment had been changing can be seen from the claim made by the Austrian foreign minister in December 1911 (in the aftermath of the Agadir crisis) that Anglo–German antagonism was 'the dominant element of the international situation', and one which seemed likely to lead to war. Yet in the course of 1912 most of the leadership in Berlin came to agree that *weltpolitik* and navalism had to yield priority to Germany's needs in continental Europe.[5] Bethmann Hollweg gloomily concluded in

December 1912, 'we have neglected the Army and our "naval policy" has created enemies around us'. Indeed the revival of the Russian army had brought anxious calls for more German troops as early as 1911. There were more reminders that the fate of the German empire in the next war would be determined 'in the first place on land'. Meanwhile the mounting defence costs were reopening bitter age-old disputes over tax policies in the Reichstag. Berghahn concludes:

> [The] tensions inside the Prusso–German monarchy which it had been possible to stave off for a while by means of a policy of manipulation and distraction rose to the surface. It became obvious that the existing order was no longer capable of coping with the problems of a rapidly changing industrial society.[6]

A fairly modest expansion in defence spending in 1912 was followed in 1913 by what has been described as 'the largest Germany had ever seen'. Bethmann was supported by both the Reich Treasury and the Foreign Ministry in refusing additional demands from Tirpitz. In naval matters in general it seemed prudent to 'let sleeping dogs lie'. The army must have priority. Jagow (the foreign minister) believed that the Russian and Slav danger was more serious than was 'generally assumed'. Here was a return to Bismarckian priorities with a vengeance – if perhaps with less rigour and imagination than the iron chancellor at his best. It is also noteworthy that – despite all the print and rhetoric recently devoted to 'world power or decline' and to the importance of new markets – the reversion to Europe should have been so rapid and relatively uncontroversial. Notwithstanding the effort devoted to the battlefleet, and for all its appeal to the middle classes, Germany remained primarily a land animal. Berghahn notes that from 1912 'most people were no longer so certain that this was the direction [the wider world] in which the country should try to expand'. The rather scrappy collection of African and Pacific island colonies even became the object of ridicule in some quarters.[7]

The ultra-nationalists fought back by urging a 'programme of expansion by stages', the *Weltreich* being reached in the second of these. The creation of a solid and substantial Europe heartland was the essential first step. Dominance in Europe should not only free Germany from the nightmare of hostile coalitions but also, in the words of Kurt Riezler, ensure greater 'world political freedom of manoeuvre'. In 1914 there was much reiteration of the fears and expectations expressed in the 1890s over the emergence of huge imperial blocs surrounded by tariff barriers so that Germany, confronted by a 'Greater Russia, World Britannia, and Pan-America', could flourish only by acquiring territory and resources on a similar scale. In February 1913 Gustav Stresemann called for the creation of 'a closed economic area to secure our need for raw materials and our exports'. Wilhelm II and Jagow at one point included in their long-term objectives a German share in partitions of the Far as well as the Near East.

Nevertheless just what *Mitteleuropa* itself might entail was still a subject for debate. Ideas ranged from a customs union to a central European confederation which included south-eastern Europe and might extend to western Europe and/or the Persian Gulf. Some progress might be made primarily by political and economic means – as in the case of the earlier *Zollverein*. But there was also a pessimistic school, a group of influential Germans who believed that it was too late to make the shift from a naval and global to an army-based and continental strategy by peaceful means. They clung to their reactionary aims and adopted tactics which ensured that they slid further into a cul-de-sac. Berghahn sees 'a strong element of inevitability ... [in] the course of pre-1914 German history'. He also adds that the retreat to a continental policy was 'even more alarming' to the Triple Entente than her overseas ventures.[8]

Once again this is only part of the story. One should note, for instance, that Russia's massive defence programme which so disturbed the Germans in 1912 dated from the start of the political and economic recovery after the external and internal disasters of 1904–6; in other words before the German 'ultimatum' of 1909, let alone the shift of policy in 1912. Russia's ambitious defence programme (while entirely understandable in the context of the spirit of the times) must be reckoned a serious contributor to the intensifying tension and rivalry in Europe. The Russians in their turn were dismayed by Austrian arms increases in 1912, while their own conduct during the First Balkan War in 1912 excited profound alarm in Berlin and Vienna. About the same time the French were changing from a defensive to an offensive war plan against Germany, encouraged by the evidence of Russia's revival. Above all France and Russia each remained convinced that its own survival was dependent upon that of the other. Poincaré went further, arguing that unless France gave both her partners strong support, they might lose heart and draw closer to Germany.[9]

In Britain there existed similar fears that too much intimacy with Germany might cause Russia and France to lose faith in the ententes (thereby greatly increasing British vulnerability in the world). An isolated Britain was also likely to find herself directly threatened by a Germany which commanded the continent. There would be no balance of power, and both Britain and her empire would be at risk. Thus even when it seemed possible by 1913–14 that some Anglo–German differences – as over the Berlin–Baghdad railway – were being eased, it was not possible to proceed from detente to entente. Germany's price would always be British neutrality in the event of a continental war. This was seen by the British as the signature of their own death warrant in the long, if not the medium, term. At the same time it was not a happy thought that Britain might be driven by such logic into war with Germany by a crisis in south-eastern Europe in which she had no interest per se.

Thus it was as if all the powers were caught in a tangle of ropes so that the more they tried to free themselves, the tighter they pulled the nooses around their necks. Early in 1914, for instance, the British made an offer of naval staff talks to reassure (not to strengthen) the Russians. This was not intended to be an anti-German move, yet – when news of this reached Berlin – it was seen as strengthening the case for action while there was yet time.

Meanwhile the most ominous developments continued to occur in south-eastern Europe. As recently as 1912 it had seemed as if Austria's historic role in Europe was still widely accepted. S. R. Williamson writes of her continuing role as a buffer state, 'a cushion against the Russians, the Balkan states and the Ottoman Empire'. He repeats the claim of the Czech historian, Palacký (1848) that, given the threat of 'Russian universal monarchy', it would have been necessary to invent Austria if she had not already existed.[10] Nationalist feelings, however, had become much more inflamed by 1914, with many taking a less critical view of Russia and showing more hostility towards the Habsburg Empire. The Balkan wars, economic setbacks and various domestic worries meant that Austrian confidence had been badly shaken. A Russian diplomat in the winter of 1913–14 thought the mood in Vienna much less optimistic than in St Petersburg. Some great financiers claimed that war was preferable to the current uncertainty. James Joll goes as far as to argue that the 'foreign policy of one country at least, Austria–Hungary, was wholly the product of its internal problems'. It is only too evident that many in Vienna feared that the empire could not go on as it was. Rumours of Russian hostility were readily believed, and the activities of certain Russian diplomats such as Hartwig in Belgrade aroused deep suspicion, as did Russia's growing contacts with Romania.[11]

Indeed it seemed to many within the Habsburg Empire that radical change was inescapable if the problems posed by its diverse peoples and cultures were to be resolved. One could not muddle along indefinitely within the present structure. Various ideas were being put forward as to how the empire might be reconstituted to achieve a more equal partnership between its 11 nationalities. Interestingly some young bureaucrats within the Foreign Ministry favoured the creation of a quasi-federation to strengthen the central government in Vienna. More ominously some diplomats believed that reform would become feasible only after a victorious war which might be expected to enhance the authority of ministers at home through the defeat of external enemies. Such belligerence increased sharply after the Sarajevo assassinations of the heir to the Habsburg throne and his wife on 28 June 1914. As the odds on war shortened, so the hopes of the militants rose of change at home. They were assisted by the disillusionment of Berchtold (their chief) with the Concert and the hostile behaviour of Russia. Thus whereas he had called for Austrian restraint in 1912, by May 1913 Berchtold had become resigned to force to settle the fate of Scutari.[12]

John Leslie argues that once war began to seem inevitable, it 'was welcomed, even deliberately by some'. None, it has been said, equalled the delight of the Austrian army chief of staff, Conrad von Hötzendorf. Another and more surprising militant, given the usual response of that department to any hint of extra expense, was the imperial finance minister. By 1914 he was describing war as the only satisfactory solution in the long run to the South Slav question, and especially to irredentism in Bosnia.[13]

Berchtold himself had concluded even before the assassination of the heir to the Habsburg Empire in Sarajevo on 28 June 1914 that Austria and Germany had to resolve their current differences in the Balkans if they were to face up effectively to the Slav danger. Although military contacts between the Austrian and German armies had been increasing since 1909, France remained the chief concern of the German generals whereas Austrian attention was centred on Serbia. War, however, was not included in the important Matscheko memorandum of 24 June drafted at Berchtold's request to suggest a political way forward in company with Germany. It did, however, reflect the conviction that Austria must somehow demonstrate that she was still a great power and capable of firm action.

Austria was under threat from Russia and perhaps a new Balkan League. Italy's behaviour was also by no means that which might reasonably be expected from an ally. Matscheko argued that the Central Powers had to find ways to win over as many south-east European states as possible – notably Bulgaria and Turkey. Berchtold himself was very anxious to isolate Serbia in order to buy time. It is not surprising, therefore, that the bloody events in Sarajevo speedily created a virtual government consensus (including the emperor) that Serbia must be reduced to satellite status, if necessary by force and even at the cost of a crisis with Russia. Otherwise, as Berchtold argued, Austria would be renouncing her 'Great Power position'. She needed to show that she could be a dangerous enemy or an effective friend.[14]

### The Outbreak of War

On 5 July the Austrian ambassador, in fateful talks with the kaiser and Bethmann Hollweg, was given the crucial 'blank cheque' which approved a decisive move against Serbia. Wilhelm spoke of 'the present time which is so favourable to us', and of the need for Austria to act swiftly. Some scholars take the view that he was hoping for no more than a localised crisis. But whatever his personal preferences at that particular moment, it is imperative to comprehend the thinking and mood in influential German circles as a whole in order to understand the casual way in which the Austrian request was discussed and German support promised.

Amid the vast literature and the many schools of thought on Germany and 1914, there are some significant areas of agreement. Thus, whether emphasis is placed on *innen* or *aussenpolitik*, on defensive or aggressive concerns, on the preservation of the existing political and social order at home or the militant pursuit of economic objectives abroad, it is evident that more and more influential individuals and groups had been reaching the conclusion that Germany's future depended on the pursuit of a more assertive and even a belligerent foreign policy. This alone seemed to promise the survival of the existing political order, the provision of sufficient employment for the masses, the availability of ample export markets and the sources of necessary imports – indeed all that was needed if Germany was to find a place in the front rank with the greatest of the other powers. As a first step Austria had to be preserved and strengthened, and Russia and France not allowed to reduce still further Germany's precious military advantages. It was not surprising that so many were so receptive to the pleas of Moltke and others for a preventive war.

The army bill of 1913, it was claimed, could provide Germany with only a temporary extension of her advantage on land. The Russian response included new strategic railways as well as additional troops. France introduced three-year military service. The general staffs in both Berlin and Vienna became increasingly pessimistic. Moltke tried to persuade Jagow in May 1914 that within two or three years the 'military superiority of our enemies would be so great that he did not know how we might cope with them'. He could see no alternative to a 'preventive war in order to defeat the enemy as long as we could still more or less pass the test'. He left it to Jagow's 'discretion to gear our policy to an early unleashing of war'.

Moltke, however, should not be seen as just another Conrad von Hötzendorff. He had assumed the post of chief of the general staff in 1906 with some reluctance. Despite his acceptance of the Schlieffen Plan, he was by no means convinced that Germany would be able to win quick and decisive victories and triumph in a short war. He doubted too if armies of a million or more men could be properly controlled. He shared the fears of Ivan Bloch that a modern people's war might prove long and arduous, with no quarter being sought until the strength of one side had been utterly broken. The elder Moltke had expressed similar fears a generation earlier. Yet although the son conceded in the spring of 1914 that neither Russia nor France seemed to be in an aggressive mood for the time being, he repeatedly argued that if Germany was to fight it had to be soon. Meanwhile speculation about the inevitability of war, especially with Russia, was becoming widespread. Germany, it seemed to many, could not solve her problems by peaceful means.[15]

Bethmann Hollweg, given the nature of his responsibilities, had most cause to try to stand back and see all these anxieties and ambitions in relation to each other and in their domestic and international contexts. Though not accepted by all historians as a 'moderate', he certainly voiced his concern at times over the growing interest in war. In 1913 he spoke with surprising frankness in the Reichstag, warning that wars could be caused by 'noisy and fanatical minorities'. He expressed private fears that unless the powers devoted themselves to the pursuit of peace there could be an 'explosion which no one desires and which will be to the detriment of all'. As late as June 1914 he predicted that a world war 'with its unforeseeable consequences will greatly strengthen the power of social democracy, since it preaches peace and will topple many a throne'.[16]

It might, of course, be said that the chancellor was expressing his views with reference to the immediate present, or was trying to gain credibility as a man of peace in anticipation of war. Yet what is evident by the summer of 1914 is how difficult it would have been for him (whatever his own preferences) to resist the powerful forces which clamoured for decisive action. These ran from the angst-ridden by way of the fatalists to the most ambitious and aggressive elements. A critical point had been reached in German history. The stability of the existing order at home and the future advance of Germany as a great power both, it was said, required a decisive international success.

Bethmann as a civilian minister was also less well placed to influence the military than his British counterparts. The latter at least had at their disposal the emergent Committee of Imperial Defence with which to probe the calculations of the service chiefs in some depth. Its members, for instance, had been able in 1911 to dismiss as nonsense the Royal Navy's ideas for an amphibious role for the army in the Baltic. Bethmann had not even been present at the notorious 'War Council' in December 1912, while Tirpitz and Wilhelm had for far too long been allowed to proceed with their naval programme without a critical analysis of the assumptions upon which it was based. Worse, the army had been left to devise a rigid two-stage battle plan which robbed the politicians and diplomats of any real flexibility once war became a probability. France must be attacked whatever the original cause of war.

Bethmann himself at the start of his chancellorship had made a bid for more room for manoeuvre by seeking British neutrality. He was, however, impeded not only by the naval obsessions of Tirpitz and the kaiser but by the fact that Germany could not hope to shift the balance of power to her advantage (especially in western Europe) without bringing Britain sooner or later into a war. The army's determination to commence a war with the defeat of France made early British entry all the more probable. If Tirpitz still wished to postpone war until his fleet was stronger, the generals were arguing that delay would favour their enemies on land. Finally Bethmann could no longer plead that there was insufficient popular support for a 'defensive' war with Russia.

There was also an irresistible temptation to see in the Sarajevo assassinations an opportunity for the Central Powers to claim the high moral ground. Better still, any serious international resistance would be headed by Russia. In the early stages Austria could be left to make the running (albeit with secret German encouragement). Bethmann himself at the very least saw an opportunity to use the crisis to test and hopefully break the Franco–Russian alignment. If a general war resulted, so be it. Even so Berghahn stresses both the 'strategy of bluff which was integral to Bethmann Hollweg's risk concept', and the 'fumbling and far from cold-blooded way' in which the July crisis was managed in Berlin.

The Germans, it might also be added, could not have been absolutely certain that Russia would choose to fight. But if she did, this would meet Bethmann's domestic needs as well as vindicate those who had argued that war was inevitable anyway. The easiest option for Bethmann was to urge Austria to seize her chance to cripple Serbia. The German general staff began some secret preparations for war with Russia, but so sure were they of their superb mobilisation plans that for the time being they could leave the main decisions to others – the ministers and monarchs in Berlin, Vienna and St Petersburg.[17]

What is also highly revealing (and incriminating) is the virtual absence of any pretence at diplomatic activity by Berlin or Vienna with regard to the third critical capital, St Petersburg. There was no initiative (on the lines, for instance, of the talks at Reichstadt in 1876) to try to control what was ostensibly a bilateral dispute between Austria and Serbia. The Crimean and even the Italian and German wars of unification had been preceded by much diplomatic activity. The last minute talk of talks at the end of July 1914 can hardly be regarded as a serious attempt by the Central Powers to find an alternative to war or capitulation by Serbia and Russia.

The thinking in Berlin and Vienna further underlines the point that even if the Austro–Serb question could somehow have been localised, little would have been settled in the longer run between the three eastern powers as a whole – unless, that is, the connections between France and Russia had been severed or weakened sufficiently to satisfy Germany. Furthermore it would still have been necessary for Russia and the Central Powers to have moderated their ambitions sufficiently for them to have devised a sequel of some kind to those understandings which had governed their relations in the Balkans and Near East for much of the period between 1871 and 1908 (something which would have required not only highly creative diplomacy but effective management of the militants at home).

In 1914, however, there was no hint of interest in another 'Alliance' ('Holy' or monarchical) or of some lesser understanding (save in the minds of such as the marginalised Witte and his allies). In Vienna and Berlin it might reasonably have been felt that Russia had had her chance in 1912–13 to try to stabilise south-eastern Europe. Thus Bethmann and the German High Command were content to launch themselves into the unknown and see what happened. The more one looks at July 1914, the more improbable the avoidance of war becomes. Even a compromise at that time would not have prevented future conflict.

Meanwhile the Austrians, somewhat to the dismay of Berlin, seemed incapable of speedy action – especially because they could not mobilise their troops quickly. Full advantage was not taken of the moral shock caused by the assassination of the archduke. Thus Vienna's deliberately unacceptable demands were not presented in Belgrade until 23 July. For its part the Serb government under Pasic both before and immediately after Sarajevo was not much influenced by Russia. In fact Pasic was by no means certain as to how much Russian support he could expect in the event of a full-scale crisis. St Petersburg was no more than hinting at military backing as late as 25 July, and Pasic of his own accord chose to follow a polite but not submissive policy towards Vienna. He leaned heavily on the argument that Serbia was and should be treated as a civilised state. Indeed he was not, he asserted, willing to bow absolutely to the will of 'friendly' powers if they tried to negotiate a settlement.[18] Greater flexibility, in any case, would have cut little ice in Vienna – although the kaiser was momentarily impressed by the concessions offered by the Serbs. Vienna broke off diplomatic relations on 25 July, and war was clearly only days distant.

On the subject of Russia, Dominic Lieven agrees that the Germans had some reason to fear her potential as a power – whatever her current conduct or immediate priorities. Social Darwinian ideas and an aggressive nationalist spirit were evident in some quarters, not least in the Duma (the same phenomena did not lack for exponents in Britain and France). On the other hand, as Lieven emphasises, Russia as a multinational empire was less cohesive than Germany. There was not the same agreement over her needs and future in the world. For all the newspaper talk in Russia of the Teutonic threat earlier in the year, Lieven concludes that 'the study of Russian internal affairs helps to explain but does not justify Germany's decision to wage war in July 1914'.[19]

Much has been made of the degree to which previous policy-making in St Petersburg had been influenced by fears of further popular uprisings and the probability of defeat in war. Thus Izvolsky had made no impression upon other ministers in January 1908 with the argument that Russia could not abandon 'her historic mission' on behalf of the Slavs and accept reduction to second-class status. But in July 1914 it was speedily agreed that 'public and parliamentary opinion' would not understand or forgive another capitulation to the Central Powers.[20] The Russians were taken aback by the violence of the Austrian note of 23 July, and within 24 hours the feeling was growing that Serbia would have to be supported, whatever the consequences. All the evidence suggested that the Central Powers were intent upon an all-out triumph.

Nor could the key policy-makers forget that past concessions had seemingly been exploited and abused by the Central Powers. These had simply whetted the Teutonic appetite for more. At first Nicholas was among the most reluctant to believe the worst (especially of the kaiser) and questioned whether Russia was ready for war. But with other early doubters he soon accepted that Russian interests and pride were at stake. This time there could be no retreat. Some preparations for war began on the 24th. Second thoughts or any later hopes of negotiations did not long survive the mounting distrust of Austria and Germany.[21] The military, though preferring delay, offered assurances that the armed forces were in a condition to fight.

The signals from France were encouraging – provided Russia was the victim of aggression. The leaders could no longer use the argument that their empire was not strong enough to take a stand, especially when the threat to their interests and influence in south-east Europe was acute.

By the end of July, although there were some last minute diplomatic moves among the powers (some perhaps tactical rather than sincere), it was evident that an Austro–Serb war could not be localised. Historians may still debate the importance or otherwise of such moves as Russia's mobilisation on 31 July, but Lieven is surely correct when he argues that Germany and Austria had gone too far to retreat.[22] This had always been likely once Austria had received a 'blank cheque' from Germany. Similarly although there were clearly those in Berlin who hoped that Britain would stand aside, most were determined to press on even if she intervened. There might have been second thoughts had Britain possessed an army with large trained reserves. But no such force existed, and had so un-British a policy as universal service been introduced earlier, it might simply have precipitated an earlier crisis. Tirpitz had lived in fear of a pre-emptive British naval attack while his own fleet was at its most vulnerable. It is not difficult to imagine the German reaction had Britain tried to create a formidable army intended to assist France.

One of the best summaries of the thinking in Berlin as the crisis deepened is provided by Admiral Müller. He observed in a diary entry of 27 July that 'the tenor of our policy' was to remain calm and allow Russia to put herself in the wrong. Then Germany should 'not shrink from war *if it were inevitable* [author's italics]'. Müller's choice of words might hint at a degree of uncertainty as to how Russia would react. What was not in doubt, however, was the determination of Bethmann, with the full agreement of the generals, to ensure that in 'all events Russia must ruthlessly be put in the wrong.'[23]

Germany and (to a lesser extent) Austria were plainly intent on major changes to the balance in Europe, and this time – if necessary – Germany would fight. All the dominoes were therefore fatally aligned and ready to be knocked over in sequence. Russia, given conditions at home and the attitude of France, felt it possible and necessary to defend the status quo in the Balkans. Germany's predetermined attack on France (in the event of war in the east) by way of Belgium put an end to the uncertainty in Britain, and relieved the fears of the service chiefs and the Foreign Office that the cabinet might opt for neutrality – at least for the time being. France, in their view, had to be supported from the outset, both to strengthen her against the initial German onslaught, but also to ensure that Britain had a prime place at the conference table when the war ended – no matter which side emerged victorious from the struggle. On 4 August Britain too was at war.[24]

# 9

# A Summing Up

The line between peace and war in Europe between 1815 and 1914 was often a narrow one – despite the long periods of peace. At the risk of oversimplification one might say that a power imbalance against France did much to keep the peace before 1854, while a power imbalance in favour of Germany had much the same effect until the later 1900s. Although there were other barriers to conflict, many of them were precarious. Despite hopes to the contrary, such developments as the growth of trade and communications did not prevent war. In the case of trade and still more the spread of nationalism, the figure of Mr Hyde was often more in evidence than Dr Jekyll. Winston Churchill in 1901 asserted that 'Democracy is more vindictive than Cabinets. The wars of peoples will be more terrible than those of kings.' Industry and ever more powerful bureaucracies further increased the capacities of the powers to wage war.

In general terms, despite the efforts of the peace movements, war remained an accepted and acceptable hazard given sufficient cause and the hope that its advantages would outweigh its costs. Images and impressions from Classical times and beyond ensured that policy-makers were steeped in a culture in which wars and empire-building were seen as a natural occupation of ambitious leaders. Admittedly talk of war did not prevent two long periods of peace. Even Nicholas I, despite his initial inclination to mobilise an army or two whenever fresh tidings of revolution reached his ears, was relatively cautious in practice (outside his own empire). He was impressed by Russia's financial if not her military limitations. Similarly, while he and other autocrats could agree that revolution had to be suppressed, it was vital that the means employed should not them-selves feed the fires rather than dowse them.

The task of the defenders of the status quo was eased for most of the years from 1815 to 1853 by the fact that the balance was tilted so heavily in their favour, and that France in particular could be iso-lated so easily. Even Louis Napoleon, when France was at the peak of her power and confidence since the fall of his uncle, did not risk war over Italy until he believed that Austrian isolation was assured. It is unlikely that he would have gone to war in the Near East in 1854 without Britain as an ally. But all these instances of leaders recoiling from war, or opting for it only when the situation seemed highly favourable, stemmed from a profound awareness of what might be the disastrous consequences of failure or mere miscalculation. Finally, in so far as there existed a diplomatic instrument to keep the peace, this was provided by the Quadruple Alliance, not by the Concert, recourse to which was normally a sure sign that the powers were already disposed towards peace and compromise. Yet even that alliance did not operate because of what had been committed to paper in 1814–15, but rather because of the frequently overlapping self-interested concerns of its four members.

Many of the earlier barriers to war broke down from the mid-1850s, not simply because of the formidable internal pressures for change within Italy and Germany, but because the overall balance of power had moved in favour of the revisionists. The Crimean War was of critical importance since it turned Russia, hitherto an arch-opponent of change in the heart of Europe, into a revisionist power. While Russia herself was not equal to war in this period, she wel-comed revisionism, especially at the expense of Austria. This was exploited by Napoleon III and Bismarck in turn. The years of war between 1854 and 1871 do much to highlight the special factors which had helped to keep the peace in the earlier period, and to expose the futility of the efforts made at the Congress of Paris in 1856 to encourage would-be belligerents to pause and exhaust the resources of diplomacy and mediation before taking up arms.

From 1871 until the mid-1900s (though still not without periods of acute tension), the advantage shifted back to the defenders of the status quo. The strongest power (Germany) due to some good judge-ment and more good luck did not provoke a solidly hostile coalition against herself. She was normally able to live with the balance as it was or to adjust it to suit her purposes short of war. It is true that

Britain and Russia might have begun a second 'Crimea' in 1878, while Bismarck did much to reduce the risk of a third in 1885. There were also groups in Germany and Austria in the late 1880s which seriously debated the option of war against Russia and perhaps France. Yet this was followed by nearly another 20 years of comparative stability during which Germany (despite the Franco–Russian alliance) again felt reasonably secure – not least because of the problems and/or extra-European distractions of the other powers. Particularly important (and instructive) were the periods of relatively good relations between the three eastern powers. Britain mattered less on the continent after 1856, while France's capacity to take initiatives (other for instance than Deceazes's defensive diplomacy against Germany in 1874–5) was greatly reduced after 1871. Russia, though interested in the survival of France, had no desire to see her return to the European revisionism practised by Napoleon III – unless that became necessary because of an even greater threat from Germany.

On the other hand the explosive potential of the Near East and south-east continued to grow. Fortunately Russia (for all her ambition and potential) was still too preoccupied with development at home and expansion in Asia to take great risks (she backed off several times from crises between 1878 and 1912). Despite their alliance, France and Russia seemed more likely to go to war with Britain than with Germany until the diplomatic revolution of the 1900s. The massive armament programmes and fierce economic rivalries constituted other threats to the peace, and yet in many respects they were the symptoms rather than the causes of tension. They did, however, often acquire a momentum of their own. Most serious of all was the situation when Germany began to fear from the later 1900s that she might be losing her advantageous position within the balance of power, a period which also coincided with growing speculation over the longevity of the Habsburg Empire and the increasing incompatibility of the interests of Russia and the Central Powers in the Balkans and the Ottoman Empire. Given that there appeared to exist no basis for a lasting compromise between the two sides, the maintenance of peace from 1909 largely turned on Russia's unpreparedness for war. By 1914 this was no longer the case, whereas the Central Powers were even more determined to assert themselves while there was yet time. The circumstances and calculations which had kept the peace in previous crises were either missing or were eclipsed by those which favoured war.

Throughout the period in question it is evident (as A. J. P. Taylor often argued) that a narrative of the policy-making in each major power does much to explain the maintenance or breakdown of peace. Rivalry was a fact of life at all times, whether driven by governments, economic interests, or popular passions. But whatever the driving forces, the deliberations of those with ultimate authority were profoundly influenced by the correlation of forces, coupled with projections as to how those might be expected to develop in the future. Paradoxically in certain circumstances a movement away from an imbalance might increase the danger of war, with those hitherto in the ascendant fearing the loss of their advantage, and those in the weaker position beginning to feel that (if the issues at stake were of sufficient importance) even a narrow chance of victory might be preferred to a humiliating retreat. Such was the situation in the high summer of 1914.

# NOTES AND REFERENCES

## 1 The 'Congress System'

1. Alan James (ed.), *The Bases of International Order* (1973), pp. 26, 97; Trevor Taylor (ed.), *Approaches and Theory in International Relations* (1978), pp. 40 ff.
2. Jeremy Black, *Eighteenth Century Europe, 1700–89* (1990), pp. 274–9, 303, 321–2, 326; see also his 'Eighteenth-Century Warfare Reconsidered', *War in History*, i, no. 2, 1994, pp. 215–32.
3. M. S. Anderson, *The Rise of Modern Diplomacy, 1450–1919* (1993), p. 233.
4. J. M. Sherwig, 'Lord Grenville's Plan for a Concert of Europe, 1797–9', *Journal of Modern History*, vol. 34, no. 3, Sept. 1962, pp. 284–93.
5. Janet M. Hartley, *Alexander I* (1994), p. 69.
6. Kenneth Bourne, *The Foreign Policy of Victorian England* (1970), p. 197.
7. B. Jelavich, *Russia's Balkan Entanglements, 1806–1914* (1991), pp. 42–4.
8. A. J. Rieber, 'The Historiography of Imperial Russian Foreign Policy', in H. Ragsdale and V. N. Ponomarev (eds.), *Imperial Russian Foreign Policy* (1993), pp. 361–3.
9. J. Hartley, *Alexander I*, p. 121; P. Grimsted, *The Foreign Ministers of Alexander I* (1969), pp. 32–4, 46.
10. W. H. Zawadski, 'Russia and the Re-opening of the Polish Question, 1801–1814', *The International History Review*, vii, no. 1, February 1985, pp. 19–44.
11. Cited in C. J. Bartlett, *Castlereagh* (1966), p. 126.
12. Franklin F. Ford, *Europe 1780–1830* (1970), p. 256.
13. J. Hartley, *Alexander I*, pp. 130–3.
14. Roger Parkinson, *Clausewitz* (1970), pp. 35, 287–8.
15. G. A. Craig, 'Wilhelm von Humboldt as Diplomat', in K. Bourne and D. C. Watt (eds.), *Studies in International History* (1967), pp. 81–102; Douglas Dakin, 'The Congress of Vienna, 1814–15', in Alan Sked (ed.), *Europe's Balance of Power* (1979), pp. 26–7.
16. G. Mann, *Secretary of Europe: the life of F. von Gentz* (1970), pp. 276–7; Grigore Gafencu, *Prelude to the Russian Campaign* (1945), p. 16n.
17. E. Hobsbawm, *The Age of Revolution, 1789–1848* (1962), pp. 127–9.
18. B. Jelavich, *St Petersburg and Moscow: tsarist and Soviet foreign policy, 1814–1974* (1974), p. 35.

19. G. Mann, *Gentz*, pp. 210 ff.
20. M. S. Anderson, *Modern Diplomacy*, p. 179.
21. G. Mann, *Gentz*, pp. 209, 215.
22. Ibid, pp. 224–30, 261, 264, 277–8.
23. Carlsten Holbraad, *The Concert of Europe* (1970), pp. 2–8.
24. F. R. Bridge, 'Allied Diplomacy in Peacetime, 1815–23', in A. Sked, *Europe's Balance*, p. 53.
25. G. Mann, *Gentz*, pp. 209, 215.
26. C. C. F. Greville, *The Greville Diaries* (1938), i. 127–8.
27. C. Bartlett, *Castlereagh*, Chapter 7.
28. F. Bridge in A. Sked, *Europe's Balance*, pp. 35–7; J. Hartley, *Alexander I*, pp. 139–41.
29. J. Hartley, *Alexander I*, pp. 144–5; F. Bridge in A. Sked, *Europe's Balance*, pp. 37–8.
30. Alan W. Palmer, *The Chancelleries of Europe* (1970), p. 18. J. Hartley, *Alexander I*, pp. 142–8 argues that the tsar's interest in disarmament stemmed in part from the need to decrease government spending. Russia's army was also inflated by the huge area it had to defend. The Congress provided ample evidence of his idealism – some of it touchingly naive, and which also included some sympathy for moderate constitutions outside Russia.
31. C. J. Bartlett, 'Britain and the European Balance', in A. Sked, *Europe's Balance*, pp. 202, 211, 216.
32. See F. Bridge, in Ibid, pp. 41–6.
33. Ibid, pp. 48–52.
34. F. H. Hinsley, *Power and the Pursuit of Peace* (1963), p. 197.

## 2  Competition Short of War

1. J. Hartley, *Alexander I*, pp. 159–60.
2. Alan W. Palmer, *Metternich* (1972), pp. 237–8.
3. A. Palmer, *Chancelleries*, pp. 45–7.
4. Paul Shroeder, *The Transformation of European Politics, 1763–1848* (1994), p. 659; Douglas Dakin, *The Greek Struggle for Independence, 1821–33* (1973), pp. 273–4.
5. M. S. Anderson, 'Russia and the Eastern Question, 1821–41', in A. Sked, *Europe's Balance*, pp. 85–7.
6. B. Jelavich, *St Petersburg and Moscow*, pp. 73, 75, 78. The Russians would have preferred the Greeks in a condition of dependence on themselves within an untouched Turkish empire.
7. R. Bullen, 'France and Europe, 1815–48' in A. Sked, *Europe's Balance*, p. 136.
8. G. Mann, *Gentz*, pp. 299–302.

9. C. L. Church, *Europe in 1830* (1983), pp. 42–3.
10. B. Jelavich, *St Petersburg and Moscow*, pp. 46–9.
11. C. L. Church, *Europe in 1830*, pp. 46–8.
12. A. Palmer, *Chancelleries*, p. 60.
13. F. H. Hinsley, *Nationalism and the International System* (1973), p. 107–8.
14. C. J. Bartlett, *Great Britain and Sea Power, 1815–53* (1963), pp. 86–7; A. Palmer, *Chancelleries*, p. 251; see also C. A. Macartney, *The Habsburg Empire, 1790–1918* (1968), p. 237; and A. Sked, *Europe's Balance*, p. 107.
15. A. Palmer, *Metternich*, p. 258; *Chancelleries*, p. 62; C. K. Webster, *The Foreign Policy of Palmerston, 1830–1841* (1951), i. 291.
16. For this crisis see especially M. S. Anderson in A. Sked, *Europe's Balance*, pp. 88–91.
17. *History Notes, 'My Purdah Lady': The Foreign Office and the Secret Vote, 1782–1909*, Historical Branch, LRD (Foreign and Commonwealth Office), no. 7, September 1994, p. 8.
18. M. S. Anderson (p. 92) and R. Bullen (p. 62) in A. Sked, *Europe's Balance*.
19. C. J. Bartlett, *Defence and Diplomacy* (1993), pp. 122–3.
20. R. Bullen, 'The Great Powers and the Iberian Peninsula, 1815–48', in A. Sked, *Europe's Balance*, pp. 69–76.
21. R. Bullen, 'France and Europe, 1815–48', in A. Sked, *Europe's Balance*, pp. 143–4.
22. A. Palmer, *Chancelleries*, pp. 61–4, and *Metternich*, pp. 262–4.
23. C. J. Bartlett, *Sea Power*, pp. 107–9.
24. A. Palmer, *Metternich*, p. 257.
25. B. Jelavich, *Russia's Balkan Entanglements* (1991), pp. 95–7.
26. M. S. Anderson in A. Sked, *Europe's Balance*, pp. 92–7. For the Russian side see H. N. Ingle, *Nesselrode and the Russian Rapprochement with Britain, 1836–44* (1976), passim.
27. C. J. Bartlett, 'Britain and the European Balance', in A. Sked, *Europe's Balance*, p. 158.
28. G. J. Billy, *Palmerston's Foreign Policy: 1848* (1993), p. 13.
29. A. Palmer, *Chancelleries*, p. 75.
30. C. J. Bartlett, *Sea Power*, p. 174.
31. Cited by H. C. F. Bell, *Lord Palmerston* (1966), i. 398; see also Bartlett, *Sea Power*, p. 185.
32. F. R. Bridge, *The Habsburg Monarchy among the Powers* (1990), pp. 38–9.
33. Bell, *Palmerston*, i. 412–3.
34. F. R. Bridge, *Habsburg Monarchy*, pp. 38–9.
35. P. Schroeder, *The Transformation of European Politics*, Chapters 13–17, but see especially pp. 797–9, 802–3.
36. W. C. Fuller Jr., *Strategy and Power in Russia, 1600–1914* (1992), Chapter 6, analyses both Nicholas I's belief that Russia was territorially sated and his awareness that she was ill-placed to fight long and expensive wars despite his fear of revolutionary infections and his anxiety to protect Russian interests in the Ottoman Empire.
37. P. Schroeder, *Transformation*, p. 801.

### 3 Revolutions and War, 1848–56

1. Ian W. Roberts, *Nicholas I and the Russian Intervention in Hungary* (1991), pp. 6–8, 12, 15–16 and passim. Nicholas personified absolutism, treating those around him as merely advisers or executors of policy.
2. G. Billy, *Palmerston*, pp. 37–47, 51–4. For later developments see pp. 142–5.
3. F. Bridge, *Habsburg Monarchy*, pp. 39–44.
4. F. J. Coppa, *The Origins of the Italian Wars of Independence* (1992), pp. 66–7. See also G. Billy, *Palmerston*, p. 140.
5. G. Billy, *Palmerston*, pp. 142–5.
6. Ibid, pp. 89–90, 111–12.
7. I. Roberts, *Nicholas I*, pp. 44–8, 56.
8. Ibid, pp. 44–8, 56
9. K. Bourne, *Foreign Policy*, pp. 277–80; G. Billy, *Palmerston*, p. 128.
10. W. Carr, *The Origins of the Wars of German Unification* (1991), pp. 99–100.
11. Ibid, p. 100.
12. I. Roberts, *Nicholas I*, p. 224.
13. On the Hungarian Refugees, see D. Goldfrank, 'Policy trends and the Menshikov mission of 1853', in H. Ragsdale, *Russian Foreign Policy*, pp. 122–4.
14. C. Bartlett, *Sea Power*, p. 272.
15. A. J. P. Taylor, *The Struggle for Mastery in Europe, 1848–1918* (1954), p. 47.
16. H. W. V. Temperley and L. M. Penson, *Foundations of British Foreign Policy, 1792–1902* (1938), p. 289.
17. C. Bartlett, *Sea Power*, p. 289; Muriel E. Chamberlain, *Lord Aberdeen* (1983), pp. 472–3.
18. M. S. Anderson, *The Ascendancy of Europe, 1815–1914* (1985), p. 18.
19. J. F. McMillan, *Napoleon III* (1991), pp. 73–6, 167.
20. F. Coppa, *Italian Wars*, pp. 66–7.
21. J. McMillan, *Napoleon III*, p. 75–81. During the ensuing war, Napoleon III was usually less ambitious than Palmerston: see above pp. 63–5.
22. D. M. Goldfrank, *The Origins of the Crimean War* (1994), pp. 5, 150, 273–4, 284; V. N. Vinogradov, 'The personal responsibility of Emperor Nicholas I for the coming of the Crimean War', in H. Ragsdale, *Russian Foreign Policy*, pp. 159–67; and I. W. Roberts, *Nicholas I*, pp. 226–8.
23. See D. Goldfrank (Chapter 5) and V. Vinogradov (Chapter 6) in H. Ragsdale, *Russian Foreign Policy*.
24. I. Roberts, *Nicholas I*, pp. 227–8. Nesselrode commented in 1851 that a war with Britain would be 'the worst of all wars' since Russia could cause no direct injury to that power (G. Billy, *Palmerston*, p. 131).
25. V. Vinogradov in H. Ragsdale, *Russian Foreign Policy*, Chapter 6.
26. M. Chamberlain, *Aberdeen*, pp. 481–2.
27. D. Goldfrank, *Crimea*, pp. 204–9; M. Chamberlain, *Aberdeen*, pp. 483–5.
28. D. Goldfrank, *Crimea*, pp. 209 ff.; M. Chamberlain, *Aberdeen*, pp. 473–86.

29. M. Chamberlain, *Aberdeen*, pp. 491–2.
30. V. Vinogradov in H. Ragsdale, *Russian Foreign Policy*, p. 170.
31. F. Bridge, *Habsburg Monarchy*, pp. 53–7.
32. W. E. Mosse, *Alexander II and the Modernization of Russia* (1958), pp. 39–41.
33. Donald Southgate, *'The Most English Minister ... ': the policies and politics of Palmerston* (1966), p. 387.
34. C. Bartlett, *Defence and Diplomacy*, pp. 56, 63, 126–7; see also Paul Kennedy, *The Rise and Fall of British Naval Mastery* (1983), pp. 174, 177–8.
35. F. Bridge, *Habsburg Monarchy*, pp. 55–60.
36. A. Palmer, *Chancelleries*, p. 109; D. M. Goldfrank, *Crimea*, pp. 290 ff.
37. C. I. Hamilton, 'Anglo–French sea-power and the Declaration of Paris', *International History Review*, vol. iv, no. 2, May 1982, pp. 166–92.

# 4 The Transformation of Europe, 1857–71

1. A. Palmer, *Chancelleries*, p. 111; N. Rich and M. H. Fisher (eds.), *The Holstein Papers* (1955), i. 21.
2. F. Bridge (*Habsburg Monarchy*, pp. 62–3), while critical of Buol (he was too self-confident and failed to establish priorities) concedes that the problems facing him were huge. See also K. Bourne, *Foreign Policy*, p. 485.
3. J. McMillan, *Napoleon III*, Chapter 6.
4. F. Coppa, *Italian Wars*, pp. 80–2. See also H. Hearder, *Cavor* (1995).
5. H. Hearder, *Europe in the Nineteenth Century, 1830–1880* (1966), pp. 166–7; F. Coppa, *Italian Wars*, pp. 87–108.
6. F. Bridge, *Habsburg Monarchy*, p. 82; W. Carr, *German Unification*, pp. 103–4.
7. K. Bourne, *Foreign Policy*, pp. 347–54.
8. F. Valsecchi, 'European Diplomacy and the Expedition of the Thousand: the Conservative Powers', in M. Gilbert (ed.), *A Century of Conflict* (1966), pp. 49–72.
9. K. Bourne, *Foreign Policy*, pp. 370–2; see also A. Palmer, *Chancelleries*, pp. 130–2.
10. W. N. Medlicott, *Bismarck and Modern Germany* (1965), pp. 35–7; Lothar Gall, *Bismarck: the White Revolutionary* (1986), i. 219–21, 230; J. H. Jensen, 'Prince Alexander Gorchakov: the politics of recovery', in R. B. McKean (ed.), *New Perspectives in Modern Russian History* (1992), Chapter 2.
11. W. Medlicott, *Bismarck*, p. 35.
12. L. Gall, *Bismarck*, i. 91–2.
13. Ibid, i. 121; see also 108–21, 126–30.

14. Ibid, i. 256.
15. W. N. Medlicott, *Bismarck, Gladstone and the Concert of Europe* (1956), p. 18 takes the duchies question (1848–64) as an example of the circumstances in which the Concert could or could not be effective.
16. W. Carr, *German Unification*, p. 121.
17. W. Medlicott, *Bismarck*, p. 44; see also pp. 46–7.
18. W. Carr, *German Unification*, p. 122. See also Chapter 3 passim.
19. Ibid, p. 129.
20. J. McMillan, *Napoleon III*, pp. 104–9.
21. L. Gall, *Bismarck*, i. 258–76; W. Carr, *German Unification*, pp. 134–5; István Deák, *Beyond Nationalism: a social and political history of the Habsburg Officer Corps, 1848–1918* (1992), pp. 52–3.
22. J. R. Vincent, *Disraeli, Derby and the Conservative Party, 1849–69* (1978), p. 262.
23. See for instance István Diószegi, *Hungarians in the Ballhausplatz: studies on the Austro–Hungarian common foreign policy* (1983), pp. 54–61, 82–5.
24. W. Carr, *German Unification*, pp. 155–60.
25. J. Vincent, *Disraeli*, pp. 281, 304.
26. W. Carr, *German Unification*, pp. 180–3.
27. Ibid, pp. 172, 182–3.
28. K. Hildebrand, *German Foreign Policy from Bismarck to Adenauer* (1989), Chapter 2.
29. W. Carr, *German Unification*, p. 178.
30. Ibid, pp. 192–203.
31. Ibid, p. 192.
32. Ibid, pp. 192–203.
33. F. Bridge, *Habsburg Monarchy*, pp. 97–9.

## 5   *Realpolitik* and Militarism, 1871–90

1. A. S. Alexandroff, *The Logic of Diplomacy* (1981), p. 21; O. Pflanze, *Bismarck and the development of Germany* (1990), iii. 83–4; also ii. 254.
2. See especially K. Hildebrand, *German Foreign Policy*, Chapters 1 and 3, especially pp. 19–29, 31–3. He notes the growing awareness in London that the German National Liberals had less concern for the balance of power, and were less interested than Bismarck in good relations between Germany and Austria–Hungary.
3. W. N. Medlicott and D. K. Coveney, *Bismarck and Europe* (1971), pp. 102–3; K. Hildebrand, *German Foreign Policy*, pp. 249–53.
4. Public Record Office, London, Lytton to Derby, no. 969, 21 Sept. 1874, FO27/2059. C. J. Bartlett, 'After Palmerston: Britain and the Iberian Peninsula, 1865–76', *English Historical Review*, cix, no. 430, February

1994, pp. 82–5. For Russia and France see W. Fuller, *Strategy and Power*, pp. 292 ff.

5. O. Pflanze, *Bismarck*, ii. 264–7, 272, 415.
6. Ibid, ii. 418–19.
7. K. Bourne, *Foreign Policy*, pp. 127–8.
8. See W. Fuller, *Strategy and Power*, pp. 311–27 for Russian policies in 1876–8. See also D. McKenzie, 'Russia's Balkan policies under Alexander II', in H. Ragsdale, *Russian Foreign Policy*, Chapter 9. especially pp. 225–6.
9. O. Pflanze, *Bismarck*, ii. 420–6.
10. Ibid, ii. 428–31; W. Medlicott and D. Coveney, *Bismarck and Europe*, pp. 93–101.
11. B. Jelavich, *St Petersburg and Moscow*, p. 181.
12. O. Pflanze, *Bismarck*, ii. 434–5.
13. Ibid, ii. 439–41.
14. Ibid, ii. 246–7; iii. 83; W. Medlicott and D. Coveney, *Bismarck and Europe*, p. 103.
15. W. Medlicott, *Bismarck*, p. 173; and *Bismarck, Gladstone*, pp. 10–17, 337.
16. O. Pflanze, *Bismarck*, iii. 92–3.
17. W. N. Medlicott and R. G. Weeks, 'Documents on Russian foreign policy, 1878–80', *Slavonic and East European Review*, 64, no. 1, January 1986, p. 81.
18. A. Palmer, *Chancelleries*, pp. 159–61.
19. W. Medlicott and R. Weeks, *Slavonic Review*, 64, no. 4, Oct. 1986, p. 566.
20. Ibid, p. 568.
21. Ibid, *Slavonic Review*, 65, i. January 1987, p. 131; see also pp. 117 ff. W. Medlicott, *Bismarck, Gladstone*, pp. 57 ff., 319–20, 323–4.
22. W. Medlicott, *Bismarck, Gladstone*, pp. 10–34; O. Pflanze, *Bismarck*, iii. 87, 510; B. Waller, *Bismarck at the Crossroads, 1878–80* (1974), pp. 249–56.
23. A. Palmer, *Chancelleries*, pp. 169–72.
24. O. Pflanze, *Bismarck*, iii. 218–25.
25. Ibid, iii. 243–8.
26. Ibid, iii. 252; N. Rich, *Friedrich von Holstein: Politics and Diplomacy in the age of Bismarck and Wilhelm II* (1963), i. 128, 204–20, 249–79.
27. Cited by G. Mann, *The History of Germany since 1789* (1974), p. 383.
28. See especially F. Bridge, *Habsburg Monarchy*, pp. 172–88. Note also I. Diószegi, *Hungarians in the Ballhausplatz*, pp. 84–5, for the enthusiasm of the Hungarian Liberal Party for war against Russia.
29. B. Jelavich, *St Petersburg and Moscow*, p. 212.
30. See O. Pflanze, *Bismarck*, iii. 257–8, 311 for Russo–German economic relations.
31. N. Rich, *Politics and Diplomacy*, i. 246–50.
32. W. Medlicott and D. Coveney, *Bismarck and Europe*, pp. 174–5.
33. K. Bourne, Foreign Policy, p. 429; C. Lowe, *The Reluctant Imperialists* (1967), ii. 85–8; Fuller, *Strategy and Power*, pp. 356–72.
34. W. Medlicott and D. Coveney, *Bismarck and Europe*, pp. 170–1, 175–7.

## 6    Imperial Rivalries and European Diplomacy, 1890–1907

1. E. Kehr, *Economic Interest, Militarism and Foreign Policy* (1977), pp. 37–8, 43–8; I. Geiss, *German Foreign Policy, 1871–1914* (1976), p. viii; V. R. Berghahn, *Germany and the Approach of War in 1914* (2nd edn., 1993), Chapters 2–3 passim, especially p. 147: '... Tirpitz's naval and world policy had posed a threat to the balance of power, which was dangerous enough to unite Germany's neighbours'.
2. M. Howard, 'A Thirty Years War? The Two World Wars in Historical Perspective', *Transactions of the Royal Historical Society*, 6th series, iii, 1993, pp. 171–84. See also W. Fuller, *Strategy and Power*, p. 347, for Schlieffen's fears of potentially disastrous wars and (pp. 350–66) for the ongoing effects of the Franco–Russian alliance.
3. K. Bourne, *Foreign Policy*, pp. 432–3.
4. M. Balfour, *The Kaiser and his Times* (1964), p. 183.
5. F. Bridge, *Habsburg Monarchy*, pp. 199, 202–10.
6. See W. Fuller, *Strategy and Power*, pp. 386–9, for the tightening of the Franco–Russian alliance against the Central Powers from 1899. Note also M. S. Anderson, *Ascendancy of Europe*, p. 45 for Delcassé's visit to St Petersburg in 1899 when he argued that the alliance should uphold the balance of power as well as keep the peace of Europe.
7. F. B. M. Hollyday, *Bismarck's Rival: a political biography of General and Admiral Albert von Stosch* (1976), pp. 65–7, 252–3, 258, 273, 278.
8. Woodruff D. Smith, *The German Colonial Empire* (1978), Chapters 9 and 11.
9. N. Rich and M. H. Fisher (eds.), *The Holstein Papers: 1837–1909* (1955–63), iii. 511–12, 528, 550–60; iv. 9–12, 22–5; B. Jelavich, *St Petersburg and Moscow*, pp. 232–49.
10. F. Bridge, *Habsburg Monarchy*, pp. 196–7, 209.
11. Ibid, pp. 210–14.
12. K. Bourne, *Foreign Policy*, pp. 440–2.
13. Ibid, pp. 446–7.
14. See e.g. A. Palmer, *Chancelleries*, pp. 182–6.
15. C. Holbraad, *Concert*, pp. 4, 173–81; K. Bourne, *Foreign Policy*, pp. 449–52.
16. F. Bridge, *Habsburg Monarchy*, pp. 221–2.
17. Ibid, pp. 225, 284–7.
18. N. Rich, *Friedrich von Holstein: politics and diplomacy in the era of Bismarck and Wilhelm II* (1965), ii. 453–6, 583, 611–14, 620–3, 669–76.
19. N. Rich, *Holstein Papers*, i. 118–19.
20. N. Rich, *Politics and Diplomacy*, ii. 565–6, 836–49; also Chapter 32.
21. N. Rich, *Holstein Papers*, i. 159 ff.; ii. 570, 814–15.
22. N. Rich, *Politics and Diplomacy*, ii. 611–14, 620–3; Chapters 40–1, 44–6.
23. Ibid, ii. 611–14; Keith Wilson, *Channel Tunnel Visions, 1850–1945* (1994), pp. 50–2.
24. C. Holbraad, *Concert*, pp. 186–190.

25. B. Tuchman, *The Proud Tower: a portrait of the world before the war, 1890–1914* (1980), pp. 236–7, 244–50; Anderson, *Modern Diplomacy,* pp. 253–65, 270–2.
26. B. Tuchman, *Proud Tower,* pp. 240–3.
27. M. Anderson, *Modern Diplomacy,* p. 262; N. Rich, *Politics and Diplomacy,* ii. Chapter 42; pp. 603–7; B. Tuchman, *Proud Tower,* p. 256; A. Palmer, *Chancelleries,* pp. 191–5.
28. K. Bourne, *Foreign Policy,* p. 472; M. Balfour, *Kaiser,* p. 238–40.
29. V. R. Berghahn, *Germany,* pp. 61–2. See also Holger H. Herwig, '*The Luxury Fleet*': the imperial German navy 1888–1918 (1980), Chapter 3.
30. H. H. Herwig, *Luxury Fleet,* pp. 75, 92.
31. W. Fuller, *Strategy and Power,* pp. 370–2, 382, 386–9 for references to Russia's interests at the Straits and the Far East, and her growing dependence on France.
32. David MacLaren McDonald, *United Government and Foreign Policy in Russia, 1900–14* (1992), pp. 78–81. See also his, 'A lever without a fulcrum: domestic factors in Russian foreign policy, 1904–10' in H. Ragsdale, *Imperial Russia,* Chapter 11, and 'A. P. Izvol'ski and Russian Foreign Policy under "United Government", 1906–10', in R. McKean, *New Perspectives,* Chapter 10, pp. 174–202.
33. K. Neilson, *Britain and the Last Tsar: British policy and Russia, 1894–1907* (1995), Chapter 9.

## 7   From the Anglo–Russian Entente to the Balkan Wars

1. Bernard Semmel, *Liberalism and Naval Strategy: ideology, interest and sea power during the Pax Britannica* (1986), p. 176.
2. D. McDonald, *United Government,* pp. 96–7, 108–9, 104–11.
3. James Joll, *The Origins of the First World War* (1984), pp. 46–7.
4. D. C. B. Lieven, *Nicholas II: emperor of all the Russias* (1993), pp. 192–4; Lieven, *Russia and the Origins of the First World War* (1983), pp. 32–7; D. McDonald, *United Government,* pp. 111–51; W. Fuller, *Strategy and Power,* pp. 418–22.
5. V. Berghahn, *Germany,* pp. 65, 91. See also Arden Bucholz, *Molke, Schlieffen and Prussian War Planning* (1991), passim.
6. C. J. Lowe and M. L. Dockrill, *The Mirage of Power: British foreign policy, 1902–22* (1972), iii. 445–8.
7. G. P. Gooch and H. W. V. Temperley, *British Documents on the Origins of the War, 1898–1914* (1926–38), ii. 397–420; vi. 738–9; R. F. Mackay, *Balfour: intellectual statesman* (1985), p. 242.
8. V. Berghahn, *Germany,* p. 137 and Chapter 7 passim.
9. See Ibid, pp. 141–2 for interesting comment on the use of imperialism in Germany to help unite the parties of the right and the centre; also

Chapters 3–7 passim. John Lowe, *The Great Powers, Imperialism and the German Problem, 1865–1925* (1994), Chapter 5 judiciously examines the scholarly debate on the importance of *weltpolitik*.

10. Lord Acton et al. (eds.), *The Cambridge Modern History* (1910), xii. 7–8, 172–3, 718–19.

11. V. Berghahn, *Germany*, p. 91, notes the forces beginning to work against Tirpitz before 1911–12, but still sees those years as the turning point.

12. D. Lieven, *Russia*, pp. 90–1.

13. Ibid, p. 134; Lieven stresses the usual subordination of economic interests to national security. See also his *Nicholas II*, pp. 94–101, 105–11, 117 ff., 190–2; A. J. Rieber, 'Persistent Factors in Russian Foreign Policy', in H. Ragsdale, *Russian Foreign Policy*, p. 353; A. Bodger, 'Russia and the end of the Ottoman Empire', in M. Kent (ed.), *The Great Powers and the End of the Ottoman Empire* (1984), Chapter 4; D. W. Spring, 'Russian foreign policy, economic interests and the Straits Question, 1905–14', in R. McKean, *New Perspectives*, pp. 203–21. Grain equalled c. 50 per cent of Russia's exports (1900s) with 75 per cent leaving via the Straits (p. 83).

14. D. Lieven, *Russia*, pp. 74–81.

15. Ibid, pp. 91–101, 153. For insight into Russian diplomats see ibid, pp. 83–91; A. Reiber in H. Ragsdale, *Russian Foreign Policy*, pp. 366–8.

16. D. Lieven, *Nicholas II*, pp. 192–4; *Russia*, pp. 153 ff.

17. A. Bodger in M. Kent, *Great Powers*, p. 87. On naval matters, see J. N. Westwood, *Russian Naval Construction, 1905–45* (1994), pp. 73–5, 92–4.

18. D. Spring in R. MacKean, *New Perspectives*, especially pp. 208–9, 218–19.

19. V. Berghahn, *Germany*, p. 150.

20. J. Joll, *Origins*, p. 52.

21. See above note 13; D. M. McDonald, *United Government*, pp. 185–7.

23. V. Berghahn, *Germany*, pp. 150–1, 179–80.

24. C. H. D. Howard (ed.), *The Diary of Edward Goschen, 1900–14* (1980), pp. 58–9.

25. F. Bridge, *Habsburg Monarchy*, pp. 312–67; L. Sondhaus, *The Naval Policy of Austria–Hungary, 1867–1918* (1994), pp. 183 ff., 232 ff. By 1910 naval expenditure had risen rapidly to almost one quarter that of the army (István Deák, *Beyond Nationalism: a social and political history of the Habsburg Officer Corps*, 1992, p. 64). For the increasing militancy in many quarters in Vienna, see pp. 73 ff.

# 8 To August 1914 and the End of an Era

1. See e.g. G. Ritter, *The Sword and the Sceptre* (1965), ii. 218–9.

2. D. McDonald, *United Government*, (1994), p. 207.

3. D. Lieven, *Nicholas II*, pp. 195–8.
4. D. McDonald, *United Government*, pp. 199–204.
5. V. Berghahn, *Germany*, p. 136. The determinants of German foreign policy in the years leading to 1914 are carefully and lucidly discussed by J. Lowe, *The Great Powers* (1994), Chapters 3 and 4.
6. V. Berghahn, *Germany*, pp. 136–9.
7. Ibid, pp. 140–2.
8. Ibid, pp. 140–5.
9. J. Joll, *Origins*, p. 8.
10. S. R. Williamson, *Austria–Hungary and the Origins of the First World War* (1991), pp. 4–6, 11.
11. Ibid, pp. 171 ff.; J. Joll, *Origins*, p. 92. John Leslie, 'The Antecedents of Austria–Hungary's War Aims', in *Archiv und Forschung*, band 20 (1993), pp. 307–94.
12. Ibid, pp. 375–89, 394.
13. Ibid, pp. 365–8. On Austria see F. Fellner, 'Austria–Hungary' in K. Wilson (ed.), *Decisions for War, 1914* (1995), Chapter 1.
14. F. Bridge, *Habsburg Monarchy*, p. 336.
15. On Moltke, see M. Balfour, *Kaiser*, pp. 263–4; J. C. G. Röhl, 'Germany' in K. Wilson, *Decisions*, Chapter 2; V. Berghahn, *Germany*, pp. 181–3. Critics of German policy ('the most complete madness') which led to war included business magnates Albert Ballin and Walter Rathenau, and the diplomat, Prince Lichnowsky (see above Röhl, 'Germany' p. 28).
16. V. Berghahn, *Germany*, pp. 175–8, 181 ff., 194–5. He stresses that policy-making was still the preserve of Wilhelm II and his advisers – a small 'strategic clique'. These were men who were guided by a narrow and dogmatic view of the world, with more than a few hints of a tendency to panic and overreact. Yet, they 'were cool enough' to try to calculate how much time they had in which to act before their position became desperate. Many scholars have underlined the growing fears of the German military and some civilian groups – notably the big landowners – at what they believed to be deteriorating prospects for the conservative order at home. War was preferable to slow death at home and abroad.
17. Ibid, p. 198–200, 211.
18. M. Cornwall, 'Serbia' in K. Wilson, *Decisions*, pp. 77–80, and Chapter 3 passim.
19. D. Lieven, *Nicholas II*, pp. 204 ff.
20. D. McDonald, *United Government*, pp. 107, 204–7.
21. D. Lieven, *Nicholas II*, p. 147.
22. W. Fuller, *Strategy and Power*, pp. 435–51; D. Lieven, *Nicholas II*, pp. 141–51.
23. V. Berghahn, *Germany*, p. 216.
24. For France and Britain, see J. F. V. Keiger, 'France', and K. Wilson, 'Britain' in K. Wilson, *Decisions*, Chapters 5 and 7; or at greater length, J. F. V. Keiger, *France and the Origins of the First World War* (1983);

Z. Steiner, *Britain and the Origins of the First World War* (1977); M. Brock, 'Britain enters the War' in R. J. W. Evans and H. P. von Strandmann (eds.), *The Coming of the First World War* (1990), pp. 145–64; and K. Neilson, *Britain and the Last Tsar*, pp. 338–40, 370–1.

# Suggestions for
# Further Reading

(Most of these works contain valuable bibliographies)

There are numerous studies of modern international statecraft and diplomacy, many of which refer – often at length – to the years 1814–1914 because of the interest it has excited as the 'classical' era in great-power relations. Some scholars, however (in the opinion of the present writer), have tended to exaggerate the contribution of statesmen and diplomats to its lengthy periods of peace and have overdrawn the degree to which there was a conscious and relatively successful search for a true 'equilibrium', quite apart from the development of 'consensual' politics within the Concert. In the context of a highly competitive world one can reverse Clausewitz's famous dictum with diplomacy becoming the continuation of war by other means. Similarly an imbalance, as long as it favoured those with a vested interest in limited and controlled change, might in practice work more strongly in favour of peace than a supposedly 'true' balance, which might be differently and wishfully interpreted by its beholders. Finally, whatever the aims of any one state (expansionist or consolidationist), its policies could not be insulated from the behaviour of others. 'Most of what states do is explained by what other states do to them.' (R. N. Rosecrance and A. B. Alexandroff (eds.), *The Logic of Diplomacy* (1981), p. 10).

On international relations, statecraft and diplomacy, the following can be no more than a sample: H. Bull, *The Anarchical Society: a study of order and world politics* (1977); Alan James (ed.), *The Bases of International Order* (1973); M. S. Anderson, *The Rise of Modern Diplomacy, 1450–1919* (1993); H. A. Kissinger, *Diplomacy* (1994); and E. V. Gulick, *Europe's Classical Balance of Power* (1955). More specific to the period under review are F. H. Hinsley, *Power and the Pursuit of Peace* (1963); E. Luard, *The Balance of Power: the system of international relations, 1648–1815* (1992); E. V. Gulick, *Europe's Classical Balance of Power* (1955); and C. Holbraad, *The Concert of Europe* (1970). See also J. L. Richardson, *Crisis Diplomacy: the great powers since the mid-nineteenth century* (1994): the crises examined include the Near East in 1839–41 and 1853–4; the origins of the Franco–Prussian war (1870); and Agadir (1911). Stress is laid on the difficulty of developing coherent policies in the absence of domestic stability, with effective interchanges between the powers requiring the pursuit of coherent policies by the participants.

Detailed overall studies of the relations of the European powers include Paul Schroeder, *The Transformation of European Politics, 1763–1848* (1994); A. Sked (ed.), *Europe's Balance of Power, 1815–1848* (1979); F. R. Bridge and R. Bullen, *The Great Powers and the European System, 1815–1914* (1980) [a new edition is promised]; Alan W. Palmer, *The Chancelleries of Europe* (1983); A. J. P. Taylor, *The Struggle for Mastery in Europe, 1848–1918* (1954); W. E. Mosse, *The European Powers and the German Question, 1848–71* (1958); J. Lowe, *The Great Powers, Imperialism and the German Problem, 1865–1925* (1994); W. L. Langer, *European Alliances and Alignments, 1871–1890* (1962); R. Langhorne, *The Collapse of the Concert of Europe* (1981); and James Joll, *The Origins of the First World War* (1984), a wide-ranging and stimulating work.

For Austria–Hungary in general, see especially F. R. Bridge, *The Habsburg Monarchy among the Powers, 1815–1918* (1990), a magisterial study; and Alan Sked, *The Decline and Fall of the Habsburg Empire, 1815–1918* (1989), who stresses the empire's viability in 1914. For discussion of specific periods see E. E. Kraehe, *The Metternich Controversy* (1971); P. Schroeder, *Austria, Great Britain, and the Crimean War* (1972); and S. R. Williamson, *Austria–Hungary and the Origins of the First World War* (1991).

Britain's role is best approached by way of M. E. Chamberlain, *'Pax Britannica'? British Foreign Policy, 1789–1914* (1988), and K. Bourne, *The Foreign Policy of Victorian England, 1830–1902* (1970) with its extensive and revealing collection of documents; and Z. S. Steiner, *Britain and the Origins of the First World War* (1977). Note also A. L. Friedberg, *The Weary Titan: Britain and the experience of relative decline, 1895–1905* (1988), which might usefully be read in conjunction with J. A. S. Grenville, *Lord Salisbury and Foreign Policy at the close of the nineteenth century* (1970) and Keith Neilson, *Britain and the Last Tsar, 1894–1907* (1995). For an extended essay on the interaction between British foreign and defence policies, see C. J. Bartlett, *Defence and Diplomacy: Britain and the Great Powers, 1815–1914* (1993).

A thoughtful introduction to French foreign policy 1815–1848 is to be found in Roger Bullen's chapters (3 and 6) in A. Sked, *Europe's Balance* (see above). The years to 1870 are covered by J. F. McMillan, *Napoleon III* (1991). For the later years note especially G. F. Kennan, *The Fateful Alliance: France, Russia and the coming of the First World War* (1984); C. Andrew, *Théophile Delcassé and the Making of the Entente Cordiale* (1968); and J. F. V. Keiger, *France and the Origins of the First World War* (1983).

On Germany before Bismarck see J. J. Sheehan, *German History, 1776–1866* (1989); and Chapters 1 and 2 of William Carr's *The Origins of the Wars of German Unification* (1991). See also Carr for the years 1862–1871, while W. N. Medlicott's *Bismarck and Modern Germany* (1965) is a good short introduction to the whole era of the Iron Chancellor. For the period before 1914 see J. Lowe, *The Great Powers: Imperialism and the German Problem, 1865–1925* (1994); L. L. Farrar, *Arrogance and Anxiety: the ambivalence of German power, 1848–1914* (1981); K. Hildebrand, *German Foreign Policy from Bismarck to*

*Adenauer* (1989); Gerhard Ritter, *The Sword and the Sceptre: the problem of militarism in Germany* (1972), 4 vols; and V. R. Berghahn, *Germany and the Approach of War in 1914* (2nd edn. 1993).

Italian foreign policy can be followed in F. J. Coppa, *The Origins of the Italian Wars of Unification* (1992); H. Hearder, *Cavor* (1995); and R. Bosworth, *Italy, the Least of the Great Powers* (1979).

On Russia see B. Jelavich, *From St Petersburg to Moscow, 1814–1974* (1974); W. C. Fuller, *Strategy and Power in Russia, 1600–1914* (1992); Janet M. Hartley, *Alexander I* (1994); N. Ingle, *Nesselrode and the Russian Rapprochement with Britain, 1836–44* (1976); H. Ragsdale and V. N. Ponomarev (eds.), *Imperial Russian Foreign Policy* (1993); D. M. Goldfrank, *The Origins of the Crimean War* (1994); R. McKean (ed.), *New Perspectives in Modern Russian History* (1992); G. F. Kennan, *The Fateful Alliance: France, Russia and the coming of the First World War* (1984); D. C. M. Lieven, *Russia and the Origins of the First World War* (1983), and his *Nicholas II, emperor of all the Russias* (1993).

## Special Topics

The era of the congresses (1814–23) is introduced by D. Deakin and R. Bridge in Chapters 1 and 2 in A. Sked (ed.), *Europe's Balance of Power, 1815–48* (1979). See also H. Kissinger, *A World Restored, 1812–22* (1957); Sir C. K. Webster, *The Foreign Policy of Castlereagh*, 2 vols. 1921 and 1931; E. E. Kraehe, *Metternich's German Policy* (1963); A. Palmer, *Metternich* (1972); P. K. Grimsted, *The Foreign Ministers of Alexander I* (1969); and J. M. Hartley, *Alexander I* (1994).

For the problems posed by the Ottoman Empire see M. S. Anderson, *The Eastern Question, 1774–1923* (1966); B. Jelavich, *Russia's Balkan Entanglements, 1806–1919* (1991); D. Dakin, *The Greek Struggle for Independence, 1821–33* (1973); M. Anderson, 'Russia and the Eastern Question, 1821–41' and bibliography, pp. 191–2, in Sked, *Europe's Balance of Power;* Sir C. K. Webster, *The Foreign Policy of Palmerston, 1830–41* (1951), 2 vols; D. M. Goldfrank, *Origins of the Crimean War* (1994), an excellent study based on a great array of primary sources from the powers and some lesser states, which also reviews in depth the debate on who or what caused the war. It is especially revealing on the conduct of Nicholas I. For the later years see W. E. Mosse, *The Rise and Fall of the Crimean System, 1855–1971* (1963); B. H. Sumner, *Russia and the Balkans, 1870–80* (1937); R. Millman, *Britain and the Eastern Question, 1875–78* (1979); C. J. Lowe, *Salisbury and the Mediterranean, 1884–96* (1965); and M. Kent (ed.), *The Great Powers and the end of the Ottoman Empire* (1984).

Recent treatments of Italian and German unification include F. J. Coppa, *The Origins of the Italian Wars of Independence* (1992) and W. Carr, *The Wars of German Unification* (1991). See also W. E. Mosse, *The European Powers and the German Question, 1848–71* (1958).

The study of Bismarck carries one into most of the great questions of the years 1862–1890. See L. Gall, *Bismarck: the White Revolutionary* (1986), 2 vols; O. Pflanze, *Bismarck and the Development of Germany* (1990), 3 vols; W. N. Medlicott, *Bismarck, Gladstone and the Concert of Europe* (1956), who ranges widely over the relations of the powers after the Congress of Berlin until the completion of the *Dreikaiserbund* in 1881; and N. Rich, *Friedrich von Holstein: politics and diplomacy in the era of Bismarck and Wilhelm II* (1965), 2 vols.

In addition to the works mentioned above on the approach to and the origins of the First World War, see John Albert White, *Transition to the Global Rivalry: alliance diplomacy and the Quadruple Entente* (1995), for details of the diplomatic revolution in the mid-1900s; K. M. Wilson, *The Policy of Entente: the determinants of British foreign policy, 1904–1914* (1985), a stimulating work which strongly supplements earlier studies which argue that Britain should not be seen as obsessed with Germany to the exclusion of all else before 1914; F. H. Hinsley (ed.), *British Foreign Policy under Sir Edward Grey* (1977); H. W. Koch (ed.), *The Origins of the First World War* (2nd edn. 1984), which includes 10 chapters examining some of the leading controversies relating to the origins of the war; and K. M. Wilson (ed.) *Decisions for War, 1914* (1995) which looks at the immediate origins with reference to each of the main participants. On Germany and Austria–Hungary in 1914 see J. H. Maurer, *The Outbreak of the First World War: strategic planning, crisis decision making and deterrence failure* (1995).

The controversial work of F. Fischer, notably his *Germany's Aims in the First World War* (1972) and *War of Illusions* (1974), is discussed by J. Joll in H. Koch, *Origins of the First World War*, Chapter 1, while Fischer makes a further contribution in Chapter 5.

# INDEX